A Surgeon's Civil War

DANIEL M. HOLT

A Surgeon's

The Letters and Diary of Daniel M. Holt, M.D.

Civil War

Edited by

James M. Greiner, Janet L. Coryell,

&

James R. Smither

The Kent State University Press

KENT, OHIO, AND LONDON, ENGLAND

© 1994 by The Kent State University Press,
Kent, Ohio 44242
ALL RIGHTS RESERVED
Library of Congress Catalog Card Number 93-34196
ISBN 0-87338-494-6
Manufactured in the United States of America

Library of Congress Cataloging-in-Publication Data

Holt, Daniel M., ca. 1819–1868.
  A surgeon's Civil War : the letters and diary of Daniel M. Holt, M.D./
  edited by James M. Greiner, Janet L. Coryell, and James R. Smither.
    p.   cm.
  Includes bibliographical references and index.
  ISBN 0-87338-494-6 (alk. paper) ∞
    1. Holt, Daniel M., ca. 1819–1868. 2. United States—History—Civil
War, 1861–1865—Medical care. 3. New York (State)—History—Civil
War, 1861–1865—Medical care. 4. United States. Army. New York Infan-
try Regiment, 121st (1861–1865) 5. United States—History—Civil War,
1861–1865—Regimental histories. 6. New York (State)—History—Civil
War, 1861–1865—Regimental histories. 7. Physicians—New York
(State)—Correspondence. 8. Physicians—New York (State)—Diaries.
I. Greiner, James M., 1954–   . II. Coryell, Janet L., 1955–   .
III. Smither, James R.   IV. Title.
E621.H76   1994   93-34196
973.7'75—dc20   CIP

British Library Cataloging-in-Publication data are available.

This work is dedicated from the following people
to the following people:

From Greiner & Coryell
to
Donald H. Stewart & Ellis A. Johnson
our teachers

From Coryell & Smither
to
David & Pat, Louise & Bob
our parents

From Daniel Morse Holt, M.D.
to my children
&
to the memory of
President Abraham Lincoln

Contents

Acknowledgments

The editors wish to acknowledge aid and sustenance from the following institutions and individuals: the Herkimer County Historical Society, through whose generosity the editors obtained access to the Holt letterbook and diary, which is printed here by their permission, with thanks particularly to Executive Director Jane Spellman, President Henry Blumberg, and Curators Mary Manion and Susan Perkins; the late Linus Ford and the Newport Lodge No. 455 Free and Accepted Masons for access to Holt's sword and sash; Robert K. Krick of the Fredericksburg and Spotsylvania National Military Parks; Susan L. Conklin, Genesee County historian in Batavia, New York, for her assistance with the Emory Upton Papers; the library staffs at Herkimer, Little Falls, and the New York State Historical Association at Cooperstown, and especially Patricia M. Di Tata, librarian at West Canada Valley Central Schools; the University of Dayton for providing clerical and computer support, particularly in the person of Amy Young; Auburn University History Department and Humanities Council for clerical, computer, and research grant support; Susan Fraysur at Auburn University for unsurpassed attention to detail in manuscript preparation; William Safire, Jeffrey McQuain, and Ann Rubin of the *New York Times* for aid in word and deed; Dr. Charles Thomas of Auburn, Alabama, for medical consultation; preliminary readers William C. Davis, John Coski, and John Hemphill for their comments and support of the project early on; Grand Valley State University for computer and clerical support; the Burnham-MacMillan Endowment Fund and the History Department at Western Michigan University for grant funds and computer and clerical support; Patrick L. Kirk for his advice and support; and Teresa Greiner, who gave up her living room for several summers to stacks of old books, loose papers, and the sounds of a typewriter.

Editors' Introduction

In the summer of 1862, in the quiet green valley of the Mohawk River in upstate New York, the Civil War seemed very far away. It was little over a year old, and the Union was losing. George McClellan, the general upon whom all had pinned their hopes of victory the year before, had withdrawn the massive forces assembled before Richmond. John Pope, his heir apparent, was soon to lose a second battle at Bull Run. Many thought the end was only a few months away. The North would surely let the Southern states secede from the Federal Union, pack up their tents and arms, and return to their homes.

But the war was not going to end. For Daniel Morse Holt, M.D., it was just beginning. A physician since 1853, he volunteered his services, he wrote, "to do my duty in the field." He was commissioned an assistant surgeon with the 121st New York on August 27, 1862, and set off for his first duty at Fort Lincoln, outside Washington.[1]

Holt was born in Herkimer, New York, the son and tenth child of printer David and Elizabeth Holt. His father became a judge in 1817 and served until 1825, when he left politics and returned to printing. He eventually moved to Madison, Wisconsin. Daniel Holt stayed in Herkimer and married Euphrasia Parkhurst in 1841, then joined his family in Madison the next year. He later left Madison for medical school in Cincinnati, where he graduated in the class of 1853. That same year both his father and Euphrasia died, only eight months apart. Two years later, Holt returned to the Mohawk Valley, this time taking up residence in Newport, a small village situated on the banks of the West Canada Creek.[2]

1. Frederick Phisterer, *New York in the War of the Rebellion*, 3433.
2. Daniel M. Holt Papers, Herkimer County Historical Society, Herkimer, N.Y. (hereafter cited as Holt Papers); Nathaniel S. Benton, *A History of Herkimer County, including the*

In 1856, Holt met and married Mary Louisa Willard, daughter of Col. Charles Willard, a distinguished veteran of the War of 1812 and one of the wealthiest men in Newport. He and Mary Louisa raised five children: Gertrude, David, and George Holt from his first marriage, and Willard and Isabel from his second. Another son, Edward Everett, died in infancy, as did a daughter, Anna.[3]

Holt's medical practice was fairly successful. Since 1856, he had worked for the Herkimer County Poorhouse as their resident physician, and in 1860 he was admitted to the county's medical society. With five children at home, the youngest only a few months old, Holt was not eager to leave when the war broke out. Herkimer County responded quickly and organized the 34th New York Volunteer Regiment in June 1861; Holt, however, did not volunteer. By the summer of 1862, another regiment was being formed in Herkimer and Otsego counties—the 121st New York Volunteers. Holt answered the call this time and traveled to Albany for examination before the State Medical Board in July. He was commissioned assistant surgeon and, at age forty-three, was the oldest member of the staff.[4] His experience would stand him in good stead. Daniel Holt was about to take his place in a regiment that would see action in nearly all the major campaigns in the eastern theater of the war.

For a country doctor from a small town, used to the simple medical problems of country folk, entering into the world of military medicine was a jolt. When the American Civil War began, the Medical Bureau of the United States Army consisted of an elderly and parsimonious surgeon general, fewer than one hundred surgeons and assistant surgeons, and a budget of $115,000. In no wise was the medical branch of the service prepared for the war that would come—a characteristic shared by most institutions and individuals in April 1861. Following the carnage and disorder of the first major battle at Manassas, Virginia, in

---

Upper Mohawk Valley, from the Earliest Period to the Present Time, 321, 484; *Mohawk Courier*, July 1, 1841; *Herkimer County Census for 1855*, 2:35, Herkimer County Clerk's Office, Herkimer, N.Y.; Sylvester Willard, *Regimental Surgeons of the State of New York in the War of the Rebellion, 1861–3*, 10; Phisterer, 3423, 3425, 3433.

3. *Herkimer County Census for 1855*, 2:35; U.S. Department of the Interior, Pension and Military Service Records, National Archives, Washington, D.C. (hereafter cited as Pension and Service Records); Joseph Willard and Charles Wilkes Walker, eds., *The Willard Genealogy*, completed by Charles Henry Pope, 289.

4. Undated newspaper clipping, Holt Papers; *Board of Supervisors 1856* (Ilion, N.Y., 1857), 11; Frederick H. Dyer, *A Compendium of the War of the Rebellion*, 3:1416; Phisterer, 3428–39.

July, it was clear that the Army Medical Department would need major reforms in order to fulfill its duties. A competent and energetic surgeon general was required, along with a vastly increased medical staff and a massive budget. Also needed were hospitals, ambulances, and a triage system, a method of supply requisition more responsive to immediate needs, and a sanitary commission capable of enforcing camp hygiene directives.[5]

When Holt arrived at Camp Lincoln to begin his duties, a few changes had been made, but much needed to be done. Surgeon General Col. Thomas Lawson, had died of apoplexy in May 1861, and was replaced by Col. Clement A. Finley, a bureaucrat more interested in cost containment than responding to the national crisis. Finley was so inept that much of the effective medical care of soldiers in 1861 came from the United States Sanitary Commission, a civilian organization. In fact, the commission led the fight to remove Finley, which was accomplished by April 1862.[6]

Appointed in Finley's place was thirty-three-year-old William A. Hammond, an assistant surgeon and a prize-winning researcher and physician. Eleven years an army veteran (his rank low because of a brief sojourn into teaching that ended when war broke out), Hammond took to his duties with the humorless zeal of a reformer. He immediately clashed with Secretary of War Edwin Stanton, angry at having to work with a man not of his own choosing, but was able to institute major reforms despite that difficult relationship. Hammond transformed the Medical Department into a professional organization capable of providing care for the hundreds of thousands of soldiers in the Union army.[7]

The Army of the Potomac, in which Holt served, benefitted from the reforms not only of Hammond but also from the work of Hammond's appointee, Medical Director Jonathan Letterman. For example, Hammond tightened examination requirements for surgeons at the state level, hoping to decrease the number of incompetents allowed to practice, a move that eventually would help in the dismissal of Holt's

---

5. Frank R. Freemon, "Lincoln Finds a Surgeon General: William A. Hammond and the Transformation of the Union Army Medical Bureau," 5–6; Mary Gillett, *The Army Medical Department, 1818–1865,* 153–54.

6. Freemon, 6–9; Bonnie Ellen Blustein, "'To Increase the Efficiency of the Medical Department': A New Approach to U.S. Civil War Medicine," 26–29.

7. Freemon, 10–13.

immediate and bungling superior, one Stephen Valentine. Hammond sought to lessen the stranglehold red tape had on supply requisitioning by allowing Letterman to bypass army requisition forms when necessary, which affected supply at the regimental level. To diminish the time the wounded went without care after a battle, Hammond fought for a separate Ambulance Corps for the entire army, a vetoed proposal that did not stop Letterman from employing the idea for the Army of the Potomac, as Holt would observe. Hammond designed more hygienic hospitals and camps and appointed medical inspectors to enforce standards that would decrease the incidence of disease caused by improper sanitation practices and hospital-borne infections. But political disagreements led to Hammond's court-martial in 1864, and the Medical Department began to decline in its effectiveness after he was arrested in January 1864.[8]

In July 1862, Holt took the Medical Department's newly instituted New York state examination to be commissioned into the service. Holt's army career paralleled Surgeon General Hammond's until the end, outlasting Hammond's by about two months. Holt's reminiscences, letters, and diary describe the medical difficulties and chaos experienced by surgeons of the Civil War, providing an insider's look at medicine as practiced in the field at the regimental level and giving occasional glimpses of the efficacy of Hammond's reforms as they affected the 121st New York Volunteer Regiment.

The 121st New York served in the Second Brigade, First Division, Sixth Corps from September 9, 1862, until the end of the war. The regiment saw action in the eastern theater at Crampton's Gap before Antietam, at Fredericksburg, Salem Church, the Mine Run campaign, the Wilderness, Spotsylvania, Cold Harbor, Petersburg, the 1864 Shenandoah Valley campaign, and Appomattox. Col. Richard Franchot recruited the regiment in New York but resigned in September 1862 to run for Congress; Col. Emory Upton replaced him. A West Point graduate, Upton was one of the finest combat commanders in the war. Under his leadership, the 121st became a first-rate fighting unit. Their finest hour came on May 10, 1864, when, in the lead of twelve handpicked regiments commanded by Upton, they cracked through the Mule Shoe at Spotsylvania.[9]

8. Ibid., 10–13, 19–21; Blustein, 32–38; Gillett, 177–92.
9. Phisterer, 3432; Bruce Catton, *A Stillness at Appomattox,* 117–28.

Dr. Holt first saw service at Crampton's Gap and Fredericksburg. He survived Gen. Ambrose Burnside's infamous "Mud March" in December 1862, and was captured by Confederates in May 1863. Before being freed by Robert E. Lee himself when Lee discovered Holt was a fellow Mason, the doctor was shot at by a young Confederate while searching the battlefield for one of his hospital workers. Never at a loss for words, Holt lectured the young "grayback" for his impulsiveness before returning to his captivity. He mourned the losses at Chancellorsville, saved lives at Gettysburg, and chased after John Singleton Mosby's Rangers in Virginia. In May 1864, Holt began keeping a diary to record Gen. Ulysses Grant's eastern campaign through the battles of the Wilderness, Spotsylvania, and Cold Harbor. He stayed with the army through much of Gen. Philip Sheridan's Shenandoah campaign but finally resigned in ill health in October 1864.

Educated and articulate, Holt described camp life and army politics with unflattering veracity. He complained of trouble getting medical supplies from "drunken and incompetent quartermasters; (a class of men above all others in the army [that] needs watching)" and of a bungling, drunken, and imperious superior, Asst. Surgeon Stephen B. Valentine: "It is utterly impossible to feel easy with such a specimen of humanity to dictate to you." Because of frequent illnesses and resignations in his outfit, Holt often served as surgeon without the increase in rank or pay he deserved. Furious at the army politics he held responsible for denying him a promotion, he vented his spleen in his letters home, writing to his wife that, "I hope you will excuse the many senseless letters which I send you; but I must let off the surplus gas or an explosion will result."

In 1867, Holt, in poor health from tuberculosis contracted in the service, compiled and copied his letters home into a bound volume. "The object in copying the written letters is to preserve them to my wife and children," wrote Holt. "Time is on the wing and the original sheets will soon be destroyed." His health was rapidly deteriorating, and although he remained cheerfully optimistic, Holt had only slightly more than a year to live. The letters he preserved for his children were a legacy that described in detail the daily routines, frustrations, and anguish Holt had experienced during his twenty-six months in service. He included a preface and an introductory narrative of his first few weeks in camp, and dedicated his work to his children and to the memory of Abraham Lincoln. Holt died on October 15, 1868, at the age of forty-seven, and was buried in the family plot in Newport, New York. His daughter, Isabel Holt Ferguson, preserved her father's remarkable letterbook and presented it to the Herkimer County Historical Society in 1930.

This edition of Dr. Holt's reminiscences, letters, and diary seeks to preserve and present the legacy the good doctor left. In recognition of the value of "un-Bowdlerized" primary sources, the editorial comments, corrections, insertions, and deletions have been kept to a minimum. Idiosyncracies in spelling and style, with the exception of geographic place names and individual persons' names, have generally been preserved. Explanatory notes to set letters in context precede the letters; illuminatory notes of specific events or individuals are at the foot of the appropriate page. Bracketed inserts are used for three things: additional identification of an item or individual; a suggested reading of an illegible word; an additional word to make a sentence grammatically intelligible. Commas have been added where needed; paragraphination has been added to break excessively long passages. In all, however, editorial impositions have been placed sparingly to preserve the spontaneity of Holt's work. A bibliography provides a list of works consulted and cited. The editors relied on standard Civil War texts and the official records, *The War of the Rebellion,* to provide information for explanatory notes. Of particular value were the following texts: Bruce Catton's trilogy tracing the actions of the Army of the Potomac, *Mr. Lincoln's Army, Glory Road,* and *A Stillness at Appomattox;* James McPherson's *Battle Cry of Freedom;* Douglas Southall Freeman's *Lee's Lieutenants;* Mary Gillett's *The Army Medical Department, 1818–1865;* and the four-volume work, *Battles and Leaders of the Civil War.*

The editorial process has been the responsibility of three individuals. James Greiner, of Herkimer, New York, discovered the letterbook and was responsible for the transcription of the work as well as the research in the local sources and the National Archives. Janet Coryell, of Western Michigan University, edited the body of the work and was responsible for the expository footnotes, explanatory notes, and the medical history. James Smither, of Grand Valley State University, served as military editor and was responsible for explanations of military strategy and tactics to help place the actions described by Holt into the overall context of the war. As with all projects with more than one cook, we share praise and blame equally. Any praise is appreciated; any errors herein are ours.

A Surgeon's Civil War

Author's Preface

The object in copying the within letters is to preserve them to my wife and children for whom they were originally written. Time is on the wing and the original sheets will soon be destroyed. Many facts are related, which perhaps in years to come, will be pleasant to look upon. Not for the *present* but for the *future* have I attempted to hand down a few incidents in my life while trying to do my duty in the field. The history of the 121st Reg. N.Y. Vols., if correctly written, would be of stirring interest. Entering at once upon a field of [War] without a month's preparation for such a change, our men fell like leaves of Autumn before the withering effects of an active campaign. It was during these exciting times—times of National distress, that I write—times such as I sincerely hope none of my kindred will ever see again. I have endeavored to speak truthfully when I took up my pen to write. [Rueing] the impulsive nature which dwells within me, I am satisfied that my friends will look leniently upon mistaken views of things as they presented themselves. Little did I think, years ago as I read exciting debate in Congress and listened to maddened political harangues, that I should be an actual participant in a war brought about by fire eaters of the South whose only object was to dissolve the Union and build upon its shattered fragments an institution whose cornerstone should be human bondage. But thus it is. I have tried to see the issue taken between freedom on the one hand and Slavery on the other, and have been happy in seeing peace and good order established. The spirit and genius of free institutions made perpetual by the emancipation of millions of human beings from the shackles of bondsmen, has placed forever in the foreground of moral reform, the chief Magistrate of the Nation—Abraham Lincoln:—and to his memory, more than any earthly thing else I am in humble admiration.

D. M. HOLT

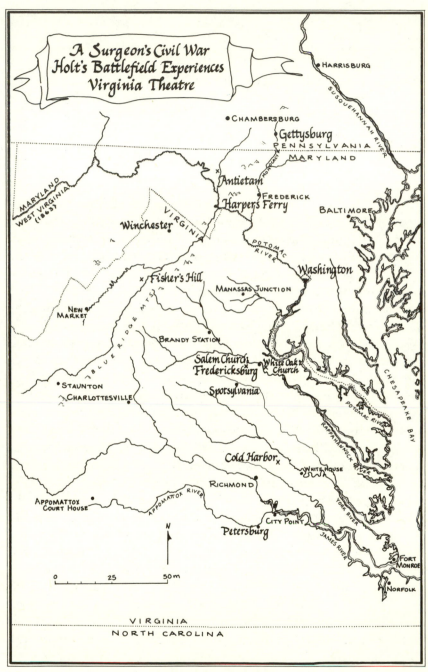

A Surgeon's Civil War
Holt's Battlefield Experiences
Virginia Theatre

HARRISBURG

CHAMBERSBURG

Gettysburg

PENNSYLVANIA

MARYLAND

SUSQUEHANNAH RIVER

Antietam

FREDERICK

Harper's Ferry

BALTIMORE

MARYLAND

WEST VIRGINIA (1863)

VIRGINIA

Winchester

POTOMAC RIVER

Washington

Fisher's Hill

MANASSAS JUNCTION

NEW MARKET

BLUE RIDGE MTS.

BRANDY STATION

Salem Church

Fredericksburg

White Oak Church

STAUNTON

CHARLOTTESVILLE

Spotsylvania

CHESAPEAKE BAY

POTOMAC RIVER

Cold Harbor

WHITE HOUSE

RAPPAHANNOCK RIVER

APPOMATTOX COURT HOUSE

APPOMATTOX RIVER

RICHMOND

CITY POINT

Petersburg

YORK RIVER

JAMES RIVER

FORT MONROE

Norfolk

0   25   50 m

N

VIRGINIA
NORTH CAROLINA

MAP BY MICAELA AYERS

Introduction by Daniel M. Holt, M.D.

During the months of July and August in the year 1862, and the second year of the rebellion, the 121st Regiment, New York Volunteers Infantry was recruited from the counties of Herkimer and Otsego, and on Saturday, the 30th day of August, left its encampment on the South side of the Mohawk River, opposite the Village of Herkimer, for the seat of war. It reached the city of Washington on Monday following (Sept. 1st), and immediately by orders marched to *Fort Lincoln,* a post on the Bladensburgh Pike seven miles from the city, where it remained for about a week, when it was ordered to march to Hall's Hill [Virginia]: but our very worthy Colonel [Richard Franchot] mistaking his order, and being rather raw and green for so fair and plump a looking personage "Kept on going" until we were picked up near Hallstown, in Maryland, by General Franklin, who then commanded the Sixth Corps and we were then brigaded in the 2nd Brigade, First Division, Sixth Corps Army of the Potomac, then under general command of George B. McClellan, after which we were compelled to keep our places and do duty by the pressing invitations of Uncle Sam's boys in blue.[1] The regiment left in camp *everything,* almost, except what was upon the backs of the men, being informed by the Colonel that we were *"going out for a fight and would be back in two days."* This was surely a very sad and disastrous

1. Richard Franchot received permission from New York's governor to raise the 121st N.Y. on July 19, 1862. An engineer and president of the Albany and Susquehanna Railroad, Franchot was no soldier but a congressman from New York. His resignation on Sept. 25, 1862, was cheered by the regiment. Commander of the Sixth Corps, William Franklin, took his command on May 18, 1862, and held the position until Nov. 16, 1862, when, just prior to the Battle of Fredericksburg, he was given command of the Left Grand Division of the Army of the Potomac. Phisterer, 3432; Mark M. Boatner, *Civil War Dictionary,* 303–4.

blunder on the part of the Colonel, for from that hour our distress began. Unprovided with tents, blankets and mess utensils, we were compelled to sleep without a roof, save that of the canopy of Heaven, and eat our food as best we could prepare it; and in storms and cold nights to endure chilling blasts and storms of rain until one-half the regiment were upon the sick list. This is not strange when we take into account the fact that our boys were tenderly cared for at home, and never, until then were exposed to hard marches (of which we early saw enough) and were properly clothed and fed. I do not wish to reflect upon Col. Franchot's humanity, but never had a regiment a *worse* commandant (unwittingly perhaps) than he. Unnecessary *"double quick"* and forced marches, when no enemy was in sight or hearing, and when *rest* was imperatively demanded for the life of the men, were made, until his name became a reproach and stench among the men of his command.[2] Shullsburgh, and many other marches made at night, when the rest of the army was still, and when our men fell from exhaustion like a line of battle under heavy fire, will long be remembered by the noble boys who composed the 121st regiment. Never was there a better appointed regiment than ours sent into the field. The Empire State showed its greatness and magnanimity in furnishing everything which could in the slightest degree, conduce to the comfort and happiness of its sons who had taken upon themselves the duty of defending our common soil from the evil machinations of an excited and desparate South who had resolved at all hazzards to perpetuate Slavery, both white and black upon us.

Nothing in the line of medical or hospital supplies was wanting. A superabundance of the choicest, purest, and most effective remedies for the cure and prevention of disease was sent into the field with us. Delicacies for the indisposed, and sick, wholesome food for convalescents, white wines, liquors and soft bedding for the sick and wounded, was piled tier upon tier until it was impossible to furnish transportation sufficient to keep it with us. The ladies of Herkimer and

2. Holt's complaints are those of a new recruit. The marches made by Union forces in the Maryland campaign were not unusually grueling by the standards of the war and were much less hard than those made regularly by their Confederate opponents. As Holt himself indicates, the soldiers' main problem was that they were not accustomed to marching, especially under a hot sun, and had a hard time keeping pace with veterans. Franchot no doubt made things worse with unnecessary orders but could not be blamed for the rawness of his troops. Stephen W. Sears, *Landscape Turned Red: The Battle of Antietam*, 120.

Otsego vied with each other to supply the best and *most* of jellies, jams, canned fruits of all kinds, dried berries and domestic wines, while both old and young worked day and night to furnish knit gloves, mittens, socks, drawers, shirts and a thousand and one little gifts which came as oil and gladness into the tired and aching hearts of those who were fighting for their firesides and loved ones at home. All these, with tents standing as they were pitched, and unguarded by anyone except a few sick who were left behind never again to be seen by us—*all* gone because of the consummate, ignorant folly of a man, whose brains were anywhere but in his head.[3] Perhaps the man can be excused upon the ground of intoxication; if such an excuse is at all admissable; but here we will let the Colonel rest; and here let him repose upon the laurels which he won upon on a *bloodless* field.

Being desirous of entering the army and feeling that I could do more good to my country in the capacity of Surgeon, than in any other, I made application to the proper authorities at Albany for such a position, and upon the suggestion of [New York State] Surgeon General S. Oakley Vanderpoel, went to Albany on, or about the 20th of July, 1862, where I underwent an examination before a medical board then in session for that purpose and in a day or two afterwards, received a note from the Surgeon General informing me that my examination had been satisfactory, and that my name had been sent into the Executive Department as a proper person to control the Surgical Department of any regiment of volunteers at that time formed or then in proccess of formation in the State.[4] I had been strongly solicited to enter the 121st which was then almost complete in its necessary quota of men and officers and that request being in harmony with my own feelings, I accepted the position of *Assistant* Surgeon of the regiment and was commissioned as such on the 27th day of August, 1862: although my

3. Supplying and outfitting the army was still, nearly eighteen months after the war began, a task left to many states instead of the federal government. States and municipal governments raised troops and equipped them as their citizens saw fit. By 1862, Q.M. Montgomery Meigs had achieved great progress in supplying enlisted soldiers all their needs in the field, but the extras that meant life with a degree of comfort were donated by home folks. Leaving those luxuries behind, particularly in the early days of a regiment's service, was not uncommon. James M. McPherson, *Battle Cry of Freedom: The Civil War Era,* 322–25.

4. Medical students took two years of lecture and then served an apprenticeship by assisting an established practitioner to earn their medical degrees. George W. Adams, *Doctors in Blue: The Medical History of the Union Army in the Civil War.*

examination was satisfactory for a *Surgeon-in-chief*.[5] In this capacity, I served the regiment until the 17th day of October, 1864—a little [under] twenty-six months—until my health became so poor, that I was compelled, against my will, to resign my commission and come home. Disease had fastened upon my lungs, and so strong was the tendency to a fatal termination, that many friends gave me up as lost; but at the date of this writing (Jan. 28, 1867) I have strong hope of being able another season to do a little business—something which I have not done to any extent since I left the Army.

The regiment, as it left the encampment at Herkimer, consisted of 1,040 men and officers, as follows:—

Officers of the 121st Regiment N. Y. Volunteers[6]

Colonel—Richard Franchot
Lieut. Colonel—Charles H. Clark
Major—Egbert Olcott
Adjutant—Thomas S. Arnold
Quartermaster—Albert Story
Surgeon—[William] Bassett
Assistant Surgeon—Daniel M. Holt
     S. B. Valentine [Stephen]
Chaplain—J. R. Sage
Company "A": Captain—H. M. Galpin [Henry M.]
     1st Lieutenant—Jonathan Burrel
     2nd Lieutenant—George W. Davis
Company "B": Captain—Irving Holcomb
     1st Lieutenant—Henry C. Keith
     2nd Lieutenant—George A. May
Company "C": Captain—Clinton A. Moon
     1st Lieutenant—Angus Cameron
     2nd Lieutenant—Charles M. Bradt

5. The administration of the Medical Department provided for several different kinds of surgeons. Each brigade had a brigade surgeon who oversaw the regimental and assistant surgeons. Contract surgeons were hired by the army to beef up the ranks whenever necessary, particularly after a big battle. (Hospital stewards, who served as apothecaries and wound dressers, and nurses made up the bulk of the rest of the medical corps concerned with primary patient care.) By July 1862, in an attempt to improve the quality of those accepted into the ranks of regimental surgeons, the volunteers were examined by boards of medical officers. Gillett, 154–56, 179–82.

6. Holt's list does contain some inaccuracies. See Phisterer, 3423.

Company "D": Captain—John D. Fish
            1st Lieutenant—Delos M. Kenyon
            2nd Lieutenant—Charles E. Staring
Company "E": Captain—Douglas Campbell
            1st Lieutenant—Theodore Sternberg
            2nd Lieutenant—Harrison Van Horn
Company "F": Captain—Nelson O. Wendell
            1st Lieutenant—Byron F. Park
            2nd Lieutenant—Frank G. Bolles
Company "G": Captain—Edwin Cook
            1st Lieutenant—James D. Clyde
            2nd Lieutenant—Charles T. Ferguson
Company "H": Captain—John Ramsey
            1st Lieutenant—U. F. Doubleday [Ulysses]
            2nd Lieutenant—Marcus R. Casler
Company "I": Captain—John S. Kidder
            1st Lieutenant—John D. P. Douw
            2nd Lieutenant—Delavan Bates
Company "K": Captain—Sackett M. Olin
            1st Lieutenant—Andrew E. Mather
            2nd Lieutenant—Frank Gorton

The object of this manuscript volume is to secure the letters to my children and friends who might take an interest in looking over the ground which I travelled while a Surgeon in the volunteer forces of the Union; and if they can find anything in here of interest, it will repay the time and labor of copying and compiling. They were written oftentimes upon the field of battle and almost always in a hurry—upon the march—in camp and in quarters, and always, at the time gave a correct idea of matters as I then beheld them; but which nevertheless, were very often incorrect in the deductions drawn from surrounding circumstances. And here let it be said at once, and in the beginning, that no man is competent (except perhaps Commandants of Corps and Divisions) to foretell what will be the issue upon to-morrow. The art of war is to a great extent a *secret* one. The plans of a campaign or a march are not communicated to officers of a low rank or to privates—*or to any one else.* He who is best at *guessing* is generally best at informing others *what is to come.* Long before I left the army I gave up all ideas of knowing anything which was to transpire. When the order came to *"pack up,"* I did so, with all the rest; and when the command to *"march!"* was given,

I seated myself in my saddle and followed on; content to know that I should find out what was meant by the move as soon as anyone else would;—I find myself, as all others did at first, prognosticating what was to be, and as often as any way, been entirely disappointed, and this must be looked for in these pages.

I have lived to see a rebellion which at first was supposed by our greatest men to be impossible to endure beyond a few days or months at most, continue through four years, during which time more blood and treasure had been expended than the world ever knew before for an equal length of time. I saw it put down so far as resort to arms is concerned, but a battle of reconstruction is going on which in its results is no less important—no less requiring, skill, courage and statesmanship. I hope to live to see our country once more settled upon the basis of freedom and equality; but if not so permitted, I shall die in the firm faith of the Nation's ability to punish treason—*"to make it odious,"* and to perpetuate its free institutions. When I see that I have felt it important that I should lend my strength and energies to put down a wicked uprising of infuriated men amongst us, I say it with all truth and candor. I lent to the country myself and what means I had to give—gave two sons who served with faithfulness a cause upon which the whole heart was placed—served with honor to themselves and family,[7] and after the clamor of war is no longer heard in the land, but instead there's the voice of peaceful industry, we have laid aside the habilaments of battle[8] and assumed the garb of a civilian ready again, should the state of the country demand it, to *"shoulder arms"* and maintain its honor.

I left home for the seat of the war on Monday Sept. 2nd, and was mustered into the Army at Albany on the same day; in the meantime staying at the Gibson House, purchasing blankets, rubber clothes &c., necessities for camp life,[9] and on the succeeding day, (3rd) started for Washington, where I arrived in due time stopping at the "Metropolitan" or "Brown's Hotel."[10] Having sent my trunk to *Fort Lincoln* (where the regiment [was] then lying) by a Negro, I started on foot to

7. Holt's sons George and David served in the army during the war. A complete genealogy of the Holt Family is found in the Holt Papers.

8. "Habilaments" meaning garments.

9. Officers were responsible for supplying their own needs.

10. Next to Willard's, Brown's Hotel was one of the most famous in Washington. Margaret Leech, *Reveille in Washington*, 8.

join it, and on the way was overtaken by Col. Franchot who was on his way out in a carriage with whom I got a ride to quarters, much to the relief of my tired feet and perspiring body. Arriving there I sent [Thomas] Huckans and [James] Cox (Neighbors of mine while at home but now soldiers of the 121st Regiment) for my trunk, which by singular and good luck happened to get there just as they issued out upon the pike, and took up quarters for the first time in my life in a tent, with [Chief] Surgeon [William] Bassett and [First] Assistant Surgeon [Stephen B.] Valentine. As an incident, the first to be related in my new life, I slept that night and each subsequent one, until we were ordered to move, in a *gun box*. I must confess that it looked something like a *coffin,* and perhaps the smell of powder put me in mind of the time when *sulphur* would be quite an ordinary diet: but I had not long to enjoy the luxury of a *gun box:*—a few days, and the ground for a bed and a *stone* for a pillow, served quite a good purpose. I thought the few days in camp *rough;* but now I see it as it is, they were among the *very best* of an exciting and eventful campaign. I must depend upon *letters* mainly for incidents which occurred during the time of my soldier life, but as many of these are lost or destroyed, but an imperfect outline can be given.

The first one written was at

> Camp Lincoln, eight miles
> out of Washington on the
> Bladensburg Pike
> September 5th, 1862.

My dear Wife:—

I sit down this morning, in my tent, having some leisure time, to write to you. I am well—better than when I left home—were it not so, I should be wholly unfit for duty; for I was, as you know, when I left home almost upon the sick list. I arrived in Washington on Wednesday night, and put up at the Metropolitan, and yesterday found my way to this fort. How long we shall remain here is entirely uncertain. Last night one hundred rounds of cartridges apiece, were issued to the men, who were ordered to "lie upon their arms" ready for instant action, we expecting an attack at any moment. The enemy, however, did not appear, and I do not know as there is any danger to be apprehended. I think there is not—yet it is necessary, I suppose, to aacustom the men to such things in order to qualify them for *real* duty. The smoke and din of Battle (Bull Run) was distinctly seen and heard from our encampment; so you can see that we are in the *vicinity* of rebels at any rate. Our men are anxious to be engaged, and I think they would fight well if an opportunity presents.[11]

As yet we have not been well supplied with provisions. The Quarter Master's Department is very imperfectly organized, and the men appeared yesterday almost ready for a revolt on account of hunger; they not having had a full ration for three days. As for myself, I fared better—eating the cakes which you so kindly put up before I left and am still eating sparingly, not knowing where the next may come from.

I am contented and should be happy but for you and the little ones. God only knows how dearly I love you all; but here I am, and here I am bound to remain, come life or come death. I do not fear the latter. The God of battles is with me still. My faith and confidence is stronger in Him than ever. I feel perfectly resigned to His will and feel great comfort in trusting Him.

Every moment the booming of cannon comes over us from different quarters; the cause I do not know—you can judge as well as I. It seems almost unreal, this great busttle and stir about me. I can hardly believe that many of these faces which are constantly passing before me, whose countenances indicate health and vigor, will soon, no doubt fill the narrow house. The question comes: shall *I* be one? I do not know. I will try to meet the grim messenger when he comes. God help me.

I will write again in a day or two and tell you where to direct your letters. As it is I cannot tell you; the post office arrangements not being fully completed and arranged.[12] Until I write again, good bye. Kiss the little ones for me.

Daniel.

11. Holt's reference is to the Second Battle of Bull Run, which had been fought Aug. 29–30, 1862. Camp Lincoln was approximately twenty–five miles from the action, northeast of Washington City up the Bladensburg Pike. By the time Holt wrote this letter, he was hearing cannon and rifle fire from skirmishes and Confederate demonstrations, probably at Falls Church, Va., and Poolesville, Md., designed to cover the Confederate crossing of the Potomac into Maryland as Gen. Robert E. Lee invaded the North. George B. Davis, et al., eds., *Atlas to Accompany the Official Records of the Union and Confederate Armies,* plate 89 (hereafter cited as *Atlas*); *The War of the Rebellion: A Compilation of the Official Records of the Union and Confederate Armies,* ser. 1, vol. 19, pt. 1:814–15, 828 (hereafter cited as *OR*).

12. Postal service during the war was provided for regiments through the quarter-master's department. Although Holt complains occasionally about poor mail service, the post office service did a remarkably good job, though problems did arise when units were located far from rail lines or roads or in action. See Allan Nevins, *The War for the Union: The Organized War, 1863–1864,* 282–83.

We were not permitted to occupy this position (Fort Lincoln) but a few days. During that time, however, I had made arrangements for mess with Surgeons Bassett and Valentine—had sent to Washington for provisions and was getting along famously—having secured the services of a first rate cook and attentive waiters, and in every way *settling down* in a foolish way to live. But how vain are the hopes of man. In an hour, the least expected, the order came to move, and to move at once, which we did on Sunday [September 7], leaving our tents standing, with our mess utensils with cooked and uncooked provisions behind, as has been previously stated—left *everything* which we could not carry on our backs and none but sick to guard the vacated quarters. Our streets, which were beginning to assume a cheerful appearance, having been decorated with pine trees and other evergreens, brought from an adjacent wood, wore an aspect of silent desertion like those of Pompeii or Herculaneum.[13] Only for *two days,* according to Colonel Franchot, were we to be absent—*going out for a fight* and then to return. But no return for us in two days or two years. The spot was left by us forever, and from the time we turned our backs upon our first encampment to the time when Uncle Sam kindly furnished us with shelter, tents and blankets, a period of over three months, we had no covering save Nature's universal sky and clouds. We began immediately to *tramp* and kept it up as long as any tramping was to be done. As for myself, I had not the good fortune (neither had Dr. Bassett or Valentine) to possess a horse, designing to purchase one of the government or some private individual after reaching the front, and so had to go afoot, like all the rest. This added greatly to the labor of my position, as in giving relief to those who fell out by the way, and administerring to the sick, I was often a mile or two in the rear and had to catch up with the column by dint of hard running. Never, in my life did I accomplish more, and never did it appear to me was I worse fed than until at last we rested near Bakersville, where we remained for about six weeks.[14] In my ignorance of duty, I did very much more than was expected or required of me; I made every soldier's case, one of my own. I carried their guns; knapsacks, and gave them the few crums which were necessary for my own support, and *what* did I get for it?—only derided as being a green

13. "Pompeii or Herculaneum" meaning two ancient Roman cities destroyed by the eruption of Mount Vesuvius in A.D. 79. Archaeological digs show that the destruction of the cities came so quickly that people were in the midst of everyday activities when life was snuffed out.

14. Bakersville was about four miles northwest of Sharpsburg, Md. *Atlas,* plate 136.

fool who would learn better after he had seen more of the service. But I never regretted it, although I now see that I was very often imposed upon by an ungrateful soldier feigning sickness to whom I gave everything I possessed, and after becoming the possessor of a horse, to seat him in my saddle, while I faintingly tugged along afoot in the dust and heat.

It was something new to me to see men fall as if shot and die almost as quickly, from sun stroke. A moment previous to falling he would be marching on as if nothing unusual was to pay, when a stagger and fall, and in some instances death, followed each other in a few moments time. No one, except experienced soldiers, are fit to command a body of troops. They know nothing of the physical endurance of their men, and are wholly unfit to judge of the extent of evil which they are inflicting by too long marches in the heat, without a rest. No troop of Infantry ought to march over a mile and a half or two miles without resting ten or fifteen minutes; but instead, we have often marched nine or ten miles, and rested only thirty or forty minutes and then up and on again. It was during one of the most intensely hot days I ever witnessed, about the time of which I am writing, that our regiment seemed to *all* give out at once. The road side was filled with lifeless men who in the morning set out hale and fresh; and behind every bush or shrub which afforded ever so little shade, there lay the prostrate forms of Herkimer and Otsego's noblest sons. Beside every rill,[15] pool or pond—anywhere a drop of water could be had, men contended as if life and death were the issue; and indeed such often was the case. I think for twenty-four hours I hardly ever suffered as I did during that time—hungry, thirsty and completely exhausted. I thought death would be a welcome call, but all suffering sometimes ends, and so did this, thank God.

It was during this day, while engaged as I have already stated, in relieving the men by carrying their guns, &c., that I took refuge for a few moments in the only ambulance which belonged to the regiment, when General Franklin who then commanded the Sixth Corps came riding past with his staff and seeing me in it, called out, "Dr are you sick?" Upon which I replied that I was not. He then ordered me out in the most abusive and profane manner telling me that "never again to let him know of my being in an ambulance while I had feet to carry

15. "Rill" meaning a small stream.

me—an order which I have strictly obeyed, taking a remarkable antipathy to such kind of riding ever since. Had I [ever] known as much then as I now do, the General would have been brought up to answer for the abuse heaped upon me before the officers of his Staff and our regiment; as he nor any other officer has a right to abuse another under any circumstances. Had I [illegible] been guilty of wrong (as no doubt I was, not knowing my duty then) it was for him to have informed me of it in a gentlemanly way, and cautioned me against a repetition of it. As it was he abused and offended me by coarse profane language such as would have cashiered him or brought upon him severe reprimand from a military courtmartial.[16] I was not long however in learning where I stood and what was proper and expected of me.

Somewhere in Maryland—near Rockville I think—we were picked up and brigaded as I before said. After forming the Brigade it was a favorite theme of the older soldiers to taunt us as having come out under a bounty of $200.00; stigmatizing us as the "two hundred dollars sons of bitches," to which we replied *we were worth it* while *they could be bought for a glass of whisky or a three cent piece.*[17] But they soon found out that we could fight as well as receive pay, and in a short time became our firm and fast friends; The 5th Maine, in particular, adopted us and we them. They stood by us through thick and thin; and so did we stand by them. If an assault was to be made—a battery charged or any dangerous and difficult task to be performed, we thought that with the cooperation of the 5th Maine we could do anything possible to be done and so it was upon their part. With the 96th Pa. (a regiment in our brigade) we were ever at variance.[18] From the first, our boys could not endure the Saerkrout illiterate lunk heads, and they appeared to

16. General Franklin was not known for diplomacy. At Second Bull Run, he replied to Gen. John Pope's desperate request for supplies by telling Pope to send in a cavalry escort to get them; after Fredericksburg, Franklin demoralized his troops by his continual bad–mouthing of the commanding general, Ambrose Burnside. Robert Underwood Johnson and Clarence Clough Buel, eds., *Battles and Leaders of the Civil War*, 2:4856 (hereafter cited as *B&L*); James M. McPherson, *Ordeal By Fire: The Civil War and Reconstruction*, 317–18.

17. By 1862, enlistments of new recruits were low enough that state, federal, and local governments encouraged volunteers by paying them bounties, sometimes up to one thousand dollars. Bruce Catton, *Glory Road*, 13.

18. The 5th Maine was made up of men from Portland. The 96th Pa. was recruited mainly from Schuylkill County outside Philadelphia. *Official Army Register of the Volunteer Force of the United States Army . . .*, 1:19 (hereafter *OAR*); William Fox, *Regimental Losses in the American Civil War 1861–1865*, 286.

equally despise us. They were cowards; and like all other cowards, were braggadocios and abusive. Until we had fairly knocked it into them by fisticuffs and blackened their eyes until we shut them out from beholding the evil that was in us, they kept up their taunts and insults; but after they came slowly to realize that a man was none the less because he could read and write, they ceased to annoy us and kept where they belonged—at the farthest verge of the brigade. Perhaps it will be well to mention the regiments which composed the Brigade at the time we entered it. All were *two* years, I think, having come out under a previous call to ours when *two* years was considered amply sufficient to put down any revolt which could be started, but we learned a lesson however not soon to be forgotten; *and the next time* when we go we shall go strong enough and long enough to make short work of it.

The regiments composing the Brigade were the 16th, 18th, 27th, and 32nd New York, 95th and 96th Penn., 5th Maine and our own. In a short time the 16th, 18th, and 32nd New York Regiments were mustered out of service, and the men whose terms had not expired on account of being mustered in after the organization of the commands, and who had several months to serve, were transferred to our regiment, thus filling it up again to nearly its original strength.[19] The number gained by this transfer was about 250—good men and true who stood by us in every danger and appeared to be as much attached to us as their former friends.

The marches through Maryland were severe enough for *old* soldiers, but ours being new recruits, suffered beyond all calculation. Our Colonel thought that because *he* could stand it in the saddle, the men ought to stand it equally as well afoot. If any fell out by the way, he swore at and abused them; and if perchance his whisky bottle came up missing he would rave like a maniac. At length we neared Burkittsville, and when within about a mile and a half of that place were ordered to load our pieces and get ready for action, as the advanced guard were already engaged, and soon we also should be. This was a poser for some who had been very valiant until then.[20] Somehow, as I have very

19. While regiments were formed in the states, brigades, made up of two or more regiments, were organized within each army by its staff. New regiments joining an army were often attached to veteran units; thus, the 121st, formed in August 1862, joined with veteran regiments from New York, Pennsylvania, and Maine, many of which had been in service since May 1861. Phisterer, 1912, 1946, 2039, 2103.

20. Burkittsville, Md., is halfway between Frederick and Harpers Ferry, Va., at the foot of Crampton's Gap. *Atlas,* plate 27. "Poser" meaning dilemma.

frequently seen since, quite a number were taken violently ill and could not proceed any further; and others were so foot sore that to go another yard was beyond all human ability. However, we were *not* brought in, but were held as reserves while the rest of the Brigade did the fighting. This was well; for being under fire once, our men were better prepared for what was to follow.

Now for letters.

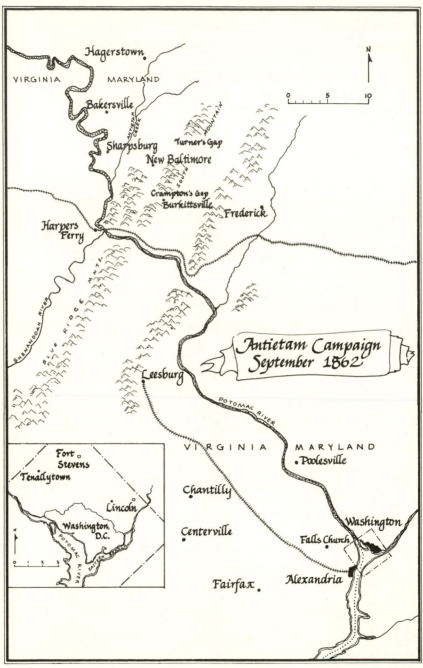

MAP BY MICAELA AYERS

ONE

Amid the din and turmoil of war

September 16, 1862 – November 7, 1862

The war had been going on for over a year before the 121st New York entered it. After the abortive attempt to end the war quickly ended in disaster in the First Battle of Bull Run in July 1861, the Federal forces at Washington had stood on the defensive while their new commander, Maj. Gen. George B. McClellan, organized and trained them, turning them into a first-quality field army, the Army of the Potomac. Having done so, McClellan was reluctant to risk his new army in battle. After much prodding from Lincoln and others, McClellan finally moved his army to the peninsula between the York and James rivers in Virginia in March, intending to attack Richmond from the east. Mistakenly believing himself to be heavily outnumbered by Gen. Joseph E. Johnston's Confederate Army of Northern Virginia, McClellan advanced at a snail's pace, taking two months to advance to the outskirts of the Confederate capital, and spending a third month sitting in front of the enemy's fortifications without attacking. While this was going on, Confederate Maj. Gen. Thomas J. "Stonewall" Jackson was driving superior Union forces from the Shenandoah Valley. In late June, Jackson brought his men back to the Richmond front and participated in the Seven Days' Battles (June 25–July 1), in which the Confederates under Gen. Robert E. Lee attacked McClellan repeatedly and drove his army all the way back to Harrison's Landing on the James. There it languished for the better part of two months, leaving Lee free to operate against Union Maj. Gen. John Pope's Army of Virginia, which was advancing on Richmond from the north. Pope quickly got himself into trouble, and his army was defeated at the Second Battle of Bull Run (August 29–30) before most of McClellan's men could be brought back to rescue it. Pope was quickly dismissed, his army merged into McClellan's, and McClellan once more set about the task of reorganizing and rallying a defeated and demoralized army. He had very little time in which to do this, however, since Lee quickly decided to

17

follow up on his victories and invade Maryland before the Union forces could recover, and by September 2 was moving large portions of his army across the Potomac.

The 121st New York entered the stage just at this point, arriving in Washington just in time to join in the campaign to drive Lee out of Maryland. Once across the Potomac, Lee boldly divided his forces to encircle the large Union garrison at Harpers Ferry, confident that McClellan would be too cautious to counterattack despite his overwhelming advantage in numbers. Lee would have been correct had not a copy of his marching orders fallen into Union hands. The prospect of defeating Lee's army in detail was too tempting for even McClellan to resist, and he immediately began to plan his response. On September 14, the leading Union columns struck the Confederate rearguards covering the passes through South Mountain. The main body of the Army of the Potomac forced its way through Turner's Gap, while the Sixth Corps, under Franklin, attacked at Crampton's Gap, with orders to try to relieve the Union forces surrounded at Harpers Ferry. The 121st was assigned to the Second Brigade of the First Division of the Sixth Corps, commanded by Col. Joseph J. Bartlett, and saw its first action that day.

Headquarters. 121st Regt. N.Y.
Vols. Crampton's Gap, Md.
September 16, 1862.

My dear Wife:—

When I last wrote you we were on the march, and so we are now. Yesterday morning we reached this place (on the crest of a mountain pass eight miles from Harpers Ferry, one from Burkittsville, and about four from Jefferson). The position was occupied after a brief but bloody conflict.[1] By nature, no site is better provided as a means of offense or defense than this. The enemy had planted upon its heights and in the gorge; a battery of Artillery and a large force of infantry occupied the sloping hill sides. From their position they were able to shell us at pleasure which they did, without our being able effectually to answer on account of their elevated position; and in order to join [Gen. Ambrose]

---

1. The Battle of Crampton's Gap was between 12,300 Union troops of the divisions of Major Generals Henry Slocum and William "Baldy" Smith and about 1,000 Confederates from Virginia and Georgia under Colonels William Parham and Thomas Munford, and Gen. Howell Cobb. Franklin, the overall Union commander, did not handle his forces effectively, letting Slocum's division do most of the fighting on its own and failing to pursue the Confederates aggressively once Slocum's men had beaten them. Sears, 145–49.

Burnside and [Gen. Edwin Vose] Sumner who were at Antietam four miles in advance, it was necessary to carry the gap and hold it, which was done in gallant style. General [Henry Warner] Slocum who commanded the Division and General [Joseph J.] Bartlett who commanded the Brigade, effected it in about three-fourths of an hour.[2] The 96th Pa. and 5th Maine were deployed as skirmishers *but failed to find the graybacks,* when General Slocum, who was sitting close by where I was lying, sprang into his saddle and calling upon his old regiment (the 27th N.Y.) soon gave notice that the ball had fairly opened. Column after column charged up the rocky declivity and the rattle of musketry which followed too plainly told that the Angel of Death was abroad in the land. In this engagement we lost 250 killed and the usual proportion of wounded. The loss of the enemy was much greater both in killed and wounded. The exact number on either side is not known owing to the consequent confusion and excitement attendant upon such a struggle. We have captured at least eight hundred prisoners and one gun which had been dealing death and destruction among our gallant boys.[3]

Battles have been raging in our front (South Mountain and Antietam) for four days past with favorable results on our side.[4] Burnside is said to have captured at least fifteen hundred rebels and others have done almost equally as well. To-day it is reported that the enemy have taken Harpers Ferry and that many of our men have been taken captive; which I hope is untrue; but supposing this is the case, we feel confident that Jackson and the rest of the rebel army will soon fall into our hands.[5] The most perfect confidence appears to be reposed in the officers

2. Burnside would command the Union army's left wing at Antietam; Sumner the Second Corps; Slocum the First Division, Fourth Corps. Colonel Bartlett continued to command the Second Brigade, First Division of the Sixth Corps; although Holt refers to him as "general" he did not make brigadier until Oct. 4, 1862. Ibid., 359–63; Boatner, 48.

3. Holt's estimate was incorrect. Federal losses were 113 killed, 418 wounded, 2 captured, with 400 Confederates taken prisoner. *OR*, vol. 19, 1:183.

4. The reference to Antietam is Holt's error. He was no doubt writing to his wife about action at Turner's Gap in South Mountain and Harpers Ferry on Sept. 14 and 15, respectively.

5. Gen. Thomas J. "Stonewall" Jackson had indeed captured Harpers Ferry on the 15th. Gen. Ambrose Powell Hill's division remained to disarm the prisoners and send off as much as possible of the enormous amount of captured supplies; Jackson joined General Lee at Antietam on the 16th. Lee summoned Hill from Harpers Ferry early on the 17th. The troops arrived less than eight hours later, after a forced march of seventeen miles, in time to push back Burnside's attack, the last Union offensive move of the day. Sears, 52–53, 195–96, 285–86.

commanding the army, and this alone is almost sure victory for us. Generals Slocum and Bartlett, under whose immediate control we are, are *gentlemen* as well as soldiers. Upon being complimented by Col. Franchot upon the brilliancy of the movement in carrying this mountain pass, General Slocum with true Christian patriotism replied, while tears filled his eyes, that his men made *him*—not he his men—that *he* directed—*they* executed. No vain glory did he covet or desire, but was willing and anxious that those who fought the battles and achieved the victory should reap the honor and applause. Such sentiments, and such expressions go far with the poor soldier. He intensely loves or hates his officers, and woe to the shoulder strapped biped who has not the good will of his men.

Louisa, I have seen what I never once expected I should see—a battle field—a field of blood and carnage—a field where brother met brother—where the closest ties of consanguinity and blood are forgotten. When the evil passions of men are let loose and hellish deeds of cruelty are perpetrated—where blind with rage and maddened with pain, men forget their God and die blasphemer. Oh! the terrible sight which met our eyes on the morning after that short and terrible conflict as we marched up those rugged steeps! (for we lay the night of the engagement on the South side of the mountain). First in the road, lay a dead horse, his federal rider having been killed and removed to the rear shortly after the engagement, then knapsacks, canteens, cartrage boxes and accoutrements of all kinds strewed the ground. Shortly a rebel with his brains blown out, arms extended, and eyes protruding from their sockets—still on, others in all manner of positions—some not yet dead but gasping the few remaining breaths away in utter unconsciousness of surrounding circumstances—others mortally wounded calling for water, knowing that eternity was separated only by a hair's breadth with thoughts of the far distant home in the South on their minds and the loved ones at home, clustering around his dying—*pillow*—did I say. ah no! mother earth to which he will soon be consigned is his only pillow now. Let his last gaze be upon the sweet forms which once bore him company and solaced every care. Let his ears no more be jarred by booming cannon and rattling small arms, but let the heavenly choir as he is about to enter the portals of the tomb, enchant his departing spirit. No more let vengeance follow our misguided brother now he is going where loyal men and rebels one are alike before a just and loving God. Surely this is no time to think of aught but mercy. Let not my passionate temper lead me to unfeeling hardships toward a fallen foe.

When we reached the crest of the mountain, we deployed to the right and left, and here we are waiting marching orders which may come at any moment or be delayed for some time. No one knows the moves upon the chess board of war but high officials or commandants of corps and divisions. To all else the changes are all a mystery and until the game is played we must be content to look on and conjecture.

Yesterday and to-day, I have passed pretty much over the whole field of battle. None but confederates were left upon the ground—our dead and wounded having been carried off during the evening and night of the conflict. Upon one spot, not larger than our house, I counted *fifteen* who had fallen in the deadly strife. Among them was an officer (Lieut. Col. Lamar of the famous Slaver *"Wanderer"* of whose course so much has lately been written) shot through the head with a minnie ball, taking off almost the entire portion of the skull.[6] His buttons, gold lace, &c. were speedily appropriated by our men as relics. I send you a small piece of lace taken by me from the coat sleeve. I cannot describe, neither can I [have you] realize what we have passed through. Hardly two weeks have elapsed since the regiment left home and here we are in the thickest of the fray, seeing and doing more than one half the regiments which went out over a year ago. It is indeed a strange and awful transition and I can scarcely realize it. To be thus transferred from scenes of quiet where the *effects* of war are not perceptable to these fields of slaughter and to become participants in the deadly contests is something which never, in the most extravagant flights of fancy can extend into my head. But this only shows how utterly oblivious the future lies before us, and how thin a veil separates it from us. Had any one told me a year ago that I could look upon such horrors and feel no mental disturbances, I should not have believed them. Yet so it is. I pass over the putrifying bodies of the dead (for they are yet not all buried, but will be by night) and feel as little unconcerned as though they were two hundred pigs. Their protruding bowels, glassy eyes, open mouths, ejecting blood and gases, the last wild expression of despair—the calm resignation of life affect me not. Whether I am indeed harder hearted or whether familiarity, ever so brief, with such scenes, tends to sear the

---

6. Charles L. A. Lamar, caught smuggling slaves from Africa to Georgia in 1858, tried to bribe witnesses against him when threatened by a Justice Department investigation. A Savannah jury returned indictments but later recanted, declaring the law against slave trading a tyrannical imposition by the North. Lamar was never tried, retrieved the *Wanderer,* and continued his heinous and profitable activities. Allan Nevins, *The Emergence of Lincoln: Douglas, Buchanan, and Party Chaos 1857–1859,* 435–37.

better feelings, I know not; but certain it is, that I slept as soundly last night in the open air, and I could almost say under the same blanket with a dead man, as I ever did.—This was no doubt due in a great measure to fatigue and exhaustion; as I was all day upon the field rendering such aid as was in my power to the wounded [who] were uncared for.

It is a hard thing, after all I have said to the contrary, to keep down the old Adam which rises within me.[7] The thought that all this has been brought upon us by brethren of the same faith and parentage as ourselves, and the issue of blood and carnage which overspreads the land is being caused by those who should have had a common interest and cause to maintain—when I see all this, and feel the unjust cruelty which they have remorselessly continued to perpetrate upon us, I feel that I cannot be too severe with them. While I know that it is improper for me to indulge in evil feelings and express so much wrath towards them, who are so closely connected to us by every tie of interest, the very knowledge of it intensifies the repugnance I bear towards them. They can plead no lack of information, and excuse themselves by no acts of oppression which the North have inflicted upon them. They have with open eyes entered into a conspiracy to break up and destroy our free institutions and entail slavery dark and eternal upon us. As a free, an enlightened and a christian people, we are bound to subdue this rebellion even though we wade through oceans of blood and empoverish the Nation. Our children, our wives and coming generations call upon us to guarantee to them the institutions which were reared and fostered by Washington, and those great lights of the Revolution, who are now sleeping the sleep which knows no waking but whose spirits inspire the hearts and nerve the arms of a people who know how to appreciate the blessings bequeathed to them. Indeed I have but little sympathy for them. This is perhaps wrong, but I cannot help having all the bitterness of my heart stirred up against them. When they tell me as I have been told by them, that they have stood up half an hour amid a shower of balls and not once fired their guns, and that for sixteen months they never have discharged their pieces at a Union man, I believe they lie and do not deserve, as surely they do not get, my respect or confidence. I can and do think better of a man who asserts his true

7. The "old Adam" is a biblical reference to the vengeful justice practiced by humanity in its depraved state prior to the arrival of the more forgiving Messiah, Jesus Christ.

sentiments under all circumstances, be they what they may, than the cringing puppy who eats his words and disowns his deeds when he happens to fall into the hands of the enemy.

I have done all the regimental duty to-day. The other Surgeons have been detailed for special duty in the hospital established at Burkittsville.[8] I expect them here to-night. A large number of our men have been detailed as nurses to take care of the wounded and also to serve as cooks and waiters. Among them is Cox and I think Huckans also.[9] I am sometimes almost famished for want of something to eat. We have no mess established as we had at Fort Lincoln, and have to depend upon sutlers or anything else to live. As we have no camp or cooking utensils, and no means of carrying provisions we are all the while upon short allowance and very often upon no allowance at all.[10] I went out to-day and bought a large gobbler but how I am to get him cooked I cannot tell. I suppose I shall have to let some of the men have it and go shares with them for a part of it. Were it not for peaches and tomatoes with an occasional onion to eat with my ginger cakes it would go hard enough I assure you. How many times I have wished that I could only be allowed to eat the crumbs which fall from your table. It makes no difference how coarse the fare if it comes at all. When others have been eating their dinners, cooked ever so

8. Regimental surgeons were detailed to temporary army field hospitals whenever major battles required such consolidation. Holt's description of the numbers of dead and wounded show just how difficult it was to get the wounded off the battlefield after such a massive engagement. By Antietam, Medical Director Letterman's reformed Ambulance Corps (with more .men, and better supplies and transport) was in place. But the Confederates destroyed the bridge over the Monocacy River at Frederick, delaying materiel brought in by rail. About eight thousand wounded had not yet been retrieved from the field twenty-four hours after the battle. Gillett, 157, 190–93.

9. James Cox, Co. C, 121st N.Y., served as a hospital cook; Thomas Huckans, also in Co. C, served as a hospital attendant until disabled in January 1863 with a double hernia. Attendants would be comparable to today's orderlies or licensed practical nurses. Nurses in the field were invariably men; Dorothea Dix and her contingent of female nurses were limited to hospital service with few exceptions. Pension and Service Records; Gillett, 155; Adams, 176–84; Ann Douglas Wood, "The War Within a War: Women Nurses in the Union Army," 197–212.

10. As a volunteer, Holt was outfitted by the county of Herkimer before he left New York. As a commissioned officer, he was not issued regular army rations but was given a cash allowance and expected to fend for himself, purchasing from the commissary. Many volunteers scavenged the countryside for food; others depended upon shipments from home; many purchased items from the ubiquitous traveling merchants called sutlers. See Bruce Catton, *Mr. Lincoln's Army*, 178–83; John D. Billings, *Hardtack and Coffee: The Unwritten Story of Army Life*.

meanly, I have stood and looked on and been ashamed to think that I with shoulder straps should fare so much worse than any of our men, for they are regularly served with government rations and good ones too, while I have to purchase the best I can and have no means of cooking it after it is purchased. I hope this will be different soon, or I am afraid I shall fall from grace and wish myself home again. Feed a man well and he will do almost anything, but starve him and you transform a kind temper to that of a beastly tyrant. I have been so hungry sometimes that I would have been willing to eat a dead mule if I could have got one.

At some subsequent time I may write more fully; but the conveniences we have for so doing are nothing. I have neither pen or paper, the supply which I brought from home being in my trunk at Fort Lincoln with all the rest of my baggage. It is said that we shall soon receive all we left behind, and I sincerely hope we shall for I begin to need a change of clothing and this cannot be done until I can get it out of the valise containing it. Our medical supplies are all gone and we feel the need of it terribly. We have not a *pound* of all—not enough to hold one surgeon's call with, and so we have been for several days past. It is hard work to get along so. Our men sicken and we have nothing to give them. They get fever and ague and they have to shake it out for all the good we can do them. They eat green apples and peaches and so are griped with colic, and they have to grunt it out in spite of what we can do. A great many of them are on the sick list with diarrhoeas and dysanteries, and so reduced that we have to get rid of them as soon as possible by sending them to hospitals. Many of them ought never to have come out, having broken constitutions or bodily defects which entirely disqualify them for the life of a soldier. Some, too, are very young—not able to carry the heavy loads necessary to be taken. They are good little fellows, full of patriotism and grit, but their little bodies are too small and delicate to endure the hardships of an active campaign. Then again we have *old* men—grandfathers without teeth—lame with rheumatism and *gout*!!! from high living in the army. *They* had better be at home thinking of death in any other shape than that of bullets. Deaf men, and men *who can talk and see too much* are here also with their aches and pains, and the worst of the whole lot. If you want to see all sorts and conditions of men, come into a regiment of raw recruits and you will be gratified. We have them all, but will get rid of a good share of them as soon as their discharge papers can be made out.[11] They have been a burden here and may be worth something at home. We should make a clean sweep soon.

I do not know as you can make this out, so imperfect are the letters and so poor the writing. I am sitting under the shade of a bush overlooking the most beautiful country I ever beheld; yet war has written in legible character its curse upon it. I will write no more of war matters at present. Other things are of importance to me. I stated to you in my last (if you were so fortunate as to receive it) that I could in no wise get along without a horse. This I have at last accomplished by purchasing of General Bartlett his mare which has passed through all the battles of the Potomac, carrying her rider through the most bloody conflicts of the war. She is a splendid beast—seven years old, dark bay, large size and perfectly calm amidst the greatest tumult. She has a minie ball now in her breast, and the mane is half gone by being cut off by a shell while the General was upon her back. A pretty close call for both horse and rider, I should judge. I purchased her for the sum of one hundred and ninety dollars. A saddle I obtained from a batteryman in the 2nd R.I. Battery[12] for six dollars; and a bridle of the Brigade Quarter Master for four dollars; so as you can see I am in for a snug little two hundred to be paid for when we are so fortunate as to get our pay. I had endured walking and heat long enough and even though I paid a large price for an animal I am persuaded it was not too much. I can now get along a little more comfortably. I can carry blankets and provisions and be something more like what I should be—a *mounted* officer. I will close this long and I fear in some respects, tedious letter by wishing you all the comfort and happiness of earth and the blessings of the Redeemer to be upon you. Love to all. Kiss the little ones for me and tell them to be good children.

Daniel.

The 121st New York did not arrive at Antietam in time to participate in the battle on September 17, but the sight of the battlefield shortly afterward and the

11. Throughout 1861, thousands of recruits in ill health or physical condition were allowed to join despite the army's best attempts to limit enrollment to those physically capable of standing the strain of war. Physical examinations of volunteers were made mandatory after August 1861, but examinations could be cursory or orders were ignored altogether. Gillett, 157–58.

12. There was no unit known as the Second R.I. Battery. Holt may have been referring to Battery B of the First R.I. Light Artillery Regiment, which had been at Turner's Gap on the 14th. Holt may have made his purchase prior to that date. *OR*, vol. 19, 1:174.

*knowledge of what had happened there had an effect on Holt. The following
letter concerns itself less with flag-waving and focuses more on the grim realities
of combat and the hardships that he and the men around him had to endure.
Several introductions are made in the following letter, the most important being
that of a twenty-three-year-old colonel, Emory Upton. One of the many "Boy
Generals," young men with military training who rose rapidly through the
ranks to fill vacancies created by casualties and cashierings among their superiors and by the expansion of the army itself, Upton attained a reputation as one
of the best combat commanders in the war and would make brigadier general at
the age of twenty-four. Holt also reveals his impression of his fellow surgeon in
the 121st, Stephen B. Valentine. A veritable thorn in Holt's side, Valentine,
whom Holt characterized as a drunken incompetent, will be the subject of many
an irate passage.*

In camp near Bakersville, Md.
September [25], 1862.[13]

My dear Wife:—

This is the *fifth* letter which I have written to you and as yet have not
heard a single word from home. When the mail arrives, which we expect
every hour, I hope to hear from you. The hours, days and weeks pass
heavily I assure you; and when almost every man in the regiment has
one and some two or three letters every delivery, I feel almost forgotten.
I have kept up courage and comfort in hoping, and still hope on.

When I last wrote we were at *Crampton's Gap* guarding the mountain
gap. Since that time we have moved further North driving the rebels
before us into Virginia; and they are now about three miles off. I attempted to give you a faint idea of the appearance of a field after battle
in my last, but it was as seeing faintly through a glass, to what I have
since beheld. No tongue can describe, nor pen write what I have seen
since then. After carrying the Gap a series of engagements ensued, resulting in the most sanguinary battles and destruction of life since the
war. Near Sharpsburg the fiercest contest took place. The booming of
cannon and the rattle of musketry was almost incessant for seven days
and nights. We could hear it and see almost all of it as it was in progress.

---

13. Holt misdated this letter as Sept. 28. Since the 121st arrived at Bakersville the "day
before yesterday"—the 23d—this was almost certainly written on the 25th. By then Lee
and his armies had withdrawn toward Shepherdstown and Martinsburg, Va., across the
Potomac River about ten miles distant. *OR*, vol. 19, 1:84–85; George B. McClellan,
McClellan's Own Story, 624–26.

At last, the Confederates under a flag of truce, asking the privilege to bury their dead, vacated their position and crossed the Potomac into Virginia where they now are. We ought to have utterly routed and destroyed their army had the effort been made, for they were completely discouraged and ready to accept any terms of capitulation or surrender had it been pressed upon them, but no! McClellan thought too much of them and let them off as they liked, into the precincts of their own state, thus giving them length of days and vitality of action which we had in our hands to withhold. It is sickening to see such parleying with rebels when we have the power to do differently. It looks almost like treason upon the part of our officers to let the bars down and tell them to get away as quickly as possible. I believe and shall ever believe, that General McClellan could have made his own terms with Lee at Antietam, but for some reason unexplained, the reverse was the case and instead of a decided brilliant victory and the end of the war, we have a doubtful victory and the enemy left to recruit at will and prolong the contest indefinitely. I am loosing all confidence and respect for McClellan—a man who a year ago I verily believed to be an agent of God to put down the rebellion in the shortest, cheapest and most approved manner. Well, I really feel sad and disgusted, and not only I but almost the entire army, for we all believed that we had the rebels in the tightest spot they ever were, and that it only required *pushing through* to complete the downfall of the confederacy. Three times we have moved expecting to follow up their retreat; and three times we have not done it.—that is, *no general engagement has taken place*—a little skirmishing and that is all.[14]

The rumor in camp now is, that we take a movement "by the right flank" and go to Hagerstown distant twelve miles. Of course I do not know as this is to be so. No one can place the least dependence upon the thousand and one idle rumors afloat among soldiers; but that we shall remain *inactive* is contrary to all past experience. Any moment we may be called upon to move. Three days halt is a long one for this division, as its commanders are active, working men. But I almost

14. Holt's sentiments regarding McClellan's "slows" were echoed in letters from soldiers dated as early as Sept. 19 and 23. To follow the Confederates and destroy them seemed commonsensical. This failure, more than any other, turned the foot soldiers against McClellan. Many of the soldiers would remain loyal to McClellan long after he was gone, but those men were mostly the ones who had been with the army when he had reorganized it in the fall of 1861 or in the late summer of 1862. Men such as Holt who had joined the army later were less likely to retain their faith in him. Sears, 313–14 n. 24.

forgot to tell you how the field of battle looked one week afterward, as the dead were almost wholly unburied, and the stench arising from it was such as to breed a pestilence in the regiment. We were ordered to bury the dead, collect arms, and accoutrements left upon the field and such other acts of cleaning up as is always necessary after an engagement. I have seen, stretched along, in one straight line, ready for interment, at least a thousand blackened, bloated corpses with blood and gas protruding from every orifice, and maggots holding high carnival over their heads. Such sights, such smells and such repulsive feelings as overcome one, are with difficulty described. Then add the scores upon scores of dead horses—sometimes whole batteries lying along side, still adding to the commingling mass of corruption and you have a faint, *very* faint idea of what you see, and can always see after a sanguinary battle. Every house, for miles around, is a hospital and I have seen arms, legs, feet and hands lying in piles rotting in the blazing heat of a Southern sky unburied and uncared for, and still the knife went steadily in its work adding to the putrid mess.[15]

As yet the 121st Regiment has had but little work for *Surgeons* as such, thank God; and I hope it will long continue although we have extracted balls, dressed wounds, and amputated perhaps a dozen limbs of those of other regiments and the secesh. It has been particularly hard upon me as Dr. Bassett has never been able to perform his duty; and consequently the weight and burden of the work has fallen upon his assistants. Day before yesterday he resigned; and yesterday Col. Richard Franchot also resigned, greatly to the relief of the regiment and a young man, (Capt. [Emory] Upton, of the *regular* army commanding a battery) was appointed in his stead.[16] So we move and so we go not knowing one day what another will bring forth; hoping and praying that soon this war will be ended and we shall see faces of loved ones once more.

15. Increasingly as the war went on, amputation was the standard treatment for any wound that broke bones into compound fractures, with the bone piercing the skin. To do otherwise, particularly in the incredibly unsanitary conditions at a battlefield hospital or station, would risk infection, gangrene, and would ultimately require more time, patient care, and work than the army could afford. Gillett, 279–86.

16. Franchot raised the volunteer regiment in August 1862; he resigned in September to return to the 37th Congress as a representative from Otsego County, N.Y. Upton moved from First Division Artillery to take command of the 121st and was promoted to colonel retroactive to Sept. 25, when Franchot's resignation went through. Upton did not actually assume command of the regiment until Oct. 23. *Biographical Directory of the American Congress, 1777–1989*, 1023; Boatner, 303, 595, 862; Phisterer, 3432.

My health, upon the whole, has been good—increasing as hard fare and active duty increased; but I have found that there is a limit to human endurance here as well as at home. Day before yesterday, when we arrived at our present encampment, I got in tired, hungry and almost overcome. Our regiment took line upon the bank of a small stream, on the edges of which grapes—large and luscious hung in great abundance. Parched with thirst and the stomach craving natural acids, induced me to partake (contrary to my knowledge of propriety) freely of them. I have, since that time, had difficulty with my bowels and am to-day almost entirely used up.

The nights are excessively cold here—frost for the last two nights being very perceptible upon the grass and herbage. Oh how cold and almost frozen I have been for a week past, sleeping in the open air with a blanket and the arch of heaven for a covering and the rough ground for a bed. It is very little like home. But upon the whole it agrees with me, and upon rising in the morning with the first faint streak of day in the East, with no fire to warm or shelter of any kind to cover you, one feels a peculiar sadness such as I never felt before. He feels, as he looks out upon the dusky forms of humanity stretched out in their blankets, beside their long lines of stacked arms, that even here, amid the din and turmoil of war, he is alone—alone as he is in the streets of a crowded city with its tens of thousands of human faces—none familiar—all strange—all alike—none caring or thinking of you—none to heave a sigh of pity or sympathy, ache the heart ever so acutely. But I stop. The mail has arrived; a soldier hands me a letter—from home?— yes, from home—sweet missive of love. It tells me I am not forgotten. Ah! I have *four*! instead of *one*—two from you and one from Gertrude and another from Eliza.[17]

Our men begin to show the effects of hard marching, imperfect clothing and deficency of camp comforts. As yet they sleep in the open air. A few brush and boughs thrown over a frame of poles is all they have for shelter. Our hospital is such a structure. When it rains, the water comes down upon the men just the same as if they were in open air. The consequence is, that sickness is greatly upon the increase. My duties necessarily become greater everyday. It has been hard enough

17. Gertrude Elizabeth Holt was Holt's eldest daughter by his first marriage. Born in Madison, Wisc., on July 12, 1842, she married Abram Fairchild on July 22, 1865, and died in 1918. Eliza's identity is unknown. Holt Papers.

here to fore, but now it requires in a [part?] exertion from morning till evening to get about. We have one hundred and fifty on the sick list, who are excused from duty, and probably double that number who come up in the morning at Surgeon's Call for temporary treatment. Unless a change takes place soon, deaths will be as frequent as the most cruel enemy could wish. We are lacking medicines. As I have already told you, we left behind everything which was calculated to relieve our men when disease got hold upon them. It requires a large amount to supply so large a demand, and I fear that we have only commenced to see trouble in this respect. There is a storm brewing in the Medical department of this regiment which when it breaks will cause somebody to leave for home. *I* cannot, and will not stand it to have a drunken tyrant lord it over me as Valentine does; and especially when he knows so little and stands so poorly both at home and here.[18] I did not come out to complain but to do my duty, and I intend to do it, but I will not allow so small a gun to kill me. *He* will be the man to leave— not me—just watch and see.

Generally speaking we are living better than now than two weeks ago. Five of us, consisting of us three Surgeons, Lieut. Keith of Company *"B"* and the Hospital Steward form a mess.[19] We have a black cook, and while in camp have three regular meals daily; but when on the march everything is changed.—Uncertainty attends every step. Sometimes we are permitted to get fuel where we please and at others, guards are established over everything, even to a straw stack. This depends upon the loyalty of the owners. If we go into Virginia, as I think we shall soon, free plunder is the word, but the country is already plundered, and the boys pray for anything but being sent into that desolate region again. We have been within eight miles of *Harpers Ferry* where we distinctly heard the uproar of the recent battles.[20] This part of Maryland is best of any over which we have passed. It resembles the Mohawk Valley in many particulars—its range of Mountains, pleasant vales and pure streams remind me of home; and were it not for the baneful curse of slavery

18. Stephen B. Valentine mustered in July 23, 1862, Holt on Aug. 27. Thus Valentine outranked Holt and apparently took full advantage of the month's superiority. Phisterer, 3438, 3433.

19. "Mess" meaning a group responsible for sharing meals and their preparation. Henry C. Keith mustered in as 1st lieutenant with Co. B, Aug. 13, 1862, and was discharged Jan. 28, 1863. Phisterer, 3434.

20. The reference is not to new action in the area, but to Harpers Ferry and Antietam.

which alike has polluted the Southern soil, I could make and enjoy a home here; but as it is, no freeman can feel like adopting in whole or in part any of the established rules which govern the peculiar institution.

If anything of importance takes place I will let you know. I am too young and green a soldier to give very correct information concerning coming events and will not try to attempt to tell what I do not know. As the mail goes out soon I will close by wishing you and the little ones good bye.

Daniel.

The difficulty of supplying medical needs was a constant problem throughout the war. On October 4, two days after Holt registered his complaints in this letter home, Jonathan Letterman, medical director of the Army of the Potomac, issued a circular to make it easier for brigades to replenish their supplies in the field and in camp. Each brigade was issued monthly a full hospital wagon; each regiment a full medical chest; each regimental officer a full hospital knapsack. The brigade surgeon kept informal track of supplies issued to officers under his command to speed up resupply and cut down on red tape.

Camp in field near
Bakersville, Md.
October 2, 1862

My dear Wife:—

Another welcome letter from home was received to-day. A thousand thanks for your kind remembrance. I thought I would write while I have a few moments leisure, not knowing when another opportunity may present itself. A few days ago I wrote you giving the general outlines of daily life, and what was true of yesterday is true also of to-day. At early dawn, we rise, wash and prepare to eat breakfast; that over, Surgeon's Call is sounded and from one hundred and fifty to two hundred patients present themselves for treatment. The time required to attend all this consumes two or three hours and then the *hospital* has to be visited and those sick in quarters:—that means, those who are too unwell to come up to call, but who are not sick enough to go into the barn which we have taken possession of for a hospital. We have to make from twenty-five to thirty of these calls daily, seeing that the medicines prescribed are faithfully given and that the condition of the men is comfortable, &c.— the diet of the sick in bed is also to be looked to—Sanitary condition of the camp must be attended to, and a general supervision of the health of the men made and reported. You may think that we have hardly time for all this, and indeed you think correctly, but it has to be done daily, and sometimes we have to see a patient several times a day. After all, the treatment the poor fellows have to accept is very little and sometimes I think amounts to almost nothing, but it is all we can give. I would have it different if I could, but my hands are tied in more ways than one. In the first place, we have but the merest apology for anything to help them with—no tents, no medicins, no clothing; and in the second place, a half drunken man [Valentine], being by date of commission— nothing else—my superior—*ranking* me as it is called; and this man who ought to co-operate with me in everything which should go to make our boys happier and more comfortable and contented, opposing every measure which I suggest for the amelioration of their condition. I some- times feel so depressed and desponding when I see how utterly futile all my efforts for their comfort are, and how little sympathetic action is vouchsafed me in their behalf by those who should be their guardians, that I feel like resigning my commission and coming home: but then I think they would perhaps fare worse and it is my duty to stay: and an- other feeling, too, prompts me to the latter course, and that is that I calculate that the greatest burden which I now bear will soon be re- moved from the situation which he now holds, and I shall be better treated in every respect. Colonel Upton is down upon him [Valentine] and I think from the general appearance of the man that when he sets his foot down upon a matter he intends to carry it out. So I live in hope. And then I might as well tell you here, too, while I am detailing griev- ances, that the Hospital Steward, Chatfield, is a man after Valentine's own heart; dishonest, sneaking, mean and *competent*.[21] He is a *good druggist* and that is all you can say of him. I do not know how he is at home; but here where he can get whisky and liquor of all kinds, like water in abundance, he is half the time unfit for duty and the other half so disagreeable in temper that it seems as if I really had got into a den of wild beasts or devils. We have plenty of company to help drink up the whisky which stands in pails and whatever can hold a gallon. From the Colonel of the regiment down to the officer's servants all stand ready to see that none of it is wasted. This one article is always sure of transporta-

21. Oscar F. Chatfield mustered in as private with Co. F on Aug. 23, 1862; he died while home on leave May 15, 1863. Phisterer, 3074; *Annual Report of the Adjutant General of the State of New York for the Year 1903*, 33.

tion let the other things go as they will. I think it would be hard to find much else than *empty bottles* after breaking camp, however much rice, beef and coffee may be left for want of means to carry it along.

Last night a man died of typhoid fever, and quite a number look as if they would soon follow. Poor fellows, when I see the way in which they lie and the lack of all earthly comforts—without wife, mother or sister to care for them or even to get a glass of cold water to cool their parched tongues, I wonder how any get well; but they appear to do about as well in the poor quarters which they occupy as those who are better cared for. I have been astonished at the *"vitativeness"* of the men— nothing seems capable of killing them. As to myself, I should be quite rugged were it not for a cough which I contracted by catching cold sleeping out nights in the cold air. I never in my life before saw such dews. They are like showers of rain; and this serves to keep the ground and grass moist all the while.

You ask me to give you special particulars about myself. This I have done at some length in former letters, which I hope you have received. Do not feel uneasy about me. I will take care of myself as well as I can and when I am unable to stand it longer, some kind hand I hope will provide for me: at any rate, I feel confident that He who has so gently dealt with me, will still continue to shield and protect me. I have firm and unshaken confidence in my Savior, and am happy to state that *all* religion is not lost in the army; for some here, as well as at home, cease not to pray. I expect to meet you again, but *when* I do not know. The Dispenser of all events only knows this, and I am willing to await his time and pleasure. It was a mournful satisfaction to learn that you had visited poor Father's grave. Oh! how I learned to love that dear old man. He sleeps, as you say, peacefully in his silent narrow house—no turmoil or battle din disturbs his quiet slumbers. In the resurrection morn we shall meet him—yes meet him—gone to his God fully ripe for the harvest. Let us try to imitate his noble example and live as pure and unspoiled a life as he lived. Poor Mother, must feel lonely enough. I pity and love the dear good soul and hope you will both be happy to- gether in our once happy home. I feel badly to think she has an idea of selling the old homestead but I do not know but it is for the best as you cannot go there.[22] Make the best of it and be contented and happy.

22. This passage refers to Louisa's father and mother. Charles Willard had died July 19, 1862. Willard and Walker, 289.

I know of nothing new or interesting to write, and I fear that you grow tired of reading so much matter with so little sense in it. You will of course have very much to do this fall in preparing for winter, but I hope you will be able to get along with it. I am sorry to have you so sorely perplexed as I feel you will be, but try to think that it is "only for a season," and that we shall soon meet again under more favorable circumstances. God bless you, dear wife. Keep up courage and believe that I feel a lively interest in all that concerns you and the little ones, and that my heart goes constantly out towards you. Until I write again, good bye. Give respects to all enquiring friends.

Daniel.

Camp in field near
Bakersville, Md.
October 15, 1862

My dear Wife:—

I have received two letters from you since I last wrote you and should have sooner answered had I time. You cannot imagine the amount of labor I have to perform. As an instance of what almost daily occurs, I will give you an account of day-before-yesterday's duty. At early dawn, while you were, I hope, quietly sleeping, I was up at Surgeon's Call and before breakfast prescribed for eighty-six patients at the door of my tent. After meal I visited the hospitals and a barn where our sick are lying, and dealt medicines and write prescriptions for one hundred more; in all visited and prescribed for, one hundred and eighty-six men. I had no dinner. At four o'clock this labor was completed and a cold bite was eaten. After this, in the rain, I started for Sharpsburg, four miles distant, for medical supplies from the Medical Purveyor at that place; but when about half way there, I met Dr. Barnes, of the 27th N.Y. returning, from there, who informed me that the department had left there for other quarters: and that the New York Sanitary Commission also located there, would dispense no supplies on a Sunday.[23] Our stock

23. Dr. Norman S. Barnes, an 1852 graduate of Berkshire College, was thirty-five years old when he enrolled in Elmira, N.Y., as surgeon in the 27th N.Y., Second Brigade, First Division, Sixth Corps. He was mustered out May 31, 1863. The Sanitary Commission, a civilian organization formed in the spring of 1861, provided medical supplies, doctors, donations, and other sorts of aid to the army in both field and hospitals. While civilian concerns such as regarding the Sabbath could render the commission's aid less than useful, overall, the Sanitary Commission and its counterparts, the Western Sanitary

of provisions having become almost exhausted, I determined to try and replenish if possible, and so turned my horses head towards Fairplay where I had previously been fortunate enough to obtain some. After dark I reached the house of my old friend who appeared to be glad to see me; and of him I purchased a bushel of potatoes, six chickens a loaf of bread, some onions, a bottle of vinegar and started for home.

The old man tried to persuade me that I had better stay until morning, alleging that the night was dark and that I would be very apt to lose my way, but having no leave of absence, and knowing that I could not be spared, we started for home. I say *we* for our Hospital Steward was with me to help in bringing in whatever I might get. We got along pretty well for about a quarter of a mile, when owing to the darkness and not well knowing the way, my horse took the wrong road and at last brought us up to a farm house "after diverse circuitous routes" through woods, corn fields, wheat fields, &c. Of the man of the house we made inquiries as to our way, who informed us, to our extreme mortification, that we were farther from camp than when we left our friends house. Up a lane for a mile—through gates and over fences we travelled until we came upon the Hagerstown Pike two miles from where we first crossed it just at dark. Having got along as far as Fairplay, we took another lane which took us out upon the road leading to Bakersville, along which we jogged for about a quarter of a mile, when we were suddenly brought up by Cavalry Videttes stationed along the road. The order was halt!! ["]Who comes there? One man dismount and advance!! Have you the countersign? What brigade do you belong to? What division?" After satisfactory explanation upon our parts, and the vidette going with us some distance, we were permitted to advance again to be halted as before. This was repeated *four* times when we were at last able to reach camp about 11 o'clock, cold, wet and tired. My green sash saved me a journey to Harpers Ferry or some other place to give an account of myself before the proper tribunal, but when they saw it, I was not long after detained.[24] After depositing chickens, &c., I was not long in crawling into my nest of straw, to be called at three o'clock to hospital to see Lieutenant [George W.] Davis die, but he is not yet

Commission and the Christian Commission, were invaluable. Willard, 5; Phisterer, 2036, 2039–40; Gillett, 160–62; William Quentin Maxwell, *Lincoln's Fifth Wheel: The Political History of the United States Sanitary Commission.*

24. Holt's reference to a green sash refers to the distinctive color used by the medical men. Billings, 348–49.

dead, although there is no hope in his case.[25] Typhoid will use him up, poor fellow, as many others who are lying near him. Next morning the same routine was to be gone over, except the night adventure and so the ball rolls on. You may ask *why* I had to do so much? It was because Valentine was sick, and I was the only man in the regiment able to do the duty. He is better now and able to do a little. I hope he will soon report as fit to do his share of work. I hate to *guess* or *insinuate* what is the matter of a man, but I cannot help thinking that if the whisky bottle had not been quite so near the head of his bed he would have been well to-day.

I do not know as I ever told you that we have new shelter tents for the men. They are better than nothing, yet not so good as those for winter quarters. Every man carries his own and at night, when they are all lighted, they present a lively and cheerful appearance. To see ten or fifteen thousand men encamped at night with their camp fires, and hear their music and singing, is no small affair, yet one soon becomes used to it and thinks but little about it. Good health and plenty to eat makes a man satisfied; but when you are poorly rationed with half rations, and more dead than alive through sickness, no wonder a person gets the blues, and longs for home sweet home. My health is better than a week ago, and spirits good. All I hope and care for is that we may have a general fight soon, and decide this dragging bloody war. If I or anyone else is to die here, the sooner the better. I hate this inactivity. I had rather be on the march day after day and fight every week than lie as we do. Most of the brigades comprising this (6th) Army Corps, have left and gone no one knows where: but we shall follow soon,[26] I have no doubt although we must guard the ford over the river until the water gets too high for crossing. I have been on picket duty since I last wrote you. I returned to camp sooner than the rest, bringing with me a wounded soldier from the town of Stratford by the name of Jacob Prame. The manner of the accident (for such it was) was by having his hand over the muzzle of his gun when by some

25. Davis died five days later on Oct. 20, 1862. He had been in service only since July. Poor sanitation and exposure to childhood diseases such as measles killed a substantial proportion of soldiers, particularly in the first two years of the war, before sanitation practices became more hygienic and more regularly enforced. Phisterer, 3431; Adams, 194–99; Gillett, 158; Freemon, 6.

26. The Sixth Army Corps was moving toward the Potomac River ford at Berlin and accomplished its move between Oct. 26 and Nov. 2. McClellan, 644.

outlandish kick he exploded the cap and the contents of the gun passed through his hand causing amputation. This was done above the wrist. It comes hard upon him as he is a poor man with a wife and two children; and the wound appears to have been through sheer careless- ness. Several such have taken place in our regiment already. We are scarcely called upon to go out on picket without someone coming in hurt more or less by carelessly handling their pieces. It is strange that men have not yet learned that Enfield rifles were made to kill people with instead of being playthings.[27]

I close my eyes—all seems like a dream. Am I here—far, far away from home and loved ones—from the sight of my native hills—from the sparkling waters and gushing fountains—its flowing streams—its holy Sabbaths—days of rest and calm repose, upon the field of carnage and hostile encounter. I cannot realize it although the clatter of arms, the report of cannon, and tramp of almost countless thousands tell but too truly that I have left them all behind. Only when I look at *myself* do I fully realize that such is the case. Nothing upon or about me indicates a civilian. Everything is warlike:—guns, swords, bayonets, flags, drums, tents and indeed all the eye rests upon is unlike home. I am at this time sitting upon a canister of black tea, with a surgical case upon my lap for a table, writing this amid almost momentary interruption. Someone comes for an excuse from duty—another for relief from guard—another does not feel well enough to attend battalion drill— still another prays for excuse from dress parade, and others still want their discharge papers made out and they sent home. This is all compe- tent[28] for the Surgeon, and these calls are as frequent as every few moments in the day. The men soon learn where to go. Dr. Valentine swears at them and sends them away. I do not so.—Although I hate the annoyance as much as he does, yet I cannot say to a sick man, or even to one who is not so violently indisposed, "return to your quarters, and do your duty or go into the guard house," when I know that he is willing to do all that is reasonably required of him. Since writing the

27. No information on Jacob Prame was found. Over 500,000 Enfield rifles were im- ported from England in the early part of the war. Popular on both sides, they were highly accurate to 800 yards, fairly accurate to 1,200. The large bullets and powerful discharge of the Enfields did such damage to human flesh and bone that amputation of the dam- aged area was common to save the life of the casualty. Boatner, 266; William B. Edwards, *Civil War Guns*, 87; Catton, *Mr. Lincoln's Army*, 186–89.

28. "Competent" meaning properly belonging to.

last word, a man has come and wants me to get him out of the guard house, he having been put there because I had not excused him from camp duty at the Surgeon's call in the morning. It appears that he was feeling too unwell to report himself sick in the morning and the sergeant not having his name among the excused, caused him to be arrested and put under guard. Learning these facts, I soon released him and again resume my writing.

Supper is almost ready. We have concluded to try *two* meals instead of *three* these short days. Our supper at 5 o'clock after battalion drills, and our breakfast *after* Surgeon's Call at 7½ A.M. It seems like a long time to wait for something to eat, but as for me, you know I have always been irregular in my diet and [this] comes like a second nature. Thinking of nothing more to write I will close by saying good bye again to you and the babies.

Daniel.

The Battle of Antietam was the single bloodiest day of the Civil War, with casualties of twenty-five thousand men. Exhausted by their efforts, the Army of the Potomac stayed in Maryland after the battle instead of following Lee into Virginia. But exhaustion changed to inertia, and McClellan's immobility tried President Abraham Lincoln's patience to its limits. The army did not move until October 30, when it slowly set out after Lee. In the meantime, Lincoln had issued the Preliminary Emancipation Proclamation. The proclamation more clearly defined the war as one to end slavery, and Holt agreed that abolition was essential to preventing a future war.

> Camp in field in the Sacred Soil
> of Virginia, Sunday evening
> [November] 2, 1862

My dear Wife:—

I write this short and hasty letter to inform you that we have again changed quarters and are now [on] the Sacred Soil of the old Dominion. We left our camp at Bakersville three days ago, and arrived here not more than two hours since. For several days previous to our leaving (we were the last division which left) the Army moved off in detachments, almost all leaving in the rain, presenting an appearance gloomy enough. With roads full of mud and water, and sleet and storm steadily pouring down upon the heads of the men, it was with no pleasant feelings I anticipated our own departure when it should be ordered.

However, when it did come, we moved off in pleasant weather, and have had it thus far, with prospects of its continuance.[29]

I did not move when the regiment went, but had to remain behind to see about an hundred of our sick (who we had conveyed to a church about two miles distant), properly cared for and disposed of. Valentine followed the column taking with him Chatfield, the Hospital Steward, and leaving me with "glass eyed Tommy Bentley" (so named because of his wearing spectacles) and about five or six others to nurse and cook for the disabled. The church which we occupied was a neat, pretty little structure, sufficient to accommodate (when the slips were taken up and bunks arranged instead) about the number we had (some 125).[30] The medical Director of the Division sent word for me to get a certain number ready by noon, which I was doing, when a train of ambulances came, sufficient, it looked to me, to transport all the sick of the army; and *we filled every one* and then some of them were uncomfortably crowded. Instead of a *part,* all went, and left me all alone except the nurses. I can tell you how it is, I *was* lonely once in my life, then if I never was before. All the army gone—sick—everything left—camps deserted and the stillness of a desert riegning over all. How to dispose of the great quantities of provisions on hand—camp kettles, clothing &c. to the best advantage I did not know. The secesh came in carts and wagons to carry it away, well knowing that I had no means of transportation. At least four or five hundred dollars worth of cotton goods such as sheets, pillow cases, ticks, shelter tents &c. dressing gowns, towels, slippers and many other articles, with pork, rice, corned beef, sugar, coffee, tea, dessicated vegetables &c., &c., &c.[31] I found a loyal man

29. A letter briefly describing skirmishing at Williamsport has been omitted. The move Holt describes came when McClellan decided he would advance on Richmond by way of either Fredericksburg or the Peninsula. McClellan was responding to substantial political pressure to pursue the enemy but moved too slowly to do any good. Lincoln would relieve him of command on Nov. 7, concerned not only about McClellan's inertia, which let the Confederate army get away, but also about his growing political appeal to those disaffected by Federal policy. Secretary of War Edwin Stanton, among others, worried about a possible coup d'etat, particularly after the Preliminary Emancipation Proclamation was issued and after McClellan was removed from command. McClellan, 645–46; Sears, 319–20, 336–39; McPherson, *Battle Cry,* 559–60, 569–70.

30. "Slips" meaning pews. Thomas H. Bentley mustered in as a private in Co. E, Aug. 23, 1862. He was promoted to hospital steward June 19, 1863, and served through the end of the war. *Annual Report,* 71.

31. Dessicated or dried vegetables, an innovation of army rations, were heartily despised by the troops. Billings, 141–42; Adams, 17.

from New York by the name of [blank] who was taking care of his sick son and Lieutenant Weaver, at a house near by the hospital, and to him I sold the whole thing for *twenty-five dollars—cash in hand paid!* Which sum I put into my pocket and shall appropriate to my own use, feeling no compunctions of conscience because of it: for the rebs stole my pocket book a day or two ago containing all my money and *teeth* beside.

When we were fairly ready for a move, the nurses took up the line of march and followed the army which was two days in advance of them:— I stopping at the head quarters of the Ambulance Department and staid over night with Capt. Robinson. In the morning, after sunrise all things having been prepared the night before, we packed up and took the pike going as fast and as direct as possible to Berlin[32] where we crossed the Potomac and in a short time came to the encampment of our men upon the Sacred Soil. On our way here we passed through Crampton's Gap and over the battlefield of Antietam. Sad reflections followed, and the same scenes and sounds appeared to come over me as upon the days when the ground was covered with dead and dying and the air filled with the putrid vapor arising from the decomposing bodies of men and horses. I do not know but I am wrong, but I cannot help feeling that the sooner this rebellion is put down the better. *Blood must flow* to a greater or less extent before it is ended, and I can see no difference whether now or at some subsequent time. My sincere, but perhaps foolish prayer is, that the next battle may decide a war which has already lasted too long. It is my firm belief that a year ago this dragging slaughter might have been ended had we shown equal energy as the rebels in prosecuting the war. I was forcibly struck with the remark of a Colonel commanding a regiment of foreigners the other day. He had been in service almost all his days in different countries—more especially his own—Prussia, and in answer to a question of mine, "how long he thought the war would last?" he very candidly and unassumingly replied that he did not think we could look for it under *five* years—that history gave no account [of] a civil war ending in less time. Too many interests are at work to perpetuate it:—heavy contracts to be filled, and the contractors growing rich out of them—government officials interested in supplying clothing, food and arms to the army —jealousies among officers—one not being willing to aid or support

32. Berlin is today Brunswick, Md., about six miles east of Harpers Ferry near the Potomac River.

the other for fear that his own reputation would suffer by advancing another—personal ambition—those who wear *one bar* wanting two—those with a leaf desiring an eagle, and those with an eagle looking for a *star:* and those of *one* star striving to obtain two and three. These are powerful incentives for protracting a conflict where so many different interests are at stake and so many different persons to satisfy.

It is generally supposed that we shall have a regular pitch fight before long. If so let it come. All I have to wish is that victory may be ours and that it may end the war. I do not desire to fight for the sake of the thing, but for the sake of closing an affair which has already lasted too long. No one desires to be at home more than I; but I am willing to remain here until my hairs are whiter than they are now and live harder and closer than I have ever done before, sooner than to wind up a job in such a manner as to require its being done over again in a few years which surely will be the case unless slavery is abolished and the Negro placed upon a basis which God designed all men to live upon—the basis of freedom and equal rights. These must be secured to them or in a few years we shall have the same bloody conflicts to go through with and the same legislative oppression to endure. Then God hasten the day of universal freedom when all the nations of the earth shall be equal before the law and bound with the hands of brotherly love.

When we are a little more settled I will write again, all the while recommending you and the little ones to the giver of every free and perfect gift, in the hope that we shall soon meet again under different and happier circumstances.

Daniel.

Camp in field near Bull Run
and on our way through
Thoroughfare Gap, Va.
November 7, 1862

My dear Wife:—

We are encamped for a few hours near the classic ground of Bull Run, and not knowing how snugly the bulls may press us at this point, I have determined to address a few lines to you. Your last letter was characteristic of yourself—full of kindness and breathing the spirit of true devotion. You do not know how much good a letter from home does me in these inhospitable regions, for such they emphatically are. You can purchase nothing even for greenbacks or gold. The whole face of the country bears the unmistakable evidence of war. Hardly a fence is standing, and the country through which we have passed for the last two or three days, resembles the Western prairies in many particulars. Large fires sweep over the meadows and woodlands, and the smoke of the burning stacks, fences, and in some instances, dwellings, I fear, fills the air with the peculiar smell of the Western country at this season of the year. Our march since we have been on this side of the river, has been constant, though not hard, averaging from twelve to fifteen miles a day. Yesterday we marched about 17 miles and encamped upon the belt of a piece of timber near a small water course,[33] where were it not for *guards,* forage for the horses might easily be attained: but as it is, our poor horses *look* and *starve,* while wheat, corn and oats are within a stone's throw of them. I am sick and tired of guarding the property of rebels; and why our men should be compelled to guard and respect anything belonging to them, is a mystery hard to solve by those who have left comfortable homes and happy firesides to endure the hardships of a soldier's life. Although strict orders have been given to the contrary, our men *do* and *will* steal from them, and I honor their judgment in so doing. Last night a man in our regiment came up to me and asked me if I was fond of apples? "Yes," of course was the answer, and he filled my pockets full of them, obtained, as he said *from one of his particular friends in a large stone house about a mile off.* He wanted a pass to visit him again in the night, asserting that he had given him a pressing invitation to do so. He went, and about twelve o'clock I was agreeably surprised to find my tent supplied with honey, fowls, &c. I shall suggest to him to visit his friend again to-night if we remain here as it appears from present indications we shall.

We have had no [bread] for several days—none in the country to be obtained. The weather is growing cold—colder—coldest! and I suffer from it past all telling. You know that I am naturally rather cold blooded; and to get up at five o'clock in the morning, eat breakfast, pack up all the duds and be off at eight, and not halt again until night except to rest the troops, wears upon a man however tough by nature he may be. You hear of people getting used to cold and sleeping upon the ground, and so they do, but I can tell you many die in toughening; and I do not believe I can ever get used to it, so as to prefer it to a good comfortable bed in a good comfortable house.

33. "Belt of a piece of timber" meaning a strip of trees near a stream.

To-day is the first day of *snow* with us, although frost and ice have been frequently seen. Since I last wrote you I have been to Harpers Ferry to convoy about eighty of our men to hospital. So you can see we are losing our men pretty fast. Only a few days since I sent one hundred to Hagerstown, and now eighty more to Harpers Ferry—in all one hundred and eighty. At this rate it will not take long to send them all off. The cause of such unprecedented sickness is the rawness of the regiment—the season of the year and above all the hardships which they have undergone. The army did not go the route I took, and perhaps I have seen what most of our men will not see—the ground upon which poor old John Brown made such a gallant and yet so unfortunate a stand against slavery.[34] The bridges over the Potomac and Shenandoah were, as you know, destroyed by the rebs and the crossing is effected by pontoon bridges. I think of all the places I ever saw, this is by nature the most sublime and romantic. Sweeping down the Valley these rivers break through mountain passes and unite to form one of the most lovely and enchanting streams the eye of man ever rested upon. All through this region the diversity of scenery is soul-inspiring, and were it not that war has rendered desolate this heaven favored region I should be willing to "live and die in Dixie." As it is, however, I have no desire to remain, and had much rather join my wife and family in the green hills of the happy North. I fear that many months will intervene e'er we shall be gladdened by the welcome news that our services are no longer required and that we may depart, never again to engage in the arts of scientifically or barbarously taking the lives of our fellow men. Although we have moving in one solid phalanx at least three hundred thousand men—enough it would seem, to eat the entire rebel army at one meal.—As we advance they retreat and continue to do so, and no doubt will unless some unforseen circumstance induces them to make a stand and give us battle.[35] The Lord incline their hearts to fight, and the Lord give us the victory, is my most earnest and sincere prayer.

34. John Brown led a raid on the Federal arsenal at Harpers Ferry in 1859 in an abortive attempt at a slave rebellion.

35. The *OR* lists the Union army's strength on Nov. 1, 1862, as 190,000 men, but admits to a likely overestimation by quartermasters. Actual strength at Fredericksburg in December was 120,000. Despite his exaggeration, Holt's assessment of the overwhelming numerical superiority of the Union army over its opponents was correct. *OR,* vol. 19, 1:97–98, and vol. 21, 1:90.

It is growing somewhat late in the season, and we shall have to think of going into winter quarters soon; not so much on account of *cold* weather, but on account of *mud!* no army can move when bound by two or three feet depth of mud. Heavy trains and artillery can no [more] move through it than a man can wade a river without getting wet. But I must close. As ever I think of you and pray for you.

Daniel.

TWO

The heart only knows
the miseries which our men endure

November 20, 1862 – January 27, 1863

O*n November 7, 1862, Gen. Ambrose E. Burnside replaced George McClellan as commander of the Army of the Potomac. Burnside regrouped the army into three "Grand Divisions," each consisting of two army corps. The Sixth Corps was part of the Left Grand Division, now commanded by Gen. William B. Franklin, who turned over command of the Sixth Corps to Gen. William F. "Baldy" Smith. Burnside's plan was to shift his army southeast from the Warrenton area to Fredericksburg, cross the Rappahannock River there, and force Lee to abandon most of northern Virginia to cover the Confederate capital of Richmond.*

The movement of the 121st that Holt discusses in this letter reflected Burnside's strategy. He wanted to move into the Tidewater area of Virginia where he could be more easily supplied by water routes, where he could bring the war closer to Richmond, and where he could draw Lee out into a battle. During the move, however, he got only as far as Fredericksburg, where he refused to cross the river until the pontoon bridges showed up, a week later. In the meantime, Lee arrived with his seventy-five thousand troops and dug in.

Camp in field near Stafford
Court House
November 20, 1862.

My dear Wife:—

I address you again from this point, having brought up here last night and encamped for the day. We have made several moves since the 7th, at which time we were lying at or near Bull Run. On the 10th we were about four miles from Thoroughfare Gap where we remained but

45

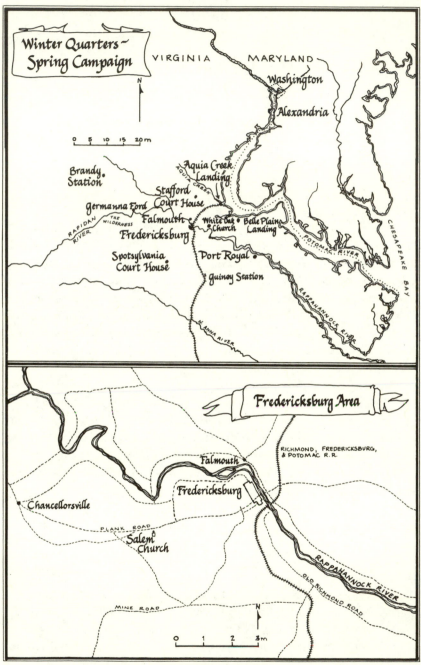

MAP BY MICAELA AYERS

a day or two and on the 15th brought up at New Baltimore.[1] No particular incidents worth relating have transpired, only that *cold* weather may be said to have fairly set in. Ice forms half an inch thick at night, and during the day when the sun shines, it all disappears again. For three days we have had seven storms of sleet and snow, and as we are not prepared for winter, it is anything but pleasant "camping it."

Unused as I am to such *open comforts,* I have suffered greatly from cold since the change in the weather. There is an awful sight of difference between a warm bed to lie in and the frozen ground on which to stretch your tired and aching body. No *pecuniary* consideration seems sufficient to pay up for loss of health and comfort of person which are almost sure to follow the life of a soldier. Were it not that *duty* calls me here I think I should not remain for pleasure or comfort. There is a certain amount of privation and all that goes to make up the disagreeable hardships and dangers of war to be endured, and I for one am willing to take my share. *Anything* which tends to shorten and put down this conflict I am in favor of employing. When the Government wakes up to its true interests to employ their natural allies, the Negroes, to fight their own battles it will be a happy and noble moment in our history. I never yet saw a disloyal black, and why they should be distrusted and kept back from fighting for their freedom now, as it is evident to my mind that total and complete emancipation must result from this outbreak, is an enigma more profound than any I have ever attempted to solve.[2] Surely the *people* must move in the matter or Congress never will. Please excuse me for running off as I so often do, from the main point, and serving up for you a dish of my own cooking. I should not be myself were it different.

1. New Baltimore was two miles southwest of Turner's Gap on the Warrenton Turnpike. The 121st then moved southeast to Stafford Court House, about seven miles northeast of Fredericksburg and Falmouth, Va. *Atlas,* plates 7, 8.

2. The decision whether to use black troops plagued the Union throughout the early years of the war. Blacks were more than willing to participate; in April 1861, Secretary of War Simon Cameron received a letter from one Jacob Dodson, offering to form a unit of black soldiers. Cameron refused. Although the Militia Act, passed in July 1862, gave Lincoln the authority to recruit black troops, the president would not support the idea wholeheartedly, fearing the border states would turn against the Union. The first official regiments were organized in Massachusetts in early 1863. Holt supported the use of black soldiers in principle fairly early on; in practice, he approved of their skills when he saw them in action late in the war. His own racism prevented his viewing blacks as social equals, however, a position characteristic of most Americans and many soldiers of the period. *OR,* vol. 3, 1:133; McPherson, *Battle Cry,* 564–65.

It is raining hard, with lightning and thunder in full chorus. Since leaving our last encampment, near New Baltimore, our march has been hard, over the roughest roads I almost ever saw, although the face of the country has been one of unsurpassable loveliness and beauty. No repairs have been made upon them since the war, but obstructions placed by both armies on their retreat, are of frequent occurrance. Baggage trains, which should keep near the column as it moves, are so delayed that they do not arrive until late at night, and perhaps not until morning. In passing over Aquia Creek night before last [November 18], the road was literally filled up with broken down wagons and supplies of all kinds. One would suppose, from the confusion and excited state of Artillery, Cavalry, Ordnance and all other moving masses that another Bull Run affair had taken place, and every man was seeking his own individual protection in his own way.

I am sometimes placed by the Division Surgeon, with an Ambulance train; at others, to see to, and control the conveyance of patients to hospital, and sometimes assigned to other duty. Diversity is the order of the day, and were it not that we are expecting the rainy season to set in every day, I should rather enjoy this sort of Gipsey life. To be sure, you often go to bed hungry and cold, and rise in the morning worse than a foundered horse, yet there is a sort of fascination about it, that compels a man on despite the hardships.

Dr. Walker has at length arrived here in partial health and pretty good spirits.[3] I was happy to see him and no mistake; for I had brought up my mind to resign unless a change had taken place in our department. I had become thoroughly disgusted with the way in which things were conducted: and under no circumstances would I have remained to have Valentine lord it over me. If I am to be *commanded*, I desire a commander who is competent or one who I can feel is my equal. This I never felt or thought of Dr. V. I do not feel like rejoicing over a fallen foe but I am the happiest man alive to see the airs taken out of him and

3. Edward S. Walker received his medical degree from New York University and established a practice at Brockett's Bridge (now Dolgeville), N.Y. When the war began, he offered his services to the first Herkimer County regiment, the 34th N.Y., to which he served as an assistant surgeon. He was promoted to surgeon of the 121st on Oct. 22, 1862. In poor health for much of his tenure with the 121st, Walker resigned six months after his arrival and served as examining surgeon of the Board of Enrollment for the duration of the war. He returned to private practice in Ilion, N.Y., until his death on July 12, 1876. Lt. L. N. Chapin, *A Brief History of the Thirty Fourth Regiment N.Y.S.V.*, 109.

he put where he belongs.[4] Let him now seek the quiet retreat of his old quarters on the Mohawk, where its murmurs will I hope so tranquilize his mind as to enable him to think of his meanness and villainies which were committed here in the army under cover and by sanction of the straps which he so disgracefully wore as an officer of the government. I am as willing as any man to do my duty, but to be made the Scavenger of a department by *such* a man as this, whose only superiority is by *date of commission,* is more than my petulant and proud nature will allow.

As you see from this, we are steadily moving South toward Richmond, distant from here about fifty miles. We are within six miles of Fredericksburg, one and a half from Stafford Court House, and about the same from the Potomac. The names are all familiar, and we are on fighting ground. At Catlett's Station, on the Orange and Alexandria Rail Road, which we crossed on our way here, General [John] Pope, as you recollect had to leave in double quick; the rebs obtaining not only all his private papers but the whole programme of the campaign; thus rendering a new plan necessary. Here also the signals, with a key to their meaning was lost, and the Union Army was disgracefully outgeneraled.[5] It is interesting to travel over this region, on very many accounts—not the least of which is its identity with the stirring events of the rebellion, but here General Washington in person surveyed the movements and planned operations against the English in the days of the Revolution; and not far from here repose the ashes of his body on the quiet banks of the stream just before us. I should like much to live here, but years will elapse 'ere the inhabitants cease to curse the *"Yankee"*—that nondescript biped to whom they ascribe all the ills which ever beset them.

I cannot comprehend these "flank movements"—first by the right—then by the left and then again by direct front; and sometimes the general direction is changed altogether. The army is moving in three

4. As Holt's superior, Valentine had been in charge since the departure of Dr. Bassett on Sept. 30.

5. Pope had numerous problems at Second Bull Run the previous August, most of which were caused by Jackson getting behind him and arriving at Manassas Junction before Pope was able to concentrate his scattered forces. Jackson's position cut Pope's communication line with Washington and put him largely in the dark regarding the disposition of his forces; as more troops arrived from several directions, his difficulties were compounded. To make matters worse, Confederate cavalry had captured Pope's headquarters, resulting in the intelligence bonanza to which Holt refers. *B&L,* 2:466–67; Boatner, 102.

grand divisions or columns;—the right under General Sumner—the center under General [Joseph T.] Hooker and the left (ours) under Gen. Smith.[6] We are trying to go somewhere—I don't know where—but inasmuch as we have pretty generally pursued a due South course since breaking camp at Bakersville [Maryland], crossing into Virginia at Berlin, and as cannonading has always been on our front and to the South, I suppose it is intended to make Richmond head quarters for the army this winter; at least I *hope* so.[7]

Our regiment is growing less and less every day from a variety of causes;—First, *sickness* has thinned the regiment very much. We have in hospitals at Hagerstown, Alexandria and other places, nearly one hundred and fifty; and desertions are also frequent.—Over *fifty* have taken French leave, without waiting to say "good bye" to the Colonel, or even to call upon their Surgeon to ascertain whether he thought it would be *healthy* for them to leave this cold weather without purse or script.[8] *Resignations* are frequent. Some companies are commanded by non-commissioned officers and some by Second Lieutenants. Thirteen have died since leaving Camp Schuyler in Herkimer county, among whom are Lieutenants Cameron of Fairfield and Davis of Otsego and several with whom you are unacquainted. You recollect young Olds—son of Carl.[9] He died at Georgetown after receiving what I considered at the time a slight injury from falling from a tree. So uncertain is life.

6. Here Holt provides evidence of his admitted lack of comprehension, confusing Maj. Gen. William F. Smith, commander of the Sixth Corps, with Maj. Gen. William Franklin, commander of Burnside's Left Grand Division. Boatner, 304, 775.

7. The flank movements Holt notes were parts of the movement of the army toward Fredericksburg. A large-scale maneuver such as this conducted in the face of the enemy was a complicated business, and units had to be assigned to cover the flanks and rear of the army, to divert his attention from the object of the move and to determine how he was responding. Orders to subordinate units were given step by step, and only the top officers knew what Burnside's plan was (for once even the Confederates were kept in the dark), so Holt does not know what is going on.

8. "French leave" meaning either desertion or simply an unauthorized departure. In an army of citizen soldiers, taking off to pursue one's interests without permission was not uncommon; desertion plagued all regiments during the war. Colonel Upton was so angry at the level of desertion he faced that he published deserters' names in the *Herkimer County Journal.*

9. Lt. Angus Cameron from Mohawk, N.Y., mustered in as second lieutenant, Co. C of the 121st on Aug. 23, 1862, and was promoted to first lieutenant eight days later. He died of typhoid fever on Nov. 9, 1862, while at Bakersville. George W. Davis enrolled at Little Falls, N.Y., and mustered in as a second lieutenant with Co. A, Aug. 4, 1862. He died Oct. 20, 1862. Orson W. Olds mustered in as a private, Co. C, Aug. 23, 1862, and died of typhoid fever on Nov. 11, 1862. *Annual Report,* 27, 47, 140.

I hope to be able to tell you of decisive action soon. Until then keep up good courage and believe me as ever your

Daniel.

Although Sumner's Right Grand Division of the Union army had reached Fredericksburg as early as November 17, the pontoon trains which Burnside and his staff felt essential to secure the supply line across the Rappahannock did not arrive until the 25th. By that time, Lee had his troops in place in Fredericksburg and had fortified Marye's Heights, the high ground overlooking the city. Burnside would then take the next two weeks, until December 11, to plan his attack.

Camp near Stafford Court
House, Va. November 27, 1862

My dear Wife:—

It seems an age since I have heard from you. Over ten days had elapsed since I received the last intelligence from home, and the days seem long and more dreary than ever. Some how or other the mails have been very irregular since we come here eight days since. *Why* we have not moved is a mystery to me. The rebels are in force at Fredericksburg and we are within eight miles of them. Dr. Walker (who is here) went to Falmouth yesterday and saw very clearly their guns planted upon the opposite side of the river, and the general impression was that to-day the ball would open in good earnest; but as yet no sound of cannon, the forerunner and harbinger of coming events, or other warlike demonstrations are heard. "All is quiet upon the Potomac" and I fear it will be, unless a strike is made speedily, as fall rains are beginning to descend and cold nights and frosts are the order of things here now. Last night was cold enough. Ice inside and outside of my tent and I almost said ice inside my heart. I sit day after day with no newspaper, book or any other reading matter to while away a weary hour. Home with all its tender endearments, will obtrude for reflection, and I wonder not that many of our men are getting sick from no other cause than dwelling too intently upon home.

Yesterday I was weighed and found that I had lost fifteen pounds since entering the service. I have not been able to get rid of that cough yet, and I fear unless we get into winter quarters soon (which God grant we *may not*) it will trouble [me] all winter. I send you a few trophies:— one a piece of our old regimental flag which has been with us through thick and thin until now—another a piece of lace taken from the coat sleeve of rebel Colonel Lamar (which I thought I sent to you previously but did not) and an old document or two which I picked up at Stafford Court House after our men had demolished the building and scattered the contents.[10] Many of the dates are very ancient—running back two or three hundred years; but I failed to get any of so great antiquity. As I have nothing to say and can think of nothing, I will not inflict the burden upon you of reading a tasteless and disagreeable re-hash of what I hope or anticipate, but stop while I have strength and breath to write again when something of greater importance transpires. You speak of the children in a general kind way, but I desire to hear particularly of them. Cannot Willie do something towards writing to me in his printing kind of way? Let him try it. Love to all.

Daniel.

Winter quarters for the army involved little action beyond defending against sharpshooters and posting pickets. Men took advantage of the lack of action by constructing more substantial buildings than their usual tents. The army did not go into winter quarters officially until after the Battle of Fredericksburg, so the house building Holt describes below must have been done by the 121st on its own initiative.

In camp near Stafford Court
House, [Va.] December 4, 1862.

My dear Wife:—

I have just finished reading your last very kind and acceptable letter, and as we are to move to-morrow or next day, I have concluded to write to-night. You do not know how consoling and comforting your letters are. As you say, "it is almost like seeing you," and they are the only things which reconcile me to my situation.

After so long tarrying here, we had almost made up our minds that we were to go into winter quarters here, and in accordance with the supposition began to erect more comfortable tenements. The 27th and

10. Stafford Court House, located near the Union supply base at Aquia Creek Landing, became one of the first places to fall victim to the Army of the Potomac's newly acquired habit of looting. Begun here in the march from Maryland, the habit would grow worse as the war continued. Bruce Catton argues that the rise in looting paralleled the change in the nature of the war—from a war to preserve the Union to a war against the South and against slavery. Confederates had thus become aliens and were therefore subject to looting, pillaging, and all the excesses of war. Catton, *Glory Road*, 16–19, 65–70.

16th N.Y. regiments, which form part of our brigade, have almost completed their log shanties, and the regularly laid out streets look cosey and cheerful. Our boys being less experienced in city building, have been looking on taking notes, and are consequently a little behind the rest, but would soon catch up, as where there is a will there is always a way to secure greater comforts. Our regimental headquarters are a little distance from the men, and in some respects, I think inconvenient; but we have the advantage of high and dry soil which is everything in locating a building. I have just begun *my* house, and if I had been permitted to finish it, should have a real comfortable one, but as it is, it must, with all the rest, be left to its own destruction or be occupied by disloyal men of whom there are not a few in this region. *All* appear to hate us, and we them; so it is fair after all. The country is poor enough, having been run over and over again by the different armies, so that there is nothing left worth fighting for. We occasionally get a fowl, pig or sheep, which unwittingly leaves the precincts of its owner's petticoats, and henceforth becomes the property of our men. The trouble in getting these little luxuries would hardly pay did not the recompense come two fold—the stomach is satisfied and *revenge*—sweet morsel, is rolled with pleasure under the tongue. In Maryland we lived pretty well; there being plenty to eat and the owners willing to sell, and in some instances to *give* you meal of victuals without wishing every mouthful to choke you.

I have, as usual, "nothing new to say," nor indeed do I expect to be able to tell you anything interesting as long as this cold weather continues. Remember me to all and especially to Mother.

Daniel.

The dreadful march Holt describes in the following letter was the first part of the movement of the Sixth Corps to its position below Fredericksburg, where the Left Grand Division was to cross the Rappahannock. Holt's complaints are indicative of the problems inherent in winter campaigning (something only Burnside would attempt in Virginia), and of the massive Union army's continuing problems in supplying itself and in finding enough competent officers to command its units.

In camp at Belle Plain
Landing, Va.
December 8, 1862.

My dear Wife:—

Since last writing to you, we have twice changed our location;— once about fifteen miles from Stafford Court House, and about one and a half from the Potomac River. Here we remained one day, and on the 6th marched again for this point, which we expect to leave again in a day or two. We came here to relieve a brigade which had been on duty at this place for a long time. Upon our arrival we became separated from our division which we must rejoin soon. Col. [Henry L.] Cake [of the 96th Pennsylvania, now Holt's brigade commander] had the honor of leading our brigade to the worst hole I ever saw, and inasmuch as there was not the least possible excuse for the suffering which was so insanely forced upon our men, we shall ever look upon this march as the most killing of any we ever experienced. Never, in a life of forty-five years, have I suffered as much in [one] year, as I have in the twenty-four hours, (or rather twelve hours) which we spent in this place. At night (for it was night when we got here) the baggage wagons had not arrived; nor did they that night—not until next day, and then not all; for many of them had been upset, stuck in the mud and broken down. Three horses belonging to our regiment died from pure exhaustion. Not a fire could be started or a bed made for our men; but upon a bleak plain, destitute of every comfort—not a tree, shrub or bush to give shelter or afford fuel, our poor men were compelled to remain all night standing in frozen pools, wet through to the skin and famishing with hunger. During the day our course had been over hills, through defiles and gorges, up and down precipitous slopes, slippery as Virginia mud could make them, with driving gales of freezing sleet and hail, until, when night closed in upon us and we were ordered to halt upon a plain covered with water, and in most places a foot deep, with here and there a little spot higher than the rest where our men congregated like rats seeking a resting place for their feet as the rising tide threatened to engulf them;—upon such a spot we were halted while the officers commanding the column held a counsel lasting two hours—consulting what was best to do under these distressing circumstances, when it was agreed that *nothing* could be done, and our men were told to *"make themselves as comfortable as possible,"* for the officers could do nothing for them. It does not require a great stretch of fancy to imagine that we were about as *un*comfortable and as unhappy a set of soldiers as ever was crowded upon a field of death, as this subsequently proved to be. About a mile and a half off, was a strip of timber upon the banks of the Potomac, where about half of the regiment went, and were comparatively comfortable, for large fires and shanties had been left by the brigade which left when we arrived. Had all followed their more fortunate comrades, it would have been better, but no one knew of the hospitalities there offered in this inhospitable spot. As for myself, I must confess that I never passed so long, dreary and comfortless a night as that. Nature gave way at last, and I fell half a dozen times upon my head as I attempted to move about to keep myself from freezing. Perfectly prostrate from fatigue and dull from desire to sleep, I remained all that night more like a dead than a live man. About midnight a wagon came up with two or three tents which we succeeded in pitching and into them as many crawled as could get within. I think that had not there been so many to seek shelter, ever so slight, under them—one lying on the top of the other, I firmly believe that some of us would have died before getting away; but as it is, we are all here at last ready for further orders, but Heaven grant that Col. Cake be not the man to give them, or to guide us to our quarters.

I am now sitting in front of a large oak fire, wondering at the endurance of mankind. It seems strange that such a sudden and complete transition from intense suffering to real comfort could take place. We remained but two nights in these uncomfortable quarters, and on Sunday morning (yesterday) struck tents and came a mile to this place where timber is plenty, but which we must leave, as I have previously said, in a day or two. It is said that we are *not* to go into winter quarters, but find them in our saddles, but if we are to experience this kind of treatment, the sooner we can make ourselves comfortable in good log huts, the better it will suit me. It is beyond the power of language to express half the suffering of the eventful day of which I write. Old soldiers say that in all their experience they never saw anything like it. I really believe that one effective company of rebels could have taken our entire brigade that night;—baggage wagons, commissary stores and all. We are much more comfortable now, and hope when we join our division again, to give you a better account of our condition.

I met with a great misfortune yesterday, but was fortunate enough to repair it the same day. I burnt my shoes so badly, in attempting to warm my feet, that they fairly fell off my feet and I had no idea where I could get any more. A soldier needs comfortable and sound covering to his feet above anything else, and it was with great pleasure that I learned that Lieutenant Frank Gorton of Company "K" had a pair of boots which he would sell for twelve dollars.[11] These I immediately seized upon, and am now in first rate trim so far as *boots* are concerned—no insignificant item I can tell you, these cold nights and mornings. I saw a ragged cavalry man this morning with pants so full of holes and covered with patches as to be hardly strong enough to hold themselves upon his body, and feet almost wholly uncovered, who told me that their regiment had not drawn any clothing for six months, and did not know when they should again. These things should not be, neither is there any excuse for it; as government has made ample and complete provision for all such cases. The blame always rests upon drunken or incompetent Quarter Masters (a class of men above all others in the army that needs watching) and who, in my opinion ought to receive no compensation for services rendered, but generally ought to pay soundly for their position, for it seems almost a necessity that they are dishonest. For instance, I am allowed two horses and forage for both; oats 12 lbs. and hay 24 [lbs.] apiece daily. This is the government ration, yet several days will elapse and not one spear of hay enters the mouths of the poor brutes, when they might just as well have it as not. Sometimes both oats and hay give out and so the animals stand at their hitching posts and gnaw away at the oak knots until their teeth are dull as crowbars. If we could obtain *full* rations when we get any, it would be some consolation, but we are short on weight as well as quality. It is seldom that both hay and oats are dispensed together. We have for instance 70 horses, all told, in this regiment. The regimental Quarter-Master reports to the Brigade, he to the Division and the Division to the Corps Quarter Master, all forage required for these 70 horses, and is credited with the amount which it is worth—no small [amount], I can tell you in the course of six months or a year; and all they can steal or withhold from us goes into their pockets; as it is never any *less* than government allowance that is reported, you see that *somebody* makes something out of it: —*surely not our poor half starved horses.*[12] I do not know as this will interest you, but has much to do with myself and *"Fannie"*.

11. Gorton mustered in as second lieutenant with Co. K, Aug. 18, 1862. He rose to captain of Co. G before being wounded and discharged Oct. 5, 1863. *Annual Report*, 76; Phisterer, 3432.
12. Although corruption regarding supplies was certainly a part of the army's experience throughout the war, the worst of it seemed to be at the regimental level rather than systemic. Allan Nevins, *The War for the Union: War Becomes Revolution, 1862–1863*, 471–82.

Perhaps next letter I can tell you more. Until then I bid you a short good bye, praying for your comfort and peace.

Daniel.

At the Battle of Fredericksburg on December 13, 1862, Burnside ordered the Right Grand Division under Sumner to attack Marye's Heights, backed up by Hooker's Center Grand Division. Franklin's Left Grand Division would cross the Rappahannock one and a half miles downstream. Burnside's written orders to Franklin were vague and confusing. Presumably, he wanted Franklin to attack and roll up the Confederate right flank under the command of Stonewall Jackson; at the least, he wanted Franklin to provide a diversion for the Federal assault on Marye's Heights. In the event, Sumner and Hooker suffered heavy losses and failed to storm the heights. Franklin did little after crossing the river with the First and Sixth corps. Only two of his divisions attacked at all, and these were driven back quickly. The Sixth Corps did not participate in these attacks and took few casualties. Holt himself remained behind with his hospital unit, barely mentioned the battle at all in his first letter following it, and does not appear to have been called upon to treat the wounded men of the other corps.

In camp at Belle Plain
Landing, Va.
December 18, 1862.

My dear Wife:—

I know that you must feel anxious to hear from me again by this time, and I should have written before only that I have no means of getting a letter to the post office, owing to our regiment, with the main army, crossing the river at Fredericksburg and the battle which ensued; a description of which you have no doubt read; if not, I cannot inform you, as I was left with thirty-two sick in camp at the time of the advance, and have not heard directly from it or any portion of it since. We were left with three days rations, expecting that in that time some provision would have been made for us, but up to this time nothing has been done—none of the sick sent to hospital—none sent to the regiment and none in any wise provided for except as I have done it. It is now ten days since I have been thus left alone—alone I say, because not a well man was left behind to take care of the sick, no medicines of any kind, and the common army rations for three days only at my service to do anything with. I have thus had to act as physician without medicines, surgeon without instruments, hospital steward without supplies,

Quarter master without means, baggage wagon without horses, and a mule team without harness. Twice I have been compelled to go to the [Belle Plain] Landing, two miles distant, and from the Post Commissary draw supplies for forty men (including myself, contraband, and four indolent pioneers left to guard government property) and upon the back of my horses and such human backs as I could press into the service, get to this station hard bread, pork, beef, sugar, rice, coffee, salt, potatoes, syrup, dried apples, candles, vinegar, tea, beans and other articles necessary for the subsistence of the men. Not a particle of hay or oats was left for poor Fannie, and must I say it? I have had to *steal* all she has Eaten since. Last night after dark I regularly *stole* a sack of oats containing three bushels, and after running over and through bushes, ditches, up hill and down, stumbling over every stump in the way for a third of a mile, came into camp more dead than alive.

During the day, wood cutting and wood toating is the order, or cold feet, fingers and body is the result. Add to all this, every ten minutes some poor soul sticks his head into my tent and wants *something*. They appear to think I am omnicient, and can supply all their wants. Can't I have some water brought from the brook for them? have some wood cut and brought up to their shanties? see that a few more boughs are put over their heads?—or a little more straw or hay placed under their aching bodies?—write a letter for them or send one to the office?—get them into a private house or sent to hospital?—settle their disputes and difficulties?—equalize their share of room in quarters, and ten thousand other requests both laughable and at the same time very annoying. Day-before-yesterday a man of Company *"I"* died of chronic diarrhoea, and the doctor must of course see to giving him his last quarters as he had failed to give him permanent ones here. I had a hole dug in the ground by dint of persuasion and threat, about three feet deep, then put some poles upon the bottom, then deposited the poor fellow with clothes all on, including overcoat and shoes, and drew his blanket around him, then some poles were placed at his side, while cracker box covers formed the ends of his narrow house, then over him other poles were placed—a handful of straw scattered upon the top, and mother earth covered the mortal remains of *Chester G. Alger*— a man beloved by all who knew him—a man beloved of God—a man who at Camp Schuyler and during our tedious marches through Maryland kept pace with his regiment and performed his part of a soldier well.[13] Poor fellow, he has made his last march; he has travelled his last weary step, and now, upon the other side of the river, he is borne on Angel's wings to join his God in glory. It is, and must be, hard to thus dispose of a fellow mortal, yet dust must return to dust—ashes to ashes; and it matters but little in what form humanity returns to its natural element, so long as the soul finds a happy lodgment with its maker.

Camp life is full of incidents. This moment a man appears and asks me what is to be done with the knapsack and accoutrements of a deserter who left two days ago.—He had appropriated his blanket and all he most desired of his effects and wanted me to take the remainder. I ordered him to return *all* and then I would decide upon the matter, [upon] which, like the rich man who went away sorrowful when our Lord touched his riches, he turned and grieved.[14]

It has been very pleasant weather since we encamped here. Last night snow to a very slight extent fell, covering the tops of the Blue Ridge and adjacent hills, yet here secluded as we are in a ravine of pine timber, we feel slightly the chilling blasts of December. It seems almost impossible that New Years is so close at hand:—that we have passed almost one-third of the winter months and seen so little frost and snow. Yet it is *cold* here, decidedly *cold*, and no stretch of fancy can persuade me that the frost King does not reign at times in the Sunny South as well as in the Frigid North. I sit here, at the door of my tent, writing upon the end of a cracker box, in ordinary clothing, looking into the cheerful fire, which I continue to keep going by the help of *"Josh"* (the contraband) and feel quite comfortable and at home, while I can hear the men at other camp fires dilating upon the comforts of home, and others cursing the *"body guards"* they are compelled to carry upon their persons and provide a living for.[15] Indeed it is a mark of distinction—the amount of *guards* who attend upon a man in the army. Most of our men could claim the highest honor, for hardly any have a less number than General McClellan and many, I mistrust, more than Alexander the Great.

13. Chester G. Alger enlisted Aug. 9, 1962, at Hartwick, N.Y., for a three-year term. He was promoted to corporal before his death of chronic diarrhea on Dec. 16, 1862. *Annual Report,* 3.

14. Holt's reference is to the biblical parable of the rich man who asked how to gain eternal life and was told to give all he had to the poor. Matt. 19:16–24 (RSV).

15. "Dilating" meaning speaking in detail; "body guards" meaning lice.

I suppose I have letters in the regiment from you if I could only get them; but as we are separated by ten or twelve miles, and I have no communication with it I do not know when I shall hear from you. Could you look into my kitchen and see the variety of cooking utensils I possess, you would envy me, and I doubt not appropriate a small stock for old acquaintance sake. Now I will give you a list of my cullinary implements, hoping you will be content with what you have, and let me enjoy my own in the quiet unobtrusive way in which my Negro and I live. In the first place let me say that the mess consists of *two*—*Josh* and myself.[16] He (Josh) is maid of all work. On him devolves the duty of rising in the morning, making fires, sweeping out the tent, making up bed, and feeding Fannie. That done, he proceeds to get breakfast; and here carries in our kit and stock in trade, which consists in all told of two dishes made of a canteen which I found upon the ground after the boys left. This I took and melted apart by placing in the fire—the two sides making two pans or basins in which we cook our potatoes, fry our meat and after cooking use as dishes to eat from. If we have a variety we place it upon a chip and eat off that.[17] As for knives, forks, spoons, etc., etc., etc., we have none. My pocket knife has to perform the duty of carving, and everything else where cutting is concerned. Looking closely over the ground, I found a can in which fruit had been preserved, and this serves as coffee pot, to boil our coffee in and cup and saucer to drink from. If the sticks which I whittled out to serve as spoons are not sufficient, I resort to nature's spoons—my fingers and get along quite well. It is astonishing *how little* is really required to serve a man. To be sure the number and quality of the conveniences for cooking are very small, yet I get along quite well, and feel no disposi-

---

16. Escaped slaves from the Confederacy were first labeled "contraband of war" by Gen. Benjamin Franklin Butler when he sought to justify his refusal to return three slaves who fled to Union lines at Fortress Monroe in Virginia after leaving their work on Confederate fortifications at Yorktown. Under military law, contraband, material essential to warfare, could be seized and did not have to be returned to the enemy. The First Confiscation Act of 1861 defined as contraband those slaves who had been employed by the Confederates, a definition important to Lincoln. If at this early juncture he had made the war one to free the slaves, he would have lost the support of the Border States. If, however, slaves were confiscated as contraband of war and became the property of the Union army or government which then freed that property, the slaves' freedom was incidental to the war, not the cause of it. In practice, most Northern regiments protected the slaves who fled to Union lines, and many used the blacks as servants. McPherson, *Battle Cry,* 355–57.

17. "Chip" meaning chip of wood.

tion to complain. You perhaps ask if this is *all* I ever have to get along with? No, by no means. When the regiment left, mess chest and every-thing else left, and I was as much dependent upon my own resources and wits as any one possibly could be. It was almost like being wrecked upon a foreign shore with nothing but your own bodily vigor to depend upon for support, only with this difference,—that here, subsistence is obtainable if you have the means of obtaining it, and in the other case it is more difficult and uncertain. I really would like to have you look in upon me during meals. It would not answer, you know, to have a *Niggar* eat at the same table with you, so to keep up the distinction which *man* has created, Josh has to keep back until his master is helped. I can sometimes hear him swearing with the men back of the tent, about the *cold victuals* he has to eat after I am through. Well, if he does not like it he will have to leave, for with all my love for a black skin I never yet saw one with whom I would be willing to be on *perfect* equality. [Illegible] and here let me say it is not because I feel that by nature I am better than they, but education—early as life itself is against it. It is engrafted in me—I cannot help it.

As to my health, I am getting along better than I expected I should after so severe a trial of my endurance. A hard, heavy cough, with great soreness of lungs and oppression of breathing, with feverish symptims generally, followed me for many days, but now a fuller, freer respiration with less pain and constriction of the chest has taken place, although rheumatism in my hips and legs does [not] allow as free locomotion as I should like. The worst difficulty I labor under now is sleepless and rest-less nights. Oh dear, how long and tedious they appear, and how I watch for the first gray streaks of morning! When after that for an hour I can generally get a little rest. All night long, for four or five in succession, I lie and listen to every cough that breaks the stillness—to every sound of moving vehicle—to every breath my darkey draws, as he snores beside the blazing pile wrapped in his old blanket and get mad at myself and him because I *cannot* and he *can* sleep. It is a real relief to hear the booming of cannon as the fight at Fredericksburg is progressing, and I have a thousand times wished I could be there instead of here, but I have as great a duty to perform here and will be content. Love to all.

Daniel.

In the following letter, Holt briefly mentions that Dr. Valentine has been ordered to Washington to stand examination regarding complaints filed against him.

Little information is available regarding the army's investigation of Valentine, but examinations by military tribunals trying to rid the army of incompetent men had begun as early as 1861.

Camp in field near
Fredericksburg, Va.
January 2n, 1863.

My dear Wife:—

I know your anxiety to hear from me, and I have felt just as anxious to write to you, but my excuse must be the old one—want of time. Since my last, dated at *"Belle Plain Landing,"* I have hardly had time for one moment respite. I suppose you were aware of the fact, as I had Mr. Huckans write to his wife to inform you of how busy I have been since joining the regiment.

Surgeon Walker has been taken sick and is now in general hospital at Washington; and Dr. Valentine was ordered there for examination[18] which left the whole running of the department upon my hands, which you must know was no small matter. In addition to the usual duties, monthly and yearly reports had to be made out, and this too, without sufficient data to work upon; which with the confusion which has ever characterized our department, it was expected that all would *appear* well if in fact it was not. Under such circumstances my ingenuity was taxed to save the concern from utter ruin.—I have now brought up all back matters—got the hospital in good running order, and regularity prevails. It was my sincere hope that I should have been left in quiet possession, when lo! and behold!! this morning Dr. Valentine reappeared having been ordered to join his regiment after having undergone the examination, and here he is again as large as life; but how long he is to remain is uncertain as no decision in his case has been made known to him. Dr. Walker I think will try to be assigned to lighter duty in some hospital if his health improves. If this takes place, a vacancy will occur and some one will have to fill it. I hope a more competent one than Valentine certainly, or I shall wish I had never been born or entered the army. It is utterly impossible to feel easy with such a specimen of humanity to dictate to you. I shall make strong efforts to leave if I am to be placed under *such* control.

18. Valentine was ordered to appear before the Medical Examining Board in Washington, D.C., on Dec. 18, 1862. Pension and Service Records.

The health of the regiment is bad. Death is upon our track, and almost every day sees its victim taken to the grave. Yesterday *two,* and to-day two more were consigned to their last resting place, and still the avenger presses harder and harder claiming as his victim the best and fairest of the men. There are quite a number waiting at the river bank to be ferried over,[19] and it makes my heart sad to think that I can in no way delay their passage. As I rode out upon the picket line to-day to see if more of our boys had been shot (for a constant fire is going on between the reb and loyal lines) or had been taken sick, I for the first time *fully* felt the dreadful effects of this cruel, wicked war. It was my mournful duty to inform the brother of one of our men who had died, and although he had expected, and for some time tried to prepare for the event, yet when the blow came, it was too severe. Nature gave way, and I left him a disconsolate, broken hearted man with his companions while I continued my round. I had time to commune with myself as I rode from post to post, and the fountain of my heart overflowed as I found relief in tears. It is a sad, sad sight to see men who at home occupied position and place, possessing wealth and homes of refined ease deposited as they are here, in the ground, with nothing but a blanket and mother earth over them—one or two only, truly mourning over them, while at home the wife and little ones count the long days and months which separate them, and pray to be again united. I cannot give you an adequate idea of the matter, but the heart feels, and the heart only knows the miseries which our men endure. I have great reason to thank my Maker that I am not yet a confirmed invalid. If I were, I should have no hope except relief in death. I never want to draw out a miserable illness here or in hospital. I have seen and know too much of army doctoring to trust much in its efficacy. Very little can be done for a man while he lies upon the ground with typhoid fever, attended by incompetent nurses. When I order one to hospital, it seems almost equivalent to ordering his grave dug.[20]

Everything indicates a move soon. The army is all excitement and agitation. The sick have been sent away to the rear—almost positive evidence that we shall advance, while the extraordinary activity of

19. The "river bank to be ferried over" phrase is a classical allusion to Charon, ferry-boat pilot who ferries the dead to Hades, land of the dead.

20. Diarrhea, scurvy, and typhoid were rampant in the camps as the weather grew more foul and supplies of food, particularly vegetables, arrived less often. For many, hospitals became charnel houses. Gillett, 207–8.

supply trains too plainly tell to experienced eyes that the repose is short and fitful.[21] I therefore write not knowing *when* or where I shall next address you. Give yourself no uneasiness on my account as I shall try to be careful in the preservation of my health which above all earthly considerations I deem the most important. I shall keep you posted in reference to all that concerns the good and prosperity of the cause, and hope to be able soon to tell you a tale more pleasing than any which I have heretofore done. Good night, I must go to bed, as it is near midnight.

Daniel.

Brigade inspection, which Holt complains of in his next letter, is the business in which everybody in the brigade lines up and is looked over by the superior officers. The goal is to determine the number of effective soldiers in each company and regiment, whether or not they have proper uniforms, equipment, supplies, and so on. For the men, it meant a lot of fussing and then a lot of standing around. Holt was not alone in his low opinion of such activity. For the officers, however, this particular inspection was no doubt to prepare for a new attempt at crossing the river, which Burnside had not yet given up on.

In camp near Fredericksburg Va
January 6th, 1863.

My dear Wife:—

As I have a few moments leisure, I think I cannot improve them better than in writing home. Our regiment is now out on Brigade Inspection and I am left alone. It is a regular bore, these inspections, and the more I can get rid of attending, the better I like it. In a day or two, I think the army will be on the move as all indications appear to point that way. It is not unpleasant to know that I shall go with and share the fate of the boys when they go. We shall no doubt cross the Rappahannock again, but not at the same point as before. A reconnoisance in force was made three or four days ago, resulting in finding a practical ford about fifteen miles higher up the river, at which point I have no doubt crossing will take place. It is thought that at the same

21. As Burnside planned his move, he set up medical facilities at Aquia Creek to avoid having to tie up men and wagons sending the wounded to hospitals in Washington. Eventually, as his campaign failed, he would send the most seriously injured to Washington and set up regimental hospitals for others. Ibid., 208.

time of a crossing above, there will be also one below the city, thus engaging the enemy upon both left and right wings, causing them to weaken or break their center, as a consequence coming out of their fortifications and engaging us upon more equal terms. You may depend upon it that a great effort will be made to wipe out the stain of our late defeat at Fredericksburg, and I am very much mistaken if a decisive battle is not fought before long. As I stated in my last, the sick and disabled have been removed to General Hospitals and everything which can or does clog the movements of an army is so far got rid of that we may be said to be in light marching order. However, when the time comes, there will be enough to impede and cause round wholesale swearing among officers and men. Why this profanity I cannot imagine. It is like water spilt upon the ground; lost to all appearances, yet watering and vitalizing evil passions and ultimately developing a nature fraught with propensities to evil, as naturally as smoke curlingly ascends the zenith.

With all the hardships of moving in cold, freezing weather, I had rather be going than to be confined in a little 7x9 tent with two or three inmates beside yourself. Take baggage, and clothing and the necessary stand or table, and the indispensable fire place or stove, and you have a den worse than that into which my illustrious predecessor Daniel was cast,[22] and sometimes I think in a Surgeon's quarters, far more dangerous. The weather is quite warm and pleasant for the season of the year, but *mud!!* ah me!—*that's the rub!* It is this we fear the most—more than rebel bullets or shells.—I hope to hear from you soon. The usual love to all.

Daniel.

Mud is always bad for armies. Wheels get stuck in it, artillery sinks in it, and roads, unless paved (these were rare in the mid–nineteenth century, particularly in the South), were impassable. Even foot soldiers and mules were slowed down considerably. Mud in the winter and spring seasons was worse than in fall and summer because there was more precipitation, the temperatures were too low, and the sun appeared too seldom to dry the mud quickly. Even minor movements could become impossible, as Holt notes below.

22. "My illustrious predecessor Daniel" is a biblical reference to the Hebrew prophet Daniel, cast into a den of lions for praying to his God in defiance of an edict of King Darius. Dan. 6:6–23 (RSV).

In camp near
Fredericksburg, Va.,
January 12th, 1863.

My dear Wife:—

All is still around the camp fire now, and inasmuch as I have been waiting for an hour or two to say a few words to you, I will immediately sit myself down to the pleasant task. Last evening's mail brought a letter for you, for which I am very thankful and will pay the debt in kind. It pleases me to learn of your general good health and that you are prospering so well.

When I last wrote you it was my firm belief that we should not be here at this present time; but "the rains have descended, the floods have come and beat upon the *ground*," and made *mud* such as only those who reside upon the Sacred Soil know anything of.[23] It is of no use opposing the combination of earth and water when properly mixed. *Mud is King!*—more of a sovereign, and a worse despot than cotton and ten thousand times more to be dreaded by such an army as ours when we want to move than all the inventions and machanations of our enemies. Of course, if it was the intention to move a few days ago, it must be abandoned now until the sun dries up the roads and ground sufficiently to allow trains to move. I hope it will soon be so. It takes but a little while when the conditions are right, to make the roads passable.

To-day I was called to see a young lady who was shot by her young brother. It was purely accidental; the boy took a loaded gun of a guard who was placed at the house, and telling her that he was going to shoot her, drew up and lodged a ball in her body, just below the heart. She cannot survive. The poor boy is nearly frantic with grief and remorse, and I think he has learned a lesson never to be forgotten—that is to be careful how he handles loaded guns. This lesson it would be well for our men to learn also; —they are exceedingly green and clumsy and hardly a time when they go out on picket but someone comes in minus a finger, hand or arm. I am now assisted by Dr. Peer, a contract Surgeon from Rochester,[24] and my beloved Dr. Valentine.

Daniel.

23. Holt's quote is a paraphrase from Matt. 7:27 (KJV): "And the rain descended, and the floods came, and the winds blew . . . ."

24. Contract surgeons were common during the war. Their nominal rank was as acting assistant surgeon; they held no other rank and served usually three to six months. Adams, 174; Gillett, 155.

Camp of the 121st Reg. N. Y. Vol.
near White Oak Church,
Virginia, January 16th, 1863

My dear Wife:—

You may think from the heading that we have changed quarters; Not a bit of it. The fact is that we are in the immediate vicinity of this venerable old church if such a name can with propriety be applied to an edifice not so good looking as my barn and wood shed. The structure is a large one story frame without steeple, spire or anything to mark its being a house of worship. Indeed it looks like a great barn, with too few windows to afford light even for that; with an exterior which never knew a painter's brush—not even white washing; at best it never had even a passable appearance, and now that troops are quartered in it and horses occupy one end where the Negroes used to be allowed to stow themselves away to hear the word of life, with clapboards off as high as a man can reach, it presents anything but a neat or decent appearance. It is from this building, then, *"White Oak Church,"* four miles from Fredericksburg that all my letters ought to have been directed. It is rumored and believed that we are to leave here for parts unknown, to-morrow, and in expectation of such an event, I have again addressed you. I hope you will excuse the many senseless letters which I send you; but I must let off the surplus gas or an explosion will result.

The box of clothing, together with knit gloves and mittens of which you speak as having been sent by the ladies of Newport and vicinity has not arrived, and I fear never will. [Confederate Gen. J. E. B.] Stuart or some other good guerilla has no doubt got them. If so, let it go— placing it to the *"D."* side of the accounts which we are to settle with these gentlemen some fine day.[25] When anything of importance turns up I will let you know. It may be in a day or two, or not at all.

Daniel.

Marching orders for January 20 would be for the army to move west to Bank's Ford, a few miles west of Falmouth, Virginia, to get behind Lee's position. If the weather had held, it might have worked, although it is difficult to tell how much

25. "D." meaning debit. In early December 1862, the *Herkimer County Journal* had published a letter from Col. Emory Upton, asking the Ladies Aid Society to knit eight hundred pairs of mittens for the regiment. Women's organizations throughout the Civil War provided supplies for soldiers. For a basic survey, see Agatha Young, *The Women and the Crisis: Women of the North in the Civil War.*

could have been gained from such a move since it took place under the eyes of the Confederates. This letter, which mentions orders to move as early as the 16th, may indicate the beginning of the shift westward.

Camp of the 121st Reg. N.Y.
Vols. near White Oak Church,
Va., January 19, 1863.

My dear Wife:—

I am uneasy as you ever was or ever will be.—No letter from home in a long time, and none, it appears to me, ever coming. I have written to you every three or four days for sometime past, and feel anxious to have you write, but I suppose donations and the necessary business of the household department is a very good and proper excuse.

We were under marching orders three days ago, and expected to move, but here we are in *status quo,* and here I hope we may remain until warmer weather comes on. Although the climate is much more mild than at home, yet it is too cold to make vigorous and healthy marches in the winter. Let an army advance and sleep upon the frozen ground for three consecutive nights, and the hospitals would be all full in no time. A soldier forgets not his nature (or rather the nature which is in him forgets not him) and he is just as amenable to disease as other men, albeit his fare and occupation is so dissimilar.

This morning, we sent off to Aquia Creek Hospital eight patients. They were to have left yesterday morning, and did get started, when an order came countermanding the previous one, and here they are sick in old quarters. This morning however, they all went, and about *seventy* more on the top of them. This wholesale sending off of the men, made Col. Upton rear like a mad bull, as well it might, for the reason was too apparent to pass the notice of the dullest mind—to get rid of the trouble of having them come up to surgeon's call in the morning. Not one-fourth of the number needed permanent treatment, and not more than eight or ten need to have been sent off. This was my beloved Dr. Valentine's work, and he alone is responsible for such an outrageous proceeding. If he is not soon dismissed dishonorably from the service, I am mistaken. *I,* if I were the commandant of a regiment would look well into such transactions and if necessity did not require it, would prefer charges against an officer so offending. Three cases of typhoid will no doubt soon pay the debt of Nature, and I fear others are close upon their track. Just as I write, the brigade band is following a poor Jerseyman to his final resting place, and these solemn rites are by no means uncommon, especially in the 15th New Jersey, a regiment in the 1st Brigade. It may not be that we are to remain here long. If we move in *such* weather I fear that coughs, catarrh[26] and pneumonia will again be rife among us. As an *army* we are in better health than a month ago; but as to discipline, *worse*. Resignations and desertions appear to be the order of the day and night. Last night, *nineteen* enlisted men and non-commissioned officers took leg bail[27] and have not been heard from since, although cavalry scouts have been sent out in pursuit.

For the last three days it has been *cold,* cold as winter, although no snow has fallen to lie upon the ground for over a month. To-day however, it is warm and pleasant, with no sign of storms. Taking one day with another, this climate is more pleasant than with us at the North; but it [is] far from being a very desirable one to live in, on account of the sudden changes which almost every week occur. Now it is blustering and blowing a gale equal to anything Herkimer county can boast of, and by to-morrow it would seem as if the lovely face of nature had never been ruffled by counter currents and unpropitious storms. I think we can boast of as fickle a minded climate as any North of the Gulf states. I should like to have you just step into my half shanty and half tent and "see how poor folks live." Perhaps you might get into the door and perhaps not; at any rate I should like to have you come and see

Daniel.

Despite the fact that he had been so soundly beaten at Fredericksburg, Burnside decided to make another effort at crossing the Rappahannock. The morale of the army was low and the weather was terrible. Rainstorms turned the dirt roads into a sea of impassible mud. Burnside's "Mud March" was the last campaign he ever directed as commander of the Army of the Potomac.

Camp of the 121st Reg. N. Y.
Vols. near White Oak Church,
Va., January 27th, 1863.

My dear Wife:—

Since I last wrote to you on the 19th, the Army of the Potomac has made a move, and here we are again at our old quarters. We advanced to the Rappahannock above Fredericksburg, were overtaken by rain, *got*

---

26. Catarrh is an inflammation of a mucous membrane, usually in the throat or nose, resulting in increased mucous production.
27. "Leg bail" meaning French leave, desertion, or unauthorized absence.

stuck in the mud and had to beat an inglorious retreat, after watching the rebels across the river for five days. *Such* mud, you nor I never saw before. Pontoon boats, batteries, ammunition trains and horses formed an unbroken mass—*all stuck in the mud.* Had the movement taken place one week sooner, I think we should have been very successful; for *all* save a very few high officials were in blissful ignorance of the contemplated move.[28] Although there were many rumors that we were soon to take up the aggressive, yet like the boy who had cried *"wolf"* so long, and no wolf coming, we had settled into the belief that it was all a sham and nothing like offensive operations was contemplated until Spring. Therefore when the order came to *"pack up and be off in half an hour,"* it came like a clap of thunder upon our unwilling ears. The weather, when we started, and for a few days previously had been all that fancy could desire or paint, but we had hardly got so far as Falmouth when the clouds overspread the heavens, and the *gentle rain* began to fall, at first, oh how warm and beautifully; but as we progressed, and night sat in, cold increased with the rain, until it *poured in torrents.* That night we went to bed—or rather to *water* without cooking our food; and in the morning, the rain still continuing, we ate our *hard tack* and salt pork and *thought* of warm coffee &c., but tasted it not. After an awful struggle we reached the river—*not* to cross over; but to be taunted by the rebels on the other side, with [the rebels] coming out with *"eight days"* rations, and after disposing of them to go back again for more.[29] For three days we lay here, all the while the rain is falling in steady streams, until the low, swampy soil on which we stood was covered in many places two feet deep, and in most others from six to twelve inches. Inasmuch as the order for marching came so sudden, I was not prepared as I should have been, with necessary provisions; and as a consequence was about as hungry as I well could be. I tried to *purchase* of the more fortunate, but got nothing but about six or eight *hard tack* and this had to last for the three days we were in this unpleasant predicament. Here again was another trial of physical endurance. During the three days of which I write, I had no tent to shield me from the rain incessantly falling so that I was perfectly wet through without the means of drying myself, as

28. Holt's assessment is probably accurate: the Confederates did not suspect a move, the weather was fine, and had Burnside moved the week of the 20th, his attempt to flank the Confederate position at Fredericksburg might very well have succeeded.

29. In other words, the Confederates were flaunting their rations by consuming them in sight of the hungry Yankees.

everything was so soakingly wet that we could not make fires, and here, against the roots of a tree I stood for three days and three nights, with a soaking wet blanket and an India rubbercap to contend against the watery element. At length the order was given—and not one moment too soon—to retrace our steps. Previous to doing so, a few head of cattle had been driven in and butcherd and by dint of perseverance and persuasion I obtained a small piece which I ate almost raw, so hungry was I that I could not wait to have it cooked over a little fire which some of our boys had succeeded in starting. Next day, and indeed the very one on which I ate it, cramps in my stomach and bowels took place to such an extent that I verily thought my last day had come. Opium, nor ether had the least effect to relieve the pain[30] and not until every part and parcel of the offending substance was ejected from the system did I get rilief. Together with wet and hunger this pain fully satisfied me with camplife; and I *now* feel that I never again will complain of poor fare at home. *Anything,* prepared in *any way* is better than I have had for a few days past.

It was truly laughable to see our boys *"play horse"* as they called it, in dragging the boats out of the mud.—A whole regiment (ours, for instance) would get hold of a long rope, and together with *sixteen mules,* snake the wagon (on which was the boat) on dryer ground. Here the whole train lay as effectually sealed from all usefulness as if they were in the Navy Yard at Washington or had never been built. Not only pontoon trains but ammunition and supply trains were in this same fix, and all had thus to be brought out. *"Corduroy roads"* had to be constructed through the woods before any could leave, and upon these our men hauled horses, wagons and all, amid screams of laughter and fun, such as I never saw before.[31] Perhaps the *commissary* could tell whether any of his *whisky* suffered that day. *I* think I saw several barrels dispensed, and in the best time any such article ever was—when men were faint, wet and fatigued as they never were before. If no worse use is ever made of liquor than this, surely the cause of temperance has no reason to complain.

Some of our men reached their old quarters at White Oak Church the same night mounted officers did; but many were until next day

30. Opium and ether are both painkillers.
31. Corduroy roads were paved with logs, sometimes split in half, sometimes paved with mud. Such roads were not very durable, but they could hold up long enough to get the army's equipment through a muddy or swampy area.

before getting back. No order was observed in marching. Every man took such a route, and such a place as suited him best. *All* were officers for the two days required in reaching home, and *all* were officers *de facto* if you should hear the cursing of the *"shoulder straps"* (and those having authority) by the men. Everyone seemed to think he had special cause of complaint, and every one for a time had it his own way; but good nature at length prevailed and the curse turn[ed] into a good natured laugh at the ridiculous appearance we all made during the few days when *"Burnside was stuck in the mud!"* Nothing more now.

Daniel.

THREE

The old familiar sound of cannon is heard

February 8, 1863 – June 5, 1863

*L*incoln *finally gave up on Burnside and removed him from command on January 26, 1863, replacing him with Joseph Hooker. Lincoln's choice of Hooker was a reluctant one, for that officer's constant complaints about Burnside and blatant lobbying for the post had not endeared him to his commander in chief, but the available options were few. Recalling McClellan was out of the question, and the only officers senior to Hooker in Burnside's army, Franklin and Sumner, had demonstrated their inadequacies at Fredericksburg. If nothing else, Hooker promised to be more aggressive than his predecessors. Perhaps "Fighting Joe" would give the Union the victories it so desperately needed.*

Cocky, ambitious, and handsome, Hooker was popular with the men because he saw to the more mundane details of army life. That meant the soldiers' needs were once again cared for more regularly. Hooker abandoned Burnside's clumsy Grand Divisions and reverted to the original corps organization, except for the cavalry, which he established as a separate corps under command of Gen. George Stoneman. He concentrated on discipline and raising the morale of the troops, particularly on increasing rations of fresh foods. He also forced or allowed many of the incompetent, alcoholic, or disabled officers that had been plaguing the Union army to resign or face discharge. In the letter below, an elated Holt reports that the incompetent Valentine has been dismissed from the service at last.

Camp of the 121st Reg. N.Y. Vols.
near White Oak Church, Va.
February 8th, 1863.

My dear Wife:—

Yesterday's mail brought another letter from home rejoicing my heart as no letter ever did before. You know that sometimes we are in

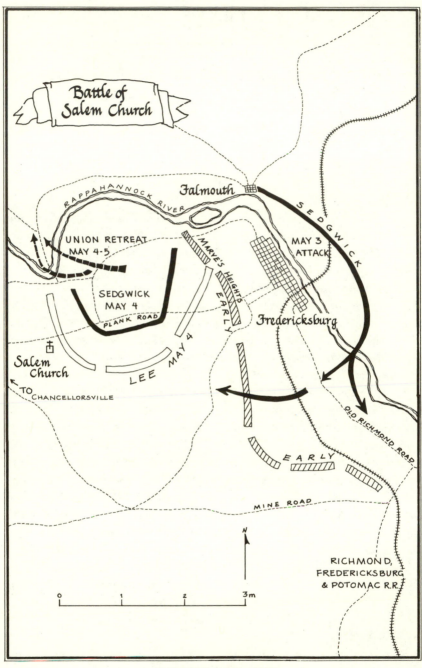

Battle of
Salem Church

RAPPAHANNOCK RIVER

Falmouth

UNION RETREAT
MAY 4-5

MARYE'S HEIGHTS

SEDGWICK
MAY 3
ATTACK

SEDGWICK
MAY 4

EARLY

Fredericksburg

PLANK ROAD

Salem
Church

LEE MAY 4

TO
CHANCELLORSVILLE

EARLY

OLD RICHMOND ROAD

MINE ROAD

N

0   1   2   3m

RICHMOND,
FREDERICKSBURG
& POTOMAC R.R.

MAP BY MICAELA AYERS

just the mood to be petted or babied or to receive reproof, admonition or what not. Well, I was feeling just right for the one you sent, and although as a letter containing news or interesting matter of any kind, it was far short of some which I have received, here was just the one for the occasion. I thank you for it, and will try to merit the confidence you repose in me.

Inasmuch as I have in my last given you a partial account of our advance and *getting stuck in the mud,* I will not again repeat it, although many incidents now present themselves which at the time of writing were forgotten. Contrary to all expectation I came out of it very well. Were it not for the raw meat which I eat as a dog would devour a meal after being half starved, and the disagreeable results which followed, I should now feel quite well: but the pain and diarrhoea which set in after eating the delicious morsel still follows me, but in a lessened degree, and I think by next time writing I shall be able to say that I am fully recovered.

I had a very fine visit from Charles Hamlin the other day. He came in company with Dr. Neely[1] and spent some hours with me: *took tea* and talked over home matters.—He looks well—is fat and healthy and to a certain extent contented: yet he would be very willing to be at home (and who would not) if it could honorably be so. I was pleased to see that his connection with the army had not corrupted him. He is a fine young man—such as a parent need not feel ashamed to own.

Dr. Valentine has been dismissed [from] the service for *incompetency and fraudulent transactions in the discharge of his duty.* In the case of young Graves, he forced his father to pay $150.00 before he would sign his discharge papers, and in the matter of the commissary, he swore he had expended out of his private funds, for the benefit of sick in hospital in the purchase of *delicacies,* $148.62; when he never, to my positive knowledge, spent one cent either directly or indirectly to better their condition. Such rascality could not be passed over lightly, and just as I expected, only not quite so severe, the blow had been struck. I am greatly relieved and shall proceed immediately to put the machine in running order again. As soon as he is gone fairly out of sight I think I shall have a day of rejoicing to which I should like to invite some of the

1. Charles Hamlin, a cousin of Holt's wife, was from the village of Herkimer and a soldier with the 57th N.Y. Volunteers. Nelson Neely was an assistant surgeon for the 57th N.Y. Infantry. Willard and Walker, 289; *OR*, vol. 19, 1:302.

men who have been so grossly swindled by him. I could tell how he stole and carried off a nice hunting case lever watch from a private,[2] but I guess he has enough to answer for, *and so will not tell you*. Let him alone. Peace to his ashes.

Dr. Walker is still at home; but he writes me that he will be here by the last of the month. I hope so, for I hate to do double and quadruple duty when others should share it. Chatfield, our Hospital Steward, is about leaving for home on a furlough of ten days.[3] *Then* I shall be absolutely left alone; for he is efficient and useful to me if so disposed and takes a great load from my shoulders in many respects. Newton Phelps acts as *Ward Master,* making out morning and monthly reports, drawing rations from the Commissary, and generally taking care of hospital arrangements. Cox and Huckans are cooks, look well, and *are* well. With all the rest who have families to support and are out of money, they are anxiously awaiting the Paymaster when they intend to let their families hear from them in a substantial manner.

I am sorry that I have to resort to such extremes to fill a small sheet, but *lack of news of interest* must be the excuse rendered. No one would feel greater pleasure in writing if I had anything to write about.

Daniel.

Camp of the 121st Reg. N.Y. Vols.
near White Oak Church, Va.,
February 17th, 1863.

My dear Wife:—

It seems almost impossible to find time to write to you, so busy have I been (and so continue to be) since my last. I am almost entirely without help; while measles and other diseases are rapidly spreading in the regiment. Dr. Walker, as you know, is at home, Valentine dismissed [from] the service dishonorably; Chatfield, our Hospital Steward, at home on furlough and no one but Phelps to lift a finger to lighten the increasing burden. It makes pretty hard and constant work, but I think

---

2. A lever watch is the cheapest non-jewel watch made. Hooker worked hard to deal with corruption and get rid of incompetent officers and medical personnel. See Catton, *Glory Road,* 140–45.

3. The furlough system, another reform Hooker implemented to improve morale, permitted limited numbers of men to be away from their units at a given time, usually for a couple of weeks. This was done to reduce the number of desertions and to persuade short-term enlistees to sign on for longer service. Ibid., 145.

I shall get through with it if help comes soon. In the morning, at 8 o'clock is Surgeon's Call; then breakfast; after which the hospital is to be visited, and sick in quarters to be seen and prescribed for, and these not a few.

The paymaster has come and gone, and our boys feel better. They were paid up to the 1st January, and very many have sent home almost every cent paid them.[4] This speaks well for the morality and virtue of the men: better than to spend it at the gambling table as many of the older regiments do—the 27th N.Y. for instance.

I have sold my mare *"Fannie"*—the one I thought so much of—the one General Bartlett rode through all the war, carrying him safely through the thickest of the fray. I purchased another for much less than I got for her, and perhaps will do as well. It is the one which Dr. Valentine rode, and which perhaps is a more decent beast of the two.— cannot be worse. As this is a letter of *items,* I might as well tell you that I sent "Josh" away yesterday. He had become insolent and saucy, and demanded an increase of pay, so I thought he had better go. I can get another as good and cheaper.—The box of mittens of which you speak has not yet arrived, and probably never will. If they were here now they would come good, but if they are delayed until spring, they had better have been kept at home, and sent another fall if the war continues so long, which God grant may *not be* the case.

I am sorry to hear of Willie's ill health.[5] Perhaps I shall be made glad next time by being told that he is better, or well.—Ever since I have been in the army, my mind has been made unhappy by the thought that diptheria, croup or some other fatal disease would fasten upon our little ones and we should be obliged to yield them up. Do be par-

4. In principle, soldiers of both armies were paid monthly in cash. The going rate at the beginning of the war was eleven dollars per month for both sides and went up a few times during the war. The Confederate wages went up more slowly, despite their higher inflation rate, and Holt talked to men whose pay was eleven dollars even as late as 1863. (The Confederacy finally raised soldiers' wages from eleven to eighteen dollars in June 1864.) In practice, payments to soldiers were often irregular, with some units or armies going for several months without pay, especially when on campaign, partly due to inefficiency, partly out of fear of having the Confederates capture the gold or the increasingly valuable greenbacks, issued after the Legal Tender Act of February 1862. Nevins, *Organized War,* 389; McPherson, *Battle Cry,* 440–48.

5. "Willie" was Willard Holt, second child of Daniel and Louisa, born on Nov. 2, 1858. Like his father, Willard became a doctor. He never married, lived his life in Newport, and died there Jan. 17, 1894. He is buried in the Holt family plot in Newport. *Herkimer Democrat,* Jan. 31, 1894, p. 4.

ticular about keeping him from the [West Canada] Creek. *I fear this more than all the rest.* Knowing his propensity to be near and in the water. Only think of the number who have been drowned in Newport, and you will I am sure, share the anxiety under which I rest. Every day of my life is one of anxiety on their account. It would be comparatively pleasant here were it not for such thoughts constantly obtruding themselves upon my mind; and I cannot help it.

George and David sent me a letter the other day, informing me that they were about to enter the army as cavelrymen and leave their situation as government nurses in Philadelphia.[6] I am sorry to hear of such a decision, for I am sure they little appreciate the duties of a soldiers life, nor the hardships incident upon it. But I must close hoping that you, my dear wife, will be cheerful and contented. My heart is with you—my all is within the precincts of my happy home. God bless and keep you until the day when we shall be again an unbroken circle around the family hearth, no more to be separated by wars or rumors of wars.

Daniel.

The importance of mail to the army's morale was inestimable. Again, Hooker's care of the soldiers was clear as his reorganization in the spring of 1863 increased the reliability of mail service.

> Camp of the 121st Regiment.
> N.Y. Vols White Oak Church, Va.,
> March 7th, 1863

My dear Wife:—

Last night I received one of those old fashioned soul inspiring letters from home. Sometimes I think I am growing childish as well as old when I find that I am so easily affected by a kind word. It is so seldom we hear them here, that when they *do* come, it seems like breathings from the spirit land—voices from the other side of the river where our loved ones have gone before and are waiting our arrival. Let them come. It makes us no worse and perhaps much better. I am firmly of

6. George (July 23, 1846–Nov. 9, 1874) and David (Nov. 27, 1843–Apr. 30, 1867) both joined the 19th Pa. Cavalry some months after this letter was written. The 19th was organized at Philadelphia between June and October 1863 to serve three years. Both brothers survived the war. George married Lottie Wilson of Chicago on Dec. 5, 1865; David died in 1867 of tuberculosis, contracted during his service. *OAR,* 3:791; Holt Papers.

the opinion that were more of such letters written to desponding soldiers, we should have less desertion and harder fighting. No man can discharge his duty so cheerfully and promptly when cries of distress and mournful regrets at leaving are constantly poured into his ears, as he can when the partner of his life and object of his affections stirs him up to action by words of patriotic fire and christian enthusiasm. No, it is only those who are the recipiants of complaining, fault-finding letters—letters worthy of no virtuous Christian mind—letters such as harrow up all the ill nature within us, and *those who receive no letters,* who are found in the rear when a battle is raging—who can see no beauty in our government—no benefits resulting from its administration and who are ready at all times to despond and talk evil when success does not attend every movement—it is this class of men, who made unhappy by home influence, is sure to turn away and disgracefully leave our country in the hands of traitors, while the loyal brother fights the battle of both. Then give me such letters as make me feel that I am a man and have a country and family to defend, and gives me an idea of freedom such as God intends all to possess.

I am plased to inform you that the box of mittens of which so much has been said and written, has arrived at last! but *such* things are a disgrace to the fair daughters of Herkimer. I am sorry to say it, but it is truth. Hardly one *knit* pair among them all. The most are made out of old cloth faded and threadbare, and in some cases *patched* at that. It looks as if they were made out of the seats of worn out satinet breeches, and two year old babies sewed them together. Our men display them upon the ends of their ramrods and bayonets, and make all manner of sport of them. It is insulting to send such things to *such* men. They deserve better treatment from friends. Rebs would give better. I am ashamed to think that after we were led to expect good comfortable articles that we should be thus—*insulted!*—yes *insulted* is the word, and no other. I have a pair in my possesion which I mean to keep as a trophy of the war—as a gift from my sisters in the North for services in the defense of their homes and perpetuity of domestic quiet. But enough. I suppose, and I *know* that no *lady*—no one who knew how to use a needle or had anything but worn out satinet pants to spare would send such things to so good and worthy a regiment of men. It has been from some back woods children, whose intentions no doubt were good, but mistook the men and object for which they were intended. I think I have said enough on this score, and perhaps too much, but we were all so disappointed when we came to receive what we had so long looked for and desired, that I cannot but express my indignation. Remember me to all.

Daniel.

> Camp of the 121st Reg. New York
> Vols. near White Oak Church, Va.
> March 13, 1863.

My dear Wife:—

Yours of the 7th containing pictures of the children was duly received. Thanks for the kind remembrance. I have looked in vain for yours. Why is it? —Are you afraid of risking your reputation for beauty in having it taken? I must confess that *such is my case*. Only to think of that beautiful, long, silver gray beard, and that *dauntless teutonic mostache* being put in jeopardy by an unskilled artist? It is more than I can think of. No, I will not run such risks. It is more to be dreaded than bullets or grape. So you need not expect to get it soon. Let your imagination drink in the beauty of that serene, angelic countenance, made divinely fair by clustering growths of hair!

I am still alone, but do not expect to be so much longer. Dr. Walker is now in Washington for the purpose, I think of resigning. I hope his place will be supplied by some competent man. So far our department has had no head. We always have had the *chief* on the sick list or in some way disconnected with the regiment. While I have had to bear the heat and burden of the day with more kicks than coppers for compensation. I have no idea who the Surgeon will be; all I know or think about it is, that *I shall not be*, for the reason that no such good fortune ever was mine. If it should be decided in *justice*, I know how the decision would be, but "Kissing goes by favor," and not being one of that kind, I shall not get it.

Newton Phelps starts this morning for home on a furlough of ten days. He will call and tell you all—more than I can write you. He, as Ward Master, has been of great benefit to me, and I am under many obligations to him for the aid afforded in keeping records &c. I shall try to have him take my trunk with him. As you know, it is in a storehouse in Washington where it has been ever since we left Fort Lincoln. It had better be at home than there, as there is no certainty of being in this region next summer. Texas, Georgia and many other places are named as probable grounds of campaigning.—However, you know as much about that as I do. No doubt I shall share the fate of the regiment go where it will, or do as it may.

Until within a month past, I was gradually and slowly going down hill. From my original weight of 140, I had lost flesh to 119—twenty-one pounds; but I am now on the gain both in flesh and weight, and I think by the time we commense operations this Spring I shall be able to stand as much as any one. I like the service, hard as it is. There is just enough excitement on the march, with change of scenery, interesting incidents &c., to make it pleasant; but this state of inaction I cannot endure. Anything is better. Men, beast and all feel better when we are *alive.* So let it come.

Daniel.

Hooker's strategy for the spring campaign of 1863 was to draw Lee out of his fortified position near Fredericksburg into the open where Hooker was sure superior Union numbers would defeat the Confederates. The movements Holt mentions in the following letter are the beginning of Hooker's plan to lighten the load so as to move the army quickly. Holt also makes clear the improvement in the army's morale.

Camp of the 121st Reg. N.Y. Vols.
near White Oak Church, Va.
March 16th, 1863.

My dear Wife:—

I do not know how I can better employ the time than in writing to you, now I have a chance; as the indications are that we shall soon leave this sacred retreat and again assume the aggressive. Perhaps by the time this reaches you, we shall be under marching orders. If not we cannot remain longer than two weeks at the farthest. Every move indicates that *very soon* we shall be "up and off." Siege guns are being placed and earth works constructed opposite and below Fredericksburg—pontoon trains are on the move to the river—officers baggage cut down and every indication that a fearful struggle will soon ensue. Let us hope and pray that when we *do* move, it will be to victory. Hooker says he will drive the rebels out of their entrenchments or he will send his army to a hotter place than they were ever in here below. We are in fighting trim and ready for the fray: Not a man speaks doubtingly or despondingly in view of the "impending crisis." All feel that this is to be a decisive battle, and all are ready for the issue. That many—very many noble sons of the Republic will be stricken down, and the soil drink deeply the blood of the truest, finest and most devoted of America's freemen there is not the shadow of a doubt, still the Nation demands the sacrifice and the sooner it is offered up the better. Let the blows fall heavy and fast until the last vestage of secession is expunged and treason seeks the dark caverns of the earth as a shelter from pursuing justice. There appears to be but one sentiment here, and that is to *fight*. Thank God no *copperheads* disgrace the field or service however plenty they may be at home.[7] Only spike their mouths and chain their tongues at the North, and we will attend to their more honorable brethrin in the South. It is hard to fight two battles at the same time—one in the front and the other in the rear; but if necessary we can attend to both. Let the *women* of our land be loyal and I will trust the men. As I have heretofore stated, it is hard to stand up against *home influence*. Let *that* be right, and I will risk the rest. I hope a righteous and holy recompense will be meted out to all the miserable cringing hypocritical cowards who oppose drafts and clog the wheels of government in every way their ingenuity suggests. I hate them worse than the enemies in front, and would sooner see a field strewn with their blackened, putrid carcasses, than those who we are fighting down here. After this long spell of quiet stillness, I long to hear the booming of cannon again. There is certainly a music in the sound of discharged artillery which to me is anything but discordant. It can be *too close* and *too near* for comfort or safety; still, like the discharge of Nature's artillery it is often more terrific than dangerous.

No treatment is so effective and so sure for secession and treason as large doses of *gunpowder tea* as a menstrum for grape and canister. We have tried the *Alternative* and *Expectant*[8] until they laugh at us, and now we begin what ought to have been administered at the onset. I can tell

7. The Copperheads were the more radical faction of the Peace Democrats. Their strength was primarily in the Midwest, particularly Illinois, Indiana, and Ohio, whence came Rep. Clement Vallandigham, their leader. Their strength in New York came from those convinced that the Emancipation Proclamation of Jan. 1, 1863, had irretrievably changed the nature of the war from one to preserve the Union to one to free the slaves. Those who would preserve the Union and yet would not fight to free the slaves argued that such a fight was an infringement of the right to private property as protected by the Constitution. Wood Gray, *The Hidden Civil War: The Story of the Copperheads*, 146–47, 215–17; McPherson, *Battle Cry*, 591–92.

8. "Menstrum" meaning a liquid that dissolves a solid; "expectant" refers to a method of medical treatment which consists of observing disease and removing any so-called "deranging influences" without prescribing medicines unless necessary.

you how it is, the South is sick and sick nigh unto death, and *"something must be did"*—you know the cooling nature of salt petre, and sulpher as a purifer, and charcoal as a preservative will save them from the fearful fever which is consuming them: —let it be given by injections through iron tubes, and the bed sores be washed with lead lotion, while as a stimulant let Sumner, Stevens and Co., make a porrige for them in their most approved manner.[9] This with the general tonic of hemp and hemlock will effect a cure if it can be had at all.

I believe, if I know myself, that if demanded and necessary, I am willing to die here in the discharge of duty. I am fully aware that it is very easy to sit here and write what you are willing to do, when no danger threatens you, but when actual jeopardy encircles you to shrink back and skulk behind anything affording shelter: but I have canvassed my feelings well and often, and I believe as I have said, that if necessary I would be willing to lay my life down here. My present feeling is, (and not myself only but *all* share it alike) *to fight!* I never was in better spirits than now—never more confident of success,—never, it appears to me, been better prepared to enter upon the blood stained battle field. God grant us all christian fortitude and heroic zeal in this our trying hour.

I am in a great hurry. I want to get this into the mail bag before it leaves for brigade head quarters, and cannot say much more. Please write as often as possible and I will do the same: hoping that the line of our communication may not be interrupted: but you *must not* expect regularity of letters from me much longer. When I can, I will write, and when I can, honorably to myself and country, return to you, I shall be the happiest man in the country. Until such a time goodbye,

Daniel.

Camp in field near
White Oak Church, Va.
March 24th, 1863

My dear wife:—

I have waited, and waited and waited, in hope of hearing from you, until I am almost frantic, and have concluded to wait no longer but sit down and write again myself.

---

9. Charles Sumner, senator from Massachusetts, and Thaddeus Stevens, leader of the Republicans in the House, were both radical abolitionists, determined to make the war a revolution that would end slavery once and for all. See David Herbert Donald, *Charles Sumner and the Rights of Man*, and Fawn M. Brodie, *Thaddeus Stevens: Scourge of the South*.

Phelps has returned and brought what you sent. I am very thankful for your little favors, and shall none the less think of you as I discuss their merits after being cooked in proper French style. It was great comfort to learn how well you were getting along, and well you were looking; for Phelps assured me that you were looking better than ever he saw you before. Really I shall begin to be proud of you. How glad I am that I shall have—a silver gray as I am—when I get home, *a young and beautiful wife!* Really such a Godsend was little expected. Perhaps *I* shall be more lovely when I get home—who knows?

Dr. Schermerhorn was here yesterday, and he gave an interesting account of home matters also.[10] The children so he says, jumped upon his lap, calling him *"Papa"* and appeared delighted to see him. How is it? Do we really look alike, or is there a *spiritual affinity* between them? I should like to see their little black eyes again at any rate, let the affinity rest where it may.

As yet, Dr. Walker has not had his resignation papers returned as accepted. Possibly they may not be and he kept in the service against his will. I like him very much. He is head and shoulders above a whole division or corps of such bipeds as Valentine. We have a 2nd Assistant appointed, but he has not yet reported. His name is *Houghtaling,* a young man from the Western part of the State, but from what particular portion I do not know.[11] I wish he was here now, as there is none too much time to learn his lesson, especially as this is his *first* experience in army life. I long to put him through—not exactly as *I* have been, but in a wholesome good-natured kind of way—such as he will always recollect as being the greatest lesson of his life—*obedience to orders!!* Ahem! *obedient to your humble servent!* Only think of it for a moment, and then do not wonder that I *am* somebody after all.

Huckans is still with me, cooking. I could not get along without him, and shall keep him as long as I can. It seems quite like home to have him and Cox so near and such good companions. Jim Kinyon is now undergoing punishment for some offense by being tied up by the thumbs.[12] It looks bad, but men must learn to do their duty although it is sometimes irksome and against their natural disposition.

10. William B. Schermerhorn, assistant surgeon of the 37th N.Y. Volunteers, was an 1854 graduate of the University of New York. Willard, 28.

11. Dr. Irving W. Houghtaling, whose name is never spelled the same way twice by either Holt or the records, was an 1863 graduate of the University of New York. He served with the 121st right out of school. Ibid., 23.

12. James P. Kenyon had enlisted at Newport on Aug. 2, 1862, for a three-year term and

The old famiar sound of cannon upon the right and center is heard, and I begin to feel that I would like to be in the mass with them. Possibly the firing is only to get range in case of action. This is necessary. Much powder is burned in this way without actual fighting. I hope to hear from you soon or I will have to come home and see what is up. Give usual quantity of love to all, and accept an unusual quantity for yourself.

Daniel.

In late March, Hooker continued to streamline the army in order to make movement easier, but the army did not yet move. Holt and the rest of the army were ready, but it would be several weeks before they would receive orders to march.

> Camp of the 121st Reg. N.Y. Vols.
> near White Oak Church, Va.
> April 2nd, 1863.

My dear Wife:—

I have just received yours of the 29th and hasten to reply. When I last wrote, I supposed that my next would be somewhere else than here; but here we are and no one knows *when* we shall be off. During the last week we have had hard storms of snow and rain which no doubt has served to keep us where we are. Had the weather been good, and the roads passable, I have no doubt that we should before this have fought a decisive battle. However, the matter is but *postponed,* not abandoned. Soon enough, many of us will have passed the portals of the grave, and soon enough the sickening sight of dead men and horses and all the *debris* of a battle field will present themselves. It is sad to contemplate such carnage, but it is inseperable from the condition of things as they now are.

I have been getting my house in order to move, packing hospital and Sanitary supplies—organizing attendants upon the Medical Staff, some as nurses, cooks, stretcher bearers, &c., &c. I am now ready to move at any time with two hours notice, and hope the coming engagement will be more decisive than the previous ons. Dr. Walker returned home last evening, his resignation as Surgeon of this regiment having

---

mustered in as a private with Co. C of the 121st on the 23d. He was discharged for disability on Dec. 23, 1863. Corporal punishments in the army varied according to commanders, and there were no set punishments for many minor infractions of the rules. Stringing men up by the thumbs, forced marches carrying knapsacks loaded with bricks, bucking and gagging—all of these sorts of punishment avoided the cost of prison and trial and made the man available for duty much more quickly. *Annual Report,* 110; Billings, 147–57.

been accepted. No one, as yet, has been appointed in his place, but probably soon will be. There is always some one ready to step forward when a vacancy occurs. All I desire is that a better one than Valentine will receive the commission.

I shall write to the boys soon. I feel a deep interest in them now that they are soldiers, and hope they will so conduct themselves as to bring no reproach upon their good name. The *regular mittens* of the Herkimer Co. ladies have come, and I am pleased to say, were "all our fancy painted them"—*good, first rate, a great improvement over the first lot sent.*

Daniel.

Camp of the 121st Reg. N.Y. Vols.
near White Oak Church, Va.,
April 6th, 1863.

My dear Wife:—

I believe I never again will write that we *expect* to move, for I have given up all such hopes or expectations. I see no more signs of an advance to-day than a month ago: yet I suppose we are liable to do so at any time. Day-before-yesterday we were ordered to strike tents which we did (as some were condemned and others were *extra*—that is more than we were allowed by orders) and we are now in shelter or *"poncho"* tents.[13]

It is Sunday today, and nearly time for the mail to leave, and I must not write much if it goes out in this mail. It closes at 4 o'clock P.M. and is within ten minutes of the time. Were it not that an occasional visit *from* a friend or *to* one, relieved the monotony of camp life, I hardly know how I should pass the tedious hours. Yesterday I went to see Dr. Schemerhorn but did not see him because of his regiment being off on picket about eight [miles?] out and he with it. I thought our encampment nothing extra, but it is a perfect paradise compared with his. Many of the old regiments have splendid quarters, especially those that are situated near pine timber. This they get and decorate their streets—setting out lines of trees and enclosing hospital and head quarters with beautiful festoons—devices masonic and otherwise—made of the small twigs and branches—the heads of streets arched; with letters of the Company occupying the street hanging in graceful

13. Holt's reference to a "poncho tent" probably refers to a tent made out of a poncho, since there was no standard army-issued tent called by that term. Army ponchos were made of unbleached muslin, then coated with India-rubber for waterproofing. Billings, 47–55.

circles over head. Of all the troops in the field for such fanciful decorations, the Massachusetts boys carry off the palm. As for us, we only thought of living as comfortably as possible without such surroundings; but we will learn another winter if we are out so long. It is better to have men employed in this way than not at all.

Daniel.

Camp of the 121st Reg. N.Y. Vols.
near White Oak Church, Va.
April 10, 1863.

My dear Wife:—

Yours of the 6th came to hand last night, having been just *three* days on its passage. This is the "shortest time on record" for a letter to start from the interior of New-York and arrive here in the heart of Virginia in so short a time. It must have made connection in every instance, for letters sent from Washington here have sometimes been *six* days in coming.

The Army of the Potomac has been reviewed by corps since my last. Yesterday Father Abraham, wife and son condescended to look lovingly upon his children in the 6th Corps.[14] As we passed in review I *smiled* at him and he *grinned* at me, he did, or *ought* to. His whiskers have fallen before the fatal stroke of the rasor, which shows a care-worn and weary look. Poor man, I pity him, and almost wonder at his being alive. The gigantic work upon his hands, and the task upon his physical frame must be very great. I have no doubt but he, as well as all the rest of us, feels the weight of the war, and as sincerely desires its end; which God grant may very soon be.

The weather for the past three days has been all that heart could wish or desire—warm and pleasant, the mud is fast drying up, and if we are *ever* to move, it seems that the day cannot be far distant. The tents of the enemy are seen in great numbers over the river opposite our encampment, and instead of *lessening* actually appear to multiply. It has been thought that Lee was transferring his men to other points, but I am fully satisfied that no withdrawal has taken place, but rather a concentration before our army here, expecting to meet us in such a way

14. The reference here is to Lincoln's review of about 12,000 soldiers of Hooker's army, which he attended with Mrs. Lincoln, Attorney-General Bates, and others. Nevins, *War Becomes Revolution*, 435.

as he never has before.[15] This is *my* opinion—none else. We shall have to meet a strong and determined foe—one worthy of our steel, and one who believing in the justness of their cause will fight like true American soldiers. When I speak of their *believing* in the rectitude and justness of their cause, of course I have reference to the *rank and file,* not to those in command of the army or those having charge of their miserable assumed government. These are *universally* almost, I believe, dishonest and have no real interest in common with their men. All their object is to secure power and place which they have lost, and which never again will be restored to them. Drowning men catch at straws, and so do these Confederate officials. Anything which for a moment offers the least hope of prolonging a worthless cause they eagerly seize upon; and by blinding the eyes of an illiterate soldiery—promising success and great prosperity after the war is over, they are induced to continue a struggle as hopeless and as surely doomed to death, as though every artery in the body were severed.

I have just finished *drinking tea*—had company and a jolly good time generally. It was rather a *surprise* party, after all. Several Captains and Lieutenants saw fit to make me a visit unexpected (at least so far as two thirds were concerned) but Tom [Huckans] contrived to help me out in good style, at least for the army. We had lemon pie, tomato catsup, ham, nuts, apples, roast beef, chicken, coffee and tea, sweatened with *maple sugar,* custard, cookies, &c. So you see that we are not entirely destitute of good things when we really set about getting them. The worst and most uncomfortable thing about it was *want of room* to seat so many— nine at a little table not over two and a half feet square. *"How did you do it?"* I hear you ask. Well it was *not* done. Every man held his plate in his lap while the viands were placed upon the board. Dishes we borrowed from those who came to visit. In this way we got along very well.

By the way I had a *grand seranade* last evening. About twenty of the men visited my quarters just before *"taps"*—sang three or four songs, cheered the *"Doctor",* and after bidding them welcome in as good style as the department would allow, bade them depart in peace, which they did, playing *"Dixie"* as they went. I tell you we have some good times

15. Holt is incorrect here. Lee was down to about 62,000 men. He had ordered Longstreet south in February to cover the Union forces that had reinforced Suffolk, Va. About 24,000 men were with Longstreet to resist any Union move against Richmond from the south; Hooker had 112,000 facing the men Lee had left. *OR*, vol. 18, 883–84; Nevins, *War Becomes Revolution,* 439.

here as well as bad ones. The only way to get along is to be cheerful and look at the brighter side of the picture all the while. I have many warm and good friends here. My heart is with the boys and the regiment: and they appear to be suited to the "old doctor" as they good naturedly call me. They take my raps at Surgeon's Call about as they take my pills, because they cannot help themselves, and because, unlike them, they never kill:—this they have found out and take both together as a necessary mixture. It does no man good to wear a long, mournful face and in a mood of despondency to hear from the Surgeon that his case is desperate and that death will probably result. Better tell him that *nothing* is the matter—that *imagination* is the disease and dismiss him, even though half sick, to do his duty. I have cured many a man who was really unwell by simply making him believe that his sickness was all in his mind.[16] I must close, as a man stands in front of the tent waiting for me to cure him of earache. So good bye.

Daniel.

On April 13, Stoneman's cavalry corps left camp to cross the Rappahannock upstream of Fredericksburg. One unit, under Brig. Gen. Grimes Davis, got across; Stoneman, with the main body of troops, hesitated at Rappahannock Bridge and lost the moment to caution and to rain. By the 15th, the Rappahannock was out of its banks, and the army's eagerly awaited chance to move was lost.

Camp of the 121st Reg.
New York Volunteers near
White Oak Church, Virginia
April 14th, 1863.

My dear Wife:—

We have at last received marching orders and I am in a perfect hubbub getting my house in order. All I have time to say is, that when I know more I will write again. The weather is propitious and I hope we

16. Psychosomatic illnesses had begun to be recognized during the Civil War as a specific medical phenomenon. Dr. S. Weir Mitchell, who served a part-time post in an army hospital in Philadelphia, specialized in the treatment of what were called "wounds of the nerves," including observation and treatment of phantom pain associated with amputation. His work attracted the notice of Surgeon-General Hammond, who established a hospital specifically for treatment of nervous disorders among the wounded. Mitchell and his associates published the results of their treatments and observations in 1864 in a work, *Gunshot Wounds and Other Injuries of the Nerves.* See David M. Rein, "S. Weir Mitchell, Pioneer Psychiatrist in the Civil War," 65–71.

shall be successful this time. Let us pray God that we shall come off with honor and victory. I had sent up an application for leave of absence, which has not yet been reported. There is not a shadow of hope of leaving now; neither would I do so if leave was granted. I did not come to skulk but do my duty as a true man, and no one shall ever say of me in truth that I was found missing when wanted. I have help now. Dr. Houghtaling has arrived, and I am relieved. Good bye. I only wrote to tell you of the joyful news that we are *probably* to move—not positively certain however, as I have sometimes found.

Daniel.

Despite Holt's impatience with the army's inactivity, he and the soldiers continued to hope that Hooker would lead them to victory and put an end to the war.

Camp of the 121st Reg. N.Y. Vols
near White Oak Church, Va.
April 20th, 1863.

My dear Wife:—

When I last wrote you on the 14th, we were under marching orders, and I was head and ears in work getting my house in order:—but here we are still, and *here I am of the opinion we shall be until we move!!* I believe I never again will place any dependense upon such orders as being final, for we are so often deceived about it, that no one can tell whether it will be so or not. *I* can see no reason why we should remain here long. The roads are getting in fine condition. Spring is fairly established and "the voice of the turtle is heard in the land."[17] The *"espirite de corps"* of the Army never was better, and to all appearance the leading of the men to battle is leading them to victory. We all hope that Hooker (fighting Joe) will knock rebellion dead this time: It is a righteous punishment this war, after all: for we as a Nation had done evil and not good. We had forgotten God and set up idols instead. As prosperity increased, so increased we in disobedience to the Divine will, until at last the wail of the oppressed reached the eternal throne, and the avenging angel swept over the land destroying our fields lying waste the heritage and killing our sons. How can we, as a Nation expect the smiles of heaven when we hold in bondage, sell and chastise our fellow man for the simple reason that the color of his skin is not like our own, though cre-

---

17. Holt's biblical quote is from the Song of Solomon 2:12 (KJV).

ated by the same hand and sustained by the same power? I tell you Louisa, *we never shall succeed until we let the oppressed go free. Never, never, never will God grant us the victory and establish our government until it can be done in righteousness.* We cannot roll the sin of slavery under our tongue as a sweet morsel and claim the divine favor. It is impious to call upon God for a blessing while we dare have such cruelty in our hearts. Then let us put away the evil from among us to be really what we profess—a God-fearing and brother-loving people. Then and not until then, will peace flow in our land like a mighty river, and Ethiopia stretching forth her hands unto God, shall be recognized and dealt with as a sister nation upon the earth.

Daniel

When Stoneman's cavalry failed in its original objective, Hooker modified his strategy slightly, splitting the army in three. The cavalry would cross upstream of Fredericksburg, then head south to cut Lee's supply lines. While the Sixth Corps, now under Maj. Gen. John Sedgwick, would attempt to distract Lee by feigning an attack at Fredericksburg, the rest of the Union army would cross the rivers to attack Lee's left flank and rear. If Lee withdrew from Fredericksburg, Sedgwick was to take Marye's Heights and pursue. Hooker was successful in his maneuvering; by April 30, seventy thousand soldiers had arrived at a spot nine miles west of Fredericksburg called Chancellorsville, well positioned to force Lee out of his entrenchments.

Camp of the 121st Reg. N.Y. Vols.
near White Oak Church, Va.
April 28, 1863.

My dear Wife:—

I have but one moment to write. The Army of the Potomac is on the move. *We* leave at 3 o'clock this afternoon. God be with you, dear one. I shall write again as soon as possible. In the meantime let us pray that our heavenly Father will be with us shielding us from all harm. Pray for your poor unworthy husband—that he may, trusting in the God of battles, escape the sad fate of many of those around me. Again dear wife, good bye. Love to all—especially the little ones.

Daniel.

Lee responded to Hooker's flanking move by marching most of his army toward Chancellorsville. Seeing this, Sedgwick assaulted Marye's Heights as ordered.

The Sixth Corps succeeded in pushing aside the small Confederate force under Maj. Gen. Jubal Early that had been left to cover Marye's Heights and then headed in the direction of Chancellorsville. Pushing westward, the corps made its way as far as a wooded area near Salem Church on May 3. Sedgwick had carried out his orders, but he was too late. Lee had already defeated Hooker at Chancellorsville and was able to send part of his army to reinforce Early and counterattack. Sedgwick's leading division barely survived the Confederate attack, and Sedgwick abandoned his hopes for an advance and deployed his corps in defensive positions near Salem Church. The next day matters grew worse as Lee continued to press Sedgwick and brought up another division. That night Sedgwick withdrew back across the Rappahannock.

The 121st took an active part in both the storming of Marye's Heights and the battle at Salem Church. During the savage fighting in the latter action, Holt was captured and detained by the Confederates for several days. In the following letter Holt assured his wife of his safety and then proceeded to inform her of his capture by the Rebels.

Camp of the 121st Reg. N.Y. Vols.
near White Oak Church, Va.
May 15th, 1863.

My dear Wife:—

Thank God, after a hard fight and many dangers, I am at last among my own people, with the little remnant of our brave and glorious regiment. You have heard, and correctly so, that I had been captured, together with twenty others who were under my command, acting as hospital attendants, &c. It was upon the evening of the 4th, next day after the sanguinary engagement at Salem Church, where we were almost totally annihilated, as the enemy was pressing upon our retreating columns, that I left my position a few rods in rear of our brigade, taking a stand a short distance to the left where I established our field hospital, and went to work dressing the wounds of those brought to the rear, when I was ordered to change quarters as the rebels were pressing and very close upon us. I did not immediately obey, but continued to dress such wounds as came to me. A Jerseyman of our brigade was bleeding profusely from the effect of a wound in the axila,[18] the artery being cut off, and in my efforts to arrest the hemorrhage by

18. "Axila" meaning armpit. Holt's reference to a "Jerseyman" is unclear. There were no New Jersey regiments in his brigade; the first brigade of the division, however, was composed entirely of New Jersey regiments.

compression, as it was too dark to do anything else, I was delayed beyond the time I ought to have been; but when at length I so far succeeded as to arrest the flow, I gathered together my squad and addressed them upon the importance of keeping together and under no circumstances to *straggle,* remarking, as I mounted my horse for them to follow *Silver Tail* (the name given to my cream colored, white mane and tail horse) and that if we went to the d——l we would all go together. Let me tell you I feared that all was not *exactly* right, because I had seen the rebels "swinging *round the circle*" and enclosing us as in a net,[19] and our forces going for sweet life to the only outlet for them— "Bank's Ford" on the Rappahannock, four or five miles above Fredericksburg. It was now after dark, so that I could not distinguish between our own men and those of the enemy: but proceeded in the direction of the sound of cheers close at hand. Not feeling quite secure, I sent out scouts, who came back reporting that nothing could be seen but *behind,* that the cheering came from our own men, as they were occupying the ground but a very short time previously. Having no alternative, I rode along, where I saw just ahead of me, not more than three rods distant, a moving line of battle, up to which I rode and asked an officer—a captain who was leading his company, *"What Brigade is this?"* to which the answer came, *"Kershaw's"!* Well, thought I, "this *is* rather queer:" but as Brigadiers were as plenty as blackberries in the army, I did not know but our own side had many such names in it, but of *that* fact, I knew nothing. After imparting to me this cheering piece of news, the officer to whom I addressed the inquiry, asked me: "To what regiment do *you* belong?" "The 121st" says I, at the same time *halting my* men who were close upon my heels. *"Halt! Halt!! Halt!!!"* ran all along the line in answer to mine for my men. It took but a moment to ascertain that the *"Kershaw"* in question was Rebel General Kershaw of the *South Carolina* forces, instead of ours. [20] *"The 121st what?"* says my interrogator. *"The 121st N. York"* says I. "What rank do you hold?" says

19. Holt's reference to "swinging round the circle" refers to Lee's march from Chancellorsville, which cut off Sedgwick from Fredericksburg. Sedgwick's position wound up being a semicircle. *B&L,* 3:158.

20. Joseph Brevard Kershaw commanded a brigade of McLaws's Division, First Corps, Army of Northern Virginia, from July 1862 until September 1863 when he transferred along with the rest of Longstreet's corps to the Army of Tennessee (excluding Pickett's division). At Chancellorsville, McLaws's division was one of two Lee took to help Early against Sedgwick while leaving Stuart to watch Hooker. Stewart Sifakis, *Who Was Who in the Civil War,* 2:360–61.

Johnny Reb, for so he was. *"Surgeon!"* says I. *"Well, doctor, I think you will have to dismount. I am very sorry to say that you have fallen into the hands of the rebels this time, and there is no help for you!"* Imagine my *disgust* at such information! Surely in *following Silver Tail,* we had all gone to the d——l together.

As I have said before, I commanded my men to *"halt!"* in the most approved style—loud and clear—and this order was given all along the rebel line, bringing to a stand still the entire rebel army—two lines being in motion at the time of my running, like a fool, into their very mouths. While still upon my horse, an officer rode up in a great rage, inquiring as he advanced, *"Who had the audacity to command a halt at that time?"* In the simplicity of my heart I answered that *"I"* had been guilty of the offense. *"By what authority did you do so?"* "No authority, only I could not well run over you, and gave my men orders to halt!" *"Who are you, sir?"* "Surgeon Holt of the 121st Reg. N.Y. Vols. of the federal Army!"—*"Federal army be damned! and you too!!* Captain place a guard over him and his men and keep them safe until morning!" It is needless to say that it was done in *"due and ancient form"* and your beloved husband from henceforth rode his own natural horses, "Silver Tail", accoutrements, blankets, &c., &c., &c., passing quietly and gently into the hands of others—*my most esteemed friends.* I never had a transfer of property more complete and thorough and with so few words, and apparently so satisfactory *on one side* as this. *It was charming.*

Into a room about eight by ten feet, twenty-one of us were packed together with three or four *guards,* who immediately began to barter our boys to swap canteens, which most of them did, receiving a difference in silver and greenbacks a sum twice the original cost of the article. This propensity to *trade* extended to pocket knives, watches, &c. and in fact to every trifle or trinket we carried with us. Talk about Yankees natural inclination to dicker! I never, in all my life saw such inveterate Yankees as these very graybacks. Not only the rank and file, but the Officers, also, wanted to possess what we happened to have— perhaps as *relics*—perhaps not; but more than one was after my green sash which happened to be upon my person at the time of capture. It was a hard thing to keep even *photographs,* they seeming to think that in the features revealed they beheld either a beauty or monster, I cannot tell which; but the fact is certain that they attached, apparently considerable importance to being the possessor of even the shadow of a d——d *"Yank"* as we are called. In the morning, I desired to be allowed to visit and relieve our boys who had been wounded in the battles of the previous two days, but more especially those of our own regiment. About three hundred had been killed and wounded and I know that many more were lying in a small brick church a short distance off.[21]

My request was complied with, and taking with me Phelps, the then Hospital Steward and the ward master, I started for the scene of action. As soon as I opened the door a score of voices cried out, "Oh doctor! doctor!! God bless you, doctor Holt, have you come to dress my wounds? Have you brought anything to eat?" and a thousand such questions until I fairly broke down, and had to weep like a child. Upon one side lay Capt. Arnold, slowly breathing life away, and beside him, the noble body of Lieutenant Upton, brother of the Colonel of our regiment, shot through the shoulder and upper portion of the right lung, and still by his side, the color bearer, Baine, with a ball lodged in his body; and all in extreme agony.[22] All over and around the building the best blood of Herkimer and Otsego was dripping away upon the rebel soil of the Old Dominion, and none were here to alleviate or in anywise to lessen the racking pain, subdue the fever, quench the thirst or fill the mouths of our dying heroes. As I took the hands of our men and felt the grip of real pleasure at seeing me, I thought how much good *one* man can do when so disposed and how much real comfort one poor soul can yield another; and there, where vows had been made before high heaven to deal justly and uprightly to all—where vows of fraternity and good will toward all had been noted by listening angels, here I renewed *my* covenant to God that I would do all in my power to give relief, and solace the pillow of death: and it was needed. Worn out by fatigue and faint through want of proper food (for I had for the three days

21. Holt is off by only a few casualties. Of the 453 men in the 121st, 276 died or were wounded at Salem Church in a battle that saw over 10,000 Confederate and just under 8,000 Union casualties. Boatner, 595; *OR*, vol. 25, 1:185, 806; Fox, 229.

22. Capt. Thomas Arnold mustered in as first lieutenant with Co. C on Aug. 23, 1862. He made captain of Co. H in October and was wounded in action on May 3, 1863, at the Battle of Salem Church. He died of his wounds on May 18. Lt. Henry Upton, who began his career as a private in the 104th Illinois Infantry, mustered in as second lieutenant, Co. G of the 121st, on Mar. 11, 1863. He transferred to Co. C in April and mustered in as first lieutenant on May 3, the same day he was wounded in action at Salem Church. He survived the fight and was discharged for disability on Feb. 27, 1864. Baine's identity is not clear. There was no man in the 121st by that name under any spelling, but the 16th N.Y. did include a Lt. Andrew C. Bayne, and the 16th was at Salem Church, so this may be the man to whom Holt refers. Phisterer, 3429, 3438; *OAR*, 2:448.

previous, neither seen meat or bread, and had slept but a very few hours during all that time) I went to work, more dead than alive, but with a will which in some degree compensated, and thus struggled on for four days longer until help arrived from our side of the river. When I now look back upon those days so full of incidents and suffering, I can hardly realize that I have passed through it, and am still alive. Yet I worked and staggered on until it seemed as if I could not drag one foot before another; and while bending over the bodies of our boys dressing their wounds, my eyes, in spite of me, would close, and I have found myself fast asleep over a dying man. Had not General Wilcox (Confederate)[23] kindly supplied me with food from his own table, and made me a *guest* rather than a prisoner, I believe I should have been compelled to throw myself down with the rest and crave the treatment I myself was yielding. As it was, I kept about, being the recipient of numerous favors from rebel officers, always treated with respect, and in very many cases with marked kindness. Here General Lee came to see me. Four times did this great man call and feelingly inquire if the men were receiving all the care that could be bestowed: at the same time remarking that it was beyond his power to yield such succor as his heart prompted. Their army, he remarked, was not supplied as ours, with Sanitary and Christian Commission supplies, neither was the Medical department as completely and thoroughly equipped—no chloroform for minor cases of Surgery—no stimulents for moderate or severe prostration, and as a consequence no means of alleviating the suffering of their men,—All that he *could,* he *did* do: he sent the Medical Director of their army to look in upon us and to supply help in amputations &c., which by this time had become imperative.[24] Death was upon our track and most nobly did these Surgeons combat it. Not alone in the breasts of our men dwell humanity. Human nature is about the same the world over, and I found just as sympathetic hearts here as anywhere. I must in justice say for an enemy, that I never was treated with greater consideration by intelligent men, than I was by these very rebs for the ten days I remained among them; and at the same time I might say I never had so hard a time. The experience of a life time was crowded into these

23. Gen. Cadmus Marcellus Wilcox commanded a brigade in Gen. Richard Anderson's division, First Corps, Army of Northern Virginia. Anderson's was the second of the two divisions Lee took to help Early against Sedgwick. Sifakis, 712–13.

24. The medical director of the Army of Northern Virginia was Surgeon Lafayette Guild, who had joined Lee's staff in the spring of 1862. Ibid., 272.

eventful days:—more of actual labor—more of real suffering, bodily and mentally—more of positive pleasure mixed up with pain in the discharge of duty.

One day as I was looking over the field to see if I could discover the body of little *"Bennie West,"* as he was familiarly called in the hospital squad to which he belonged previously to the time of crossing the river, but into whose hands a musket had been placed upon the morning of that fatal day,[25] I was halted by a young grayback who presented his piece at my breast and pulled trigger, but the musket for some reason would not go off. After expostulating with him upon the enormity of shooting a man in cold blood and giving him as good a lesson as I was capable of upon the recklessness of not knowing or caring what he was doing, he candidly informed me that he was acting from the impulse of the moment—not expecting to see a Union Officer then and supposing that he was in the line of duty, he concluded to add one.more to the mass of decaying putrid humanity around us. I was realy thankful that I had thus escaped, and concluded that hereafter when I visited the field it would be under the protection of a guard or in company with a Confederate Officer. On another occasion, as I stood with two other surgeons at the operating table inside the church, a soldier who was examining the arms which were stacked against the building, with a view of getting a gun better then his own, by accident discharged the piece, the ball passing just beside my head and wedged in the pillar supporting the gallery within a foot [of] me. Seeing the danger of having several hundred guns, as they were picked up after a battle,— some loaded, others not, standing where anyone desiring to get one through necessity or fancy, an application was made to have them removed which was done; and from henceforth our lives were no more in jeopardy from that cause.

As you may imagine, after assistance arrived from our side, I had time to take a little refreshment and ease:—With the supplies came wine, brandy, whiskey and delicacies for the sick, which very soon became known to our brethren of the Confederacy. It is truly wonderful what a change of feeling takes place in a man's *agreeableness* when made happy and pleasant by good cheer. The house became crowded

25. Benton "Bennie" West enlisted in August 1862 at age eighteen. He served as a private in Co. B until his death in action at Salem Church on May 3. A legal minor, West's enlistment had to be approved by his parents. His papers listed his occupation as "teacher." Clinton Moon Papers, Herkimer County Historical Society; *Annual Report*, 200.

sometimes, with Army Officials, all of whom, to [all] appearance, left well satisfied that the Surgical Department of the loyal army, if no other, was well supplied and *better officered.* Then it was my good fortune to become acquainted with Dr. Todd, a Brigade Surgeon, and a brother of Mrs. Lincoln.[26] Upon remarking to him that I had the pleasure of seeing the President and his sister at a corps service a few days previous, he remarked "Well, I don't know as I feel any the better or worse for that. She is a poor weak-minded woman anyhow."—A rather light estimate I thought of her character, but one in which if I did not express it, I fully concurred. This Dr. Todd is anything but a pleasing personage— short, rather inferior looking with an impediment in his speech, the first impression as to intelligence is unfavorable; but subsequent acquaintance reveals quite a different man. He is pleasant when engaged in lively conversation, and much of the hesitation in speech is overcome as he becomes interested in the matter under discussion:—I think I should like him very much even though he is thoroughly rebel in every particular: still the gentleman within him prevents all allusion to unpleasant topics such as discussions upon the political questions of the day, and relative merits of Confederate and loyal soldiers.

Prices of everything here are very high:—for instance, I gave *fifty cents a piece* for three small *dipped* tallow candles, and this in greenbacks. The common price is $3.00 per pound. Ham $1.35 lb., Eggs $2.00 dozen. Whiskey $160.00 per gallon! I was offered $20.00 in Confederate rags for a quart, but had none to sell. Calico $4.00 per yd., and everything in proportion! Feeling a desire for a small piece of veal, we (the Surgeons) thought we would buy a small calf which I heard was for sale at a house just at hand. We delegated Phelps (Hospital Steward) to make the purchase if possible, and report the cost. This he did as follows:—Price—$150.00 in greenbacks and a *gallon of Whiskey!* $160.00 more!! leaving the snug little sum of $310.00!! sufficient to move a large family from the East and locate it upon a farm in the West of 160 acres, or a quarter section, of as good land as lies within the limits of the United States, and all for a paltry little lousy calf not weighing more than sixty pounds, all told. And the most singular of all was, that the man did not appear to be anxious to get rid of it for that: as-

26. Todd's service with the Confederacy began in 1861 and was one of the reasons Mary Todd Lincoln suffered from accusations that she sympathized with the Confederates. Most of her relatives retained their Southern sympathies. Jean Baker, *Mary Todd Lincoln: A Biography,* 223–24.

serting that by carrying it to Richmond he could realize a much greater sum; and I have no doubt of it, knowing what I do of the *quantity* and *quality* of the confederate shin plasters.[27]—

It may be asked *how* the common soldiery subsist upon the pittance of eleven dollars in their miserable scrip, which we know they receive and no more. I answer they get their *rations* and *clothing* such as it is, and with economy, enough to support *themselves;* but when a *family* has to live out of the *per diem* of a soldier, it is folly to think that it serves to eke out a life for a week. The difference between *their* currency and ours, as reported at present, is as twenty to one: thus leaving in reality in *cash,* less than fifty cents a month for fighting such battles as we compel them to fight, and destroying every vestage of a living left them when we came upon it. Surely, the life of a rebel soldier is no *sinecure* letting alone the agreeableness of it.[28] In conversation with a very intelligent man—a common soldier of their army, I asked him how it was that such a state of things could exist—how a man receiving eleven dollars in confederate rags could support a wife and children at home? He answered by saying, "Here you have a fair example. *I get eleven dollars a month and spend it the same day I draw it, for a pint of whisky!* I never think nor do any of the rest of us, of sending home money: but on the contrary we have to send home for funds to keep us going in the army. If we want anything more than hard tack and corn meal, we have to pay for it, and then our wages go in no time. We can *live* on what we are allowed, and when you say that, it is all. During the last year, my wife has sent to me from Tennessee, over eighteen hundred dollars, and last week I sent home for seven hundred more. I am a printer by trade and have an office at Memphis, but fight with my body here; while my wife runs the machine and fights you Yanks at the South." Well, here it is all in a nutshell—as clear as day! and no wonder such men fight hard. They appear to really believe that their homes and firesides demand the sacrifice of life and every comfort as much as even our revolutionary sires believed it their duty to oppose tyrants.

It was amusing in the extreme to see the different vehicles which composed the baggage and supply trains. Fully one-half had the *"U.S."* mark upon them, having been captured from our army. These were the *best,* but *all* looked old and rickety—such as we would have condemned long

27. "Shin plasters" meaning paper money made worthless by inflation.
28. "Sinecure" meaning an office with remuneration but no duties.

ago. The balance was made up of all sorts of country wagons with "prairie schooner"[29] boxes rearing their lofty forms and sterns heavenward, while beside their venerable companions moved the family carriage drawn by a couple of mules, upon the back of the nigh one, riding the everlasting *"Nigger"* with his long whip and one line, feeling as important as the most lordly. In keeping with their trains are their troops—of all ages, heights and complexions, not a more motley or grotesque troupe could by possibility be got together. Beside the old grandfather marched the grandson, and beside the tall lank tar boiler of the Carolinas trudged the lilliputian drummer boy scarcely strong enough to carry the load which swung upon his shoulders. Officers dressed in splendid uniforms, mounted upon steeds ready to stumble through weakness, afforded a striking contrast between our well fed animals and theirs. No *grain* of any kind, so I was informed enter the mouths of the poor brutes; that having to go down the throats of the rank and file. A little hay, straw and corn fodder, together with pasturage when the army was lying in camp was all that the horses and mules were allowed.

I find that I might spin this out to an untold and indefinite length, but will abruptly close, leaving for future letters a fuller synopsis of the days while I was a prisoner in rebeldom. Had not General Lee, through influences which may be inferred, when it is Known that we are both masons, seen fit to let me off very easily when the other surgeons returned by flag of truce across the river, after having sent the wounded before them (in all amounting to about one hundred) and in the height of his excellence restored to me, horse, blankets, sword and accoutrements, I might now be an inmate of Libby; but thanks to General Lee and the rest of the Confederate officers I never was better and more handsomely treated, and shall ever feel a debt of gratitude toward them, hard to liquidate.[30]

You have asked me to give a description of a battle—of a field after the angel of death has passed over it; but I can no more do so than I can give you an idea of anything indescribable. You must stand as I have stood, and hear the report of battery upon battery, witness the effect of shell, grape and canister—you must hear the incessant discharge of

29. "Prairie schooner" meaning a large covered wagon such as those used by pioneers going across the western prairies of the United States.
30. "Libby" meaning the Confederates' Libby Prison in Richmond. In June 1862, both armies had agreed that noncombatants, including physicians, would not be held as prisoners of war. The order was only sporadically obeyed. Gillett, 181.

musketry, see men leaping high in air and falling dead upon the ground—others without a groan or a sigh yielding up their life from loss of blood—see the wounded covered with dirt and blackened by powder—hear their groans—witness their agonies, see the eye grow dim in death, before you can realize or be impressed with its horrors. Notwithstanding all this, you do not see it in its true light. You become excited, enraged, and the only feeling is that of retaliation and revenge. You will scarcely believe me when I say, that during that awful conflict I forgot that my office and duty was to care for the wounded—that I longed to be in the fray and unnecessarily exposed myself to dangers such as I now shrink from. I have been covered with dirt and stones thrown over me by the bursting of shells within a few feet of me—had balls pass in unpleasant proximity to my head, and still felt no disposition to change position. The only feeling then, was, to avenge the death of those who a few hours previously were by my side and had apparently as many happy days as I to live, and as many old scores to settle. But when cool reflection comes—when exhausted nature gives place to repose—when reason resumes her throne, you begin to realize the awful tragedy. I hope never again to be in such a fight; yet to-day, if necessary, I am willing to follow our noble boys and share their fate, in the effort to redeem our common country. This is a terrific war! A war where brother meets brother—father a son, and son a neighbor. Oh when will these battling elements cease? I see no speedy termination— I would that I could: but the sable clouds still hover—the heavens are hung in black—no cheering light penetrates the gloom of contending elements. I see only through the eye of faith, a brighter day. The natural eye discovers no faint streak of morning light—all, all is dark, around, above, before, on every hand. Still I do not despair. The hurricane must expend its violence—the raging elements be still—order must be restored out of chaos. That time may be nearer than I suppose. I hope it is. I am satisfied with human gore; and no one would be more willing than I to leave this spot if it could be done with honor to ourselves and justice to the Nation: but sooner than recede an inch from the God-inspired principle of freedom which incites to action this noble army of men, or compromise the weight of a feather with rebels in arms, I would still see the same scenes of bloodshed re-enacted everyday, until a perpetual and honorable peace is secured.

It is rumored that we are to cross or *attempt* to cross the river again very soon: If so, there is but little hope of seeing you for a long while.

I do not know, but I am becoming demoralized, for when I think how hard I have to work and get so little pay—assuming the duties and responsibilities of surgeon with neither *rank* or *pay*, and this too, for months and months together, my patience is pretty nearly exhausted, and unless a change takes place pretty soon, I shall resign my commission in this regiment, and try for another.[31] No other command would suit me as well, so far as *social* connections are concerned, and none would be more joyfully left, if burden and responsibility are to come into the account. Perhaps I shall feel better next time I write: as I am now, nothing looks hopeful or cheerful. To see the miserable little remnant of our full, noble regiment as it was, when we left Herkimer less than a year ago—to see scarcely a corporal's guard going out on dress parades with colors so torn and shattered as to be unfit to unfurl (if indeed it could be) and feeling that these little companies, some of them not larger than *fifteen* in number will soon be still further reduced, and your own life correspondingly unsafe, is a thought not pleasant to dwell upon nor profitable either: so I will try to think as little of it as possible and again return to duty.

Daniel

In the following letter, Holt continued the saga of the 121st's adventures during the Chancellorsville campaign, detailing the advance across the river the night of April 29. This had been the first major engagement of the 121st. Upton drilled and trained his men precisely for a moment such as this. They put up a stubborn resistance at this strategic point in the battle, but a price was paid. The 121st New York suffered more casualties than any other regiment in the Army of the Potomac, a loss of 278 men killed and wounded. Holt was particularly saddened by the death of Capt. Nelson Wendell, a man with whom he spoke just before the battle.

Camp of the 121st Reg. N.Y. Vols,
near White Oak Church, Virginia
May 17th, 1863.

31. The differences between the duties of assistant surgeon and surgeon were not that great medically but entailed much more administrative work on the part of the surgeon. The point here is that clearly Holt was doing the work of the surgeon and had been for some time because of the illness of Bassett and Walker, and the incompetence of Valentine. He deserved promotion; in fact, he had passed the examination to be ranked as surgeon prior to his assignment with the 121st. Willard, 10.

My dear Wife:—

I do not intend, as a day-before-yesterday to inflict upon you the pain of reading a *sixteen* page letter, but simply to inform you in what manner I have sent money and by whom. It is a great relief to get rid of it, as I had, during my captivity among the rebels about fifteen hundred dollars upon my person—money left in my hands, the [most?] of it, as being safer than in the hands of those who owned it. I had about $250.00 belonging to Captain Wendell who was killed in the engagement at Salem Church,[32] and *this* was saved to his friends who will in a short time become possessed of it. Only a day or two previous to the fight he gave it to me, remarking that he had been in a great many engagements before and came out all right, and never felt until then that there was danger of being killed; but *now* a strange foreboding of evil attended him, and he wanted me to take charge of his effects until after the battle.—He would keep only *five* dollars—a sum sufficient for a few days requirements, and a sum sufficiently large to fall into the hands of the enemy. Poor fellow, I saw him with about two hundred others, stretched out before a trench half full of water, into which they were to be thrown at the convenience of their captors. *Entirely naked,* his greenbacks would have served a poor purpose towards clothing him for the tomb, and as I looked upon all that remained of so pure and worthy a man as he, I thought how well it was that in life he had provided against such a contingency as I now saw in his death.

As I have not given you an account of our march down to, and crossing the river, I will, in as few words as possible, try to tell you how it was effected. On the day of our breaking camp at this place, it was in a drizzling, sleety rain, arriving at (or near) the river after dark. About a mile below the city (Fredericksburg) it was contemplated to lay the bridges, and the columns were ordered to halt and make themselves as comfortable as possible, without fire, until 11 o'clock when it was anticipated the boats would be shoved into the river, and a portion of the troops embark for the other side. After partaking of a previously prepared meal, our men rolling themselves in their blankets prepared to consign themselves to sleep—a sleep, as it proved to

32. Nelson O. Wendell mustered in as captain with Co. F, Aug. 23, 1862. He was killed in action on May 3, 1863. Emory Upton later recalled that Wendell was standing beside Upton in the line of battle when a minie ball struck him in the shoulder, throwing him several feet. Wendell rose from the blow but was struck again, this time in the head, and killed instantly. Emory Upton to W. A. Johnson, Oct. 25, 1879, Emory Upton Collection, Genesee County Department of History; Phisterer, 3439.

many, the last natural one, of earth—and at the appointed hour were all upon their feet ready to obey any order promulgated from head quarters. The line having been re-formed, moved on a few rods and waited for a long time after coming to a halt to receive orders to move again. At length it came when another advance of a few feet was made, and another halt. This alternate moving a few rods and halting for an hour or half hour continued until all became thoroughly tired and many again lay upon the ground, declaring that when they were *ready* to move they would arise and go, and not until then. After about four hours spent in this manner, the column began to move in earnest, and passed down the ravine in which we were lying, at almost a *"double quick.*["] Arriving at the bank of the river, we waited another hour for the boats which just arrived, to be launched into the stream. Not a word was spoken above a whisper; not a match allowed to be struck to light a pipe—indeed hardly a breath to be drawn for fear of exciting the suspicion or revealing to our foes the close proximity of their dreaded Yankee friends. Wrapped in the stillness of a clear and cloudless night, the white tents of our enemies could be seen upon the opposite hills, while upon the river as a winding sheet, lay a deep impenetrable fog shutting out the outlines of the shore which lay but a few feet in advance. All was still as the chamber of death, save an occasional dull splash as boat after boat was lifted from the wagon which bore it, and found a resting place upon its natural element below. Not a ray of light dispelled the thick shade which hung over our heads, although in the East, the King of day was sending out an occasional herald proclaiming his approach. No voice or sound from the other side, where we knew our enemies were strongly entrenched and ready to receive us—not even a murmur or ripple of the waters, fell upon our ear: but here, with the eyes straining into the darkness, and ears anxiously and keenly bent upon catching a sound, even the most faint and imperfect to conceive, we stood in silent wonder whether our approach was known or not. Not long were we to remain thus in doubt: for just as the last boat load of *forty* had departed from our shore, a line of fire and report of musketrey broke the stillness of the morning air. Never, since I was born, did such a sudden transition from the silence of the tomb to confusion of Babel, fall upon me.[33]

---

33. "Babel" is a biblical reference to the origin of different languages. According to this tradition, when the descendants of Noah built a tower to reach to heaven, God de-

The 16th N.Y. just upon our right returned the volley, and amid the excitement our men were landed and after a short and decisive conflict, took possession of the rifle pits and defenses of those who had until a few moments previous, occupied and constructed them. Our regiment was the second one to pass over; but I could not go with them because of my horse and their being full to overflowing. However, as soon as the bridges were constructed, (three in number) I passed over, with hospital squad and drum corps, being the *first surgeon* to cross the river at the battle of Fredericksburg [Chancellorsville]. It was not long before I found my regiment and had the satisfaction to learn that the crossing had been effected as far as *we* were concerned, without loss. Indeed the loss to the Union Army was small—not more than half a dozen killed and three or four times that number wounded. For two days not much but skirmishing took place—no decisive action was fought, but feeling of our foes position was the principal thing arrived at. At length on the third day, a general advance was made, and dearly we paid for all we got. After carrying the outer line of works, those upon Mary's Hill [Marye's Heights] were attacked and captured, and we moved on to the vicinity of Salem Church, where *"Bully Brooks"* [Brig. Gen. William Thomas Harbaugh Brooks] ordered us in without shelling the woods, and the result was that we came out almost perfectly annihilated. Loss in killed outright 190, wounded 200. There was a total loss of about 400 besides priseners. The 121st exsists no more in *fact*—the *name* glorious and abiding will remain, but how poorly compensated by such renown, are the wives, sisters and mothers of these heroes:—this glorious band of martyrs will long be known in story and children's children shall call them blessed! Better thus to die than fill a traitor's grave; but with all the glory there remains a sadness which all the honors of earth cannot alleviate or wipe away.[34]

It is a splendid sight to witness the silencing of battery after battery by superior gunnery—to see the precision with which shot and shell

---

stroyed the tower and caused them all to speak different languages to prevent such a cooperative effort in the future. Gen. 11:1–9.

34. Salem Church was the first real battle for the 121st. Holt's shock at seeing so many of his friends dead no doubt left him angry, bitter, and eager to find a reason for the losses. Blaming the commander for not shelling the woods gave him a way to explain the losses that did not reflect badly on his friends. But no one was to blame for the losses of the 121st at Salem Church, unless it was Hooker himself, whose failure at Chancellorsville had put Sedgwick in danger in the first place. *OR*, vol. 25, 1:566–70, 579–85.

can be thrown, and the destruction attendant upon their bursting. You probably will never see it, but I have often wished that you might from some safe standpoint drink in the enthusiasm of our men as success follows success, and cheer after cheer breaks upon your listening ear. I can never forget that exciting time. It is worth a whole life time to live for. But enough. I must go to tea. Huckans says it is ready. I hope it will be a good one, but from what I know is on hand I cannot expect much. Love to all until I write again.

Daniel.

Camp in field near
White Oak Church, Va.
May 31st, 1863.

My dear Wife:—

This must be a short letter. It is written for two purposes—one to keep *your* spirits up and another to keep *mine* up. With the wounds and accidents of the regiment come increase of labor on my part. The hospital is full to overflowing and many in quarters are about as badly off. As to myself I am pretty well used up. Something akin to chronic diarrhoea just for pastime is running me, while the plague of scrofula has broken out with threats to render me useless.[35] I need relaxation and respite from the constant strain upon my system. I fear I shall become thoroughly unwell unless I can in someway be relieved from so much care and hardship. It is work, work, work, from dawn to dark and no thanks from anyone. Good bye; From poor old worn out

Daniel.

John O. Slocum, brother of Gen. Henry Warner Slocum, arrived in June under appointment as surgeon. Holt was greatly displeased at the choice, arguing that since he had been performing the duties of surgeon all along, he deserved the promotion. Holt threatened to resign but remained with the regiment.

Camp of the 121st Reg. N.Y. Vols.
near White Oak Church, Virginia
June 5th, 1863.

35. Scrofula, a skin disease, is a secondary symptom of tuberculosis. It was called the "king's evil" because French kings were supposed to have the ability to cure it with "the king's magic touch."

My dear Wife:—

Last night yours of the 31st was received. I am grieved to hear of your illness but hope e're this reaches you that you will be so far recovered as to enjoy your usual health.

I was in hopes of seeing you soon, but no such prospect is in view, nor do I see any chance of getting home except through resignation—a step which I mightily hate to take, but one, nevertheless, which may become necessary. You ask *why* I am not promoted? remarking that it is the wonder of my friends. Why, if I am qualified, I am so often and so unceremoniously set aside. I will tell you, and in a very few words—*favoritism.* It is in this wise. Colonel Upton owes his promotion from *Lieutenant* in the *regular* service, to Colonel of *Volunteers,* to the influence of General Slocum, a regular army officer, and he (Upton) to reciprocate the favor, recommends Slocum's brother, who is an Assistant in the 122nd N.Y. to Surgeon in this regiment.[36] Having none to press my claims or in any way to interest themselves in my behalf, I remain where I started with all the work to do—responsibility to carry and none of the advantages arriving from the increase of labor. This I feel unwilling to endure any longer. I have been pack horse long enough and think I ought to get a little more compensation for the service I bestow. I have written to [New York State] Surgeon General Quackenbush on the subject stating all the facts, saying that unless I am promoted or transferred to another regiment, I should resign.[37] He replies that *my services are appreciated and I shall be promoted very soon.* We shall see.

We are lying upon our arms, ready to move at a moment's notice. The river is very low, and a visit from General Lee may take place at any time. Well, let him come if he so desires; but he will find quite a difference between fighting behind fortifications and entrenchments, to that of making assaults upon scientific defences.

Daniel.

36. Slocum, an 1847 graduate of Castleton Medical College, had been appointed assistant surgeon with the 122d N.Y. (from the Syracuse area), then was promoted to surgeon with the 121st on June 4, 1863. After the war, he set up a practice in Camillus, N.Y.

37. Quackenbush, the new surgeon-general of the State of New York, was appointed Jan. 1, 1863, by new governor Horatio Seymour and was responsible for examining surgeons and determining their fitness to serve. Willard, 29; Phisterer, 39, 3437; *Syracuse Standard,* Mar. 6, 1885.

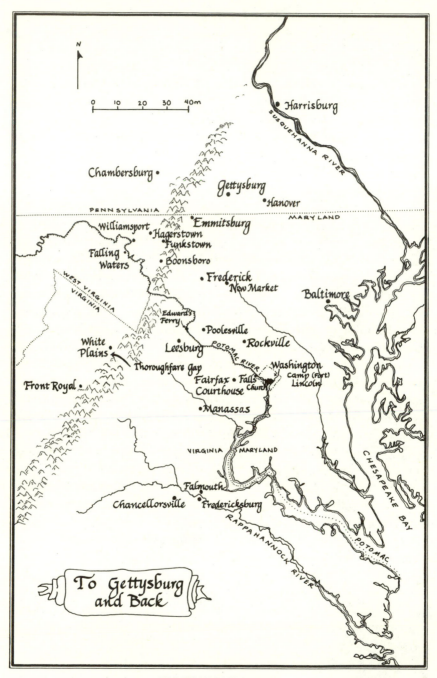

To Gettysburg and Back

MAP BY MICAELA AYERS

FOUR

It cannot be that we shall remain inactive for long

June 12, 1863 – August 25, 1863

"**M**y God!" said Abraham Lincoln after the Battle of Chancellorsville, "What will the country say?" The Union army had suffered seventeen thousand casualties in a battle which by all rights it should have won. The Union forces spent a month recuperating after the battle; so did the Confederates, who had thirteen thousand casualties. Hooker lost whatever nerve he possessed, and the Union momentum for the push for Richmond once again vanished.

Lee, on the other hand, used the month to rest, re-equip, and reinforce his army with the addition of Longstreet's divisions. Called to Richmond by Jefferson Davis for a strategy session in May, Lee proposed another invasion of the North to draw the Army of the Potomac away from Richmond, to resupply his troops with Northern food, to obtain foreign recognition for the Confederacy, to hand the Peace Democrats the Union's fall elections; in short, to end the war by making the North quit.

Holt was at the Corps Hospital near Fredericksburg. Many support services of the Union army were organized at the corps level, following the system of the Napoleonic wars, wherein each corps possessed all necessary resources for independent campaigning. Medical Director Letterman had reorganized the hospital system for the Army of the Potomac late in 1862. Field hospital systems were organized by division, but were grouped eventually by corps. Letterman's goal was to decentralize the administration of care, thus ensuring personnel would know exactly whom they were working for and where they were supposed to be. By issuing medical supplies to brigades and regiments for distribution instead of using supply bases, Letterman's system also served to prevent wholesale destruction or abandonment of massive amounts of medical supplies when the army *was threatened. By 1863, each corps had its own hospital to care for the seriously injured and relieve the combat units of those they could not care for.*

At the time he wrote the following letter, Holt anticipated that the army would move soon. Union cavalry had scouted out the Confederates on June 9, and found they had already begun preparing for their second Northern invasion.

Camp of the 121st Reg. N.Y. Vols.
opposite Fredericksburg,
Virginia, June 12th, 1863.

My dear Wife:—

A week ago to-morrow, I wrote you from our old encampment at *White Oak Church,* saying that we were under marching orders. On Saturday we broke camp and arrived here where we have been ever since. As many rumors as men are afloat. I used to suppose that a tea party of ladies, old and young, was of all place upon the earth, the most fruitful for news, but when compared to camp life, our dear sisters are so far in the shade that ages of incessant gabble will be necessary to fetch them within hailing distance. It is said, and pretty generally believed, that the whole army is soon to leave for parts unknown—that the movement in front of the city is only a feint to cover important demonstrations in another direction, but I cannot see the propriety of erecting such heavy forts and mounting 100 lb siege guns if we are to leave without a struggle. It seems easy enough to get across the river:— indeed our Southern friends appear to be pleased at our friendliness and oppose but few and feble barriers to our approach: but when we want to shake hands and fall upon their necks, embracing them in love, they retire within their domiciles and give us to understand that "familiarity breeds contempt"—that "*distance* lends enchantment to the view," and that the sooner we get back again into our tents this side of the Rappahannock, and attend to the manufacture of wooden nutmegs, clocks, &c., the better it will suit them: and if peradventure we should insist, Jonathan like,[1] to look into their quarters for very laudable purposes—to gratify a curiosity—to see how much hog and hominy their larder contained, ten to one, we should be invited to retire with a piece of leather in unpleasant proximity to *our* quarters.

1. "Jonathan like" meaning "an In-di-vid-u-al not only remarkably qualified for attending to his own business, but who has a *penchant* for looking a little into the business of his neighbors." Richard H. Thornton, *An American Glossary: Being An Attempt to Illustrate Certain Americanisms Upon Historical Principles,* 1:500.

Daniel M. Holt, Assistant Surgeon of the 121st New York Volunteers from September 2, 1862, to October 16, 1864. From Isaac O. Best, *The History of the 121st New York Infantry* (Chicago, 1921).

The Antietam battlefield. Holt wrote, "I have seen, stretched along, in one straight line, ready for interment, at least a thousand blackened, bloated corpses . . . ." *Courtesy of the Library of Congress.*

Maj. General Emory Upton. From Isaac O. Best, *The History of the 121st New York Infantry* (Chicago, 1921).

This picture, taken in 1887, is of a reunion of Sixth Corps Veterans at Salem Church. Holt operated on Union and Confederate soldiers at this church, and it was here that he was captured. Col. C. C. Sanders of the 24th Georgia described the scene: "The amputated limbs were piled up in every corner almost as high as a man could reach; blood flowed in streams along the aisle and out at the doors . . ." ("Chancellorsville," Southern Historical Society Papers 20 [1892]: 171–72). Photograph courtesy of the National Park Service.

John O. Slocum. Originally an assistant surgeon with the 122d New York, Slocum was transferred to the 121st as surgeon, much to the displeasure of Holt. His brother was Maj. Gen. Henry Warner Slocum. It was Slocum who insisted that Holt resign from the regiment and return home to save his health. From Isaac O. Best, *The History of the 121st New York Infantry* (Chicago, 1921).

Gettysburg, Pennsylvania. Holt wrote, "Every house and every barn for a dozen miles

Egbert Olcott. After the war, he was pronounced insane due to the head wound he suffered at the Battle of the Wilderness. Holt disliked his gambling and drinking habits. From Isaac O. Best, *The History of the 121st New York Infantry* (Chicago, 1921).

Reverend John Adams offered his services to the 121st at the age of sixty-two. He had been the regimental chaplain of the 5th Maine. Holt attended his prayer meetings whenever possible. From Isaac O. Best, *The History of the 121st New York Infantry* (Chicago, 1921).

So it is with these firey pork eaters. They cannot endure any inspection or question as to their mode of living.

I have not been with the Regiment since it came here; but was detailed to Corps Hospital—a matter of distinction—none but the most competent being thus detailed.[2] I have very often been so taken from our own regiment, and always with regret on my part. It is no pleasure to be separated from my men, any more than having a home, and being absent from it half the time. An attachment springs up between you and those who are your daily companions, and for whom you are in a greater or less degree constantly looking out for opportunities to benefit and relieve of their burdens. In a short time they learn to look up to you as their father, or dispenser of good things to them, and you, in turn, look to them for little acts of kindness which none so well as a good and faithful soldier knows how to bestow. There is a fraternal link which binds you stronger than all the ties of oaths and obligations which can be taken on the face of the earth. You cannot make a man love you if his heart is not with you, any more than you can unite oil and water, even though he may swear by all the powers above and below, that he will be your friend through thick and thin, and *never, never, never* desert you. There must be something more than the utterance of vows by lips—something more substantial than hollow words—something beside "sounding brass and tinkling cymbals"[3] to unite and cement the sympathies:—heart must respond to heart—while true brotherly love, overlooking and forgiving all faults, forms the basis of action.

Last night an order came to move, the whole army of the Potomac was under arms, and some corps are said to have left during the night. The Sixth Corps, as usual is left, to cover the retreat, (if retreat it is) and keep the column steady.[4] So on the advance. If severe, heavy work is to be done, requiring energy, skill, endurance and fortitude, this corps is the one for it; always leading an advance, or covering a retreat—posts of honor and danger delegated only to the best and most reliable of the army.

2. The terminology that Holt used to describe the hospital as a corps hospital rather than a division hospital is technically inaccurate, but does reflect the way the system worked in practice. Gillett, 193, 201–11.

3. "Sounding brass and tinkling cymbals" is a biblical reference to describe one's voice if one speaks without charity or love. 1 Corinthians 13:1.

4. The Sixth Corps here was covering the Union rear while the rest of the army moved to block Lee. The Union army did rather a better job of this than Lee expected, thanks in part to the effectiveness of the Union cavalry in screening their movements, as well as Jeb Stuart's decision to ride around the Union army instead of tracking its

My health is anything but good. I cannot get over the difficulty of my bowels, nor check the tendency to lung disease. Sometimes it causes me real uneasiness. I fear that I may become permanently disabled; and this at such a time in my life, with so poor a prospect of making money after the war, is anything but pleasant to dwell upon. Perhaps it is more my fears than anything else. I will try to think so, but *facts* are stubborn things.

Daniel.

Camp in field, near
"Fairfax Court House, ["]
June 19th, 1863.

My dear Wife:—

You can hardly imagine my happiness in being able to address you from this point. The monotony of camp life is relieved and we are enjoying the comforts of fresh air and diversified scenery. The army, (or a portion of it) is now lying here for the day resting after several intensely hot marches with clouds of dust, dense and suffocating, filling your eyes, mouth and ears, and indeed covering the body so thickly that when men strip to go into the water to bathe, they resemble crocodiles more than human. No one knows better than we the benefit of frequent and close contact with the pure element. Nothing more refreshing—nothing more condusive to health and comfort, nothing more inspiring. *Cold water* any time before whisky for me or my men.

The country through which we have passed since leaving Fredericksburg, has been diversified as our section in New-York, and in the generality of its features, very much alike. No mountain ranges nor extended lowlands, but hills moderate in altitude and vallies corresponding with the height of the highlands mark the face of the country. As a consequence, pure water, flowing over pebbly bottoms is abundant and lavishly appropriated by our thirsty, dusty troops. The order to "halt", for ever so brief a period beside one of the numerous streams which water and fertilize the soil, is hardly given, when gun, knapsack, haversack, blanket, cartridge boxes—all—all that in anywise interfere with perfect locomotion, is thrown aside, and into the pure

---

movements and screening Lee's advance. Edwin B. Coddington, *The Gettysburg Campaign: A Study in Command,* 52, 107–13, 186.

element a thousand naked men plunge in mirthful glee, for a while forgetful of everything but the pleasurable emotions of the passing hour. Faint, hungry and careworn they enter to come out refreshed, invigorated and ready to resume a march in broiling sun at a temperature almost high enough to cook eggs. Blistered feet are forgotten, a spirit of insubordination never thought of—grumbling gives way to songs, and on the Army of the Potomac moves as if going to festive entertainments rather than to fields of bloody carnage. So easily is a man made hopeful or desponding by pleasant or unpleasant surroundings, that one hour finds him ready to desert and forever to tarnish a reputation on which he places as much value as his life, and in the following hour no sacrifice or hardship is sufficient to induce him for a moment to harbor a disloyal thought, much less to utter it.—So we are constituted and so cannot we help the workings of the mind.—

The little village of *"Stafford Court House,"* unlike many of the Southern towns and cities, resembles our Northern villages.[5] Neat, white *painted* instead of *whitewashed* houses and fences, the structure of which betokens advancement in the right direction, with churches in keeping with the quiet loveliness of all around, favorably impress the mind as you proceed through this naturally fine region of country. To be sure the baneful effects of war are to be noted here, as almost everywhere I have been in Virginia, in the destruction of fences, public buildings, rail roads and their depots, while none but blacks are left to tell the tale of suffering which they have brought upon themselves. Notwithstanding there is an unmistakable evidence left behind that in days when the tramp of hostile armies of men was not heard upon their soil—when tears of mourning moistened not the eye, or coursed its way down the cheek of a prosperous people, they were blessed indeed. But enough. There is no use of concealing it—*they* as well as *all* here, are anything but a happy people *now,* and this unhappiness all their own folly and wickedness.

This, to me, appears to be the culminating point in the rebellion. Lee and his generals are risking their all upon a single die. If successful, Heaven knows what disgraceful compromises may be made:—if unsuccessful, the last hard blow will be struck, and we shall have to go to work and clean up, like a good housewife her house after the day's

5. This is a scrivener's error by Holt. The 121st was at Fairfax Court House.

work is over. If a successful invasion of the soil of Pennsylvania or any Northern State takes place, it will give eclat[6] to a sinking, desponding cause which will prolong the contest, but not, (in my mind) establish secession, or divide the Union. The North, although wide awake, is not thoroughly aroused to its perilous condition. I verily believe it would be a benefit to our cause if the rebs should march firebrand and sword in hand, into the interior of New-York lying waste its villages, cities and hamlets—giving to the fiery element its wealth in grain, manufactures and home industry of whatsoever nature. Not until they learn that there is no compromising with traitors and rebels in arms—that they have no feeling or intention other than the downfall of the Republic, setting up instead, an absolute monarchy—not until they have learned this and much more upon which it closes its eyes and stops its ears, will it furnish what it should long ago have sent, instead of *money and prayers—men!*[7] Yes, men, who can load and fire a musket— men to fill up the ranks when their brothers are shot down, men to *fight* instead of standing afar off and wonder "Why the Army of the Potomac does not move!" Let them come and see and both they and we will be better off and the sooner the war will cease. Two hundred dollars in greenbacks cannot fire a gun, although it may buy it together with powder and ball, and all that is necessary to kill a man. We want the *men* and not their money. It is no worse for certain mutual friends of ours to expose their lives and bodies than for me, and they are no better or will be no more deeply mourned than I, *"even though I say it."* There is no mistake as to our *ability* to crush out and forever silence the monster secession, if you give us the material—*men* to do it with. We have *more* than the South, and can fill up *more* and *oftener* than they. Even though everything else were equal, on *this* alone, we can beat them, and will, in spite of them; but want them *now.*

I have good news to tell you. My horse, saddle, and *everything* captured by the rebels was regained the day we left White Oak Church. They were returned by flag of truce within four days from the time I addressed

6. "Eclat" meaning acclaim, renown, or notoriety.

7. By 1863, Union recruitment failed to attract enough soldiers to fight, and many regiments' enlistment periods were expiring. The Conscription Act of March 1863 allowed men to buy a substitute's service or to pay a commutation fee of three hundred dollars that exempted them from the results of the draft. The commutation fee tended to set the fees paid for substitutes at about the same price. Commutation was only good for one draft, however (there were four Union drafts altogether); a substitute's service meant the service requirement was filled for the duration. McPherson, *Battle Cry,* 600–603.

General Lee on the subject. They were with our Provost Marshal General over a month, and not until the very hour of leaving did he inform me that they had been there, and I could get them by calling. Of course I went and now have an extra horse to sell. There will be no trouble about this. Horses are scarce and high. I will write again soon.

Daniel.

Camp of the 121st Reg. N.Y. Vols
Stafford Court House, Va
June 24th, 1863[8]

My dear Wife:—

From some inexplicable cause we are still at this place slightly engaging the enemy every day. Our men rush from their quarters to see a captured squad of Jonnies[9] as they are being conveyed to the rear, with as much curiosity as our children do to see a caravan of wild animals.— I have sometimes thought them greater curiosities, with their long, lank, sinewey arm and sullen features, that were the rest of their bodies as liberally supplied with hair, they would beat a gorilla all to death in physiological proportions and developements. On the other hand, we are regarded with like wonder and I presume *contempt* by them. When I, with my little troupe of drumer boys and officers servants became a prey to their rapacious maws, it was with the greatest difficulty that we could secure ground sufficient to lie down upon, so eager were they to see a veritable live *"Yank"* with pockets full of dicker. [10]

I have seen my new boss, Dr. [John O.] Slocum. He came here day before yesterday and staid an hour or two talking over matters connected with the regiment. He appears to be a good fellow, and if inclined to be half decent, we shall get along well enough. If not, I plainly told him I should be anything but an *assistant* to him. But I apprehend no difficulty and will think none. I presume we shall be on the move again soon, as it is evident to my mind Lee does not intend to fight us in Virginia if he can help it, but will get as far North as he can before being halted. This he can do if he sets his mind upon it, and you may perhaps have fighting nearer home than

8. This letter is either misdated or mis-placed by Holt. By the 24th, the 121st was at Fairfax Court House, not Stafford Court House. Isaac O. Best, *History of the 121st New York State Infantry,* 85–86.

9. "Jonnies" meaning Johnny Reb, the Confederate soldiers.

10. "Dicker" meaning goods for barter.

many suppose. As I have told you all in previous letters, I will not trouble you with recitals and reiterations in this.

Daniel.

In mid-June 1863, Lee had begun his move north, and by the end of the month he had almost his entire army in Maryland and Pennsylvania. Hooker, in pursuit of Lee as the Confederates headed north into Pennsylvania, believed himself far outnumbered by Lee. Unable to convince Halleck of his need for more men, Hooker angrily submitted his resignation on June 27. Halleck and Lincoln, who had lost all confidence in Hooker since the debacle at Chancellorsville, accepted the resignation and hurriedly notified Gen. George Gordon Meade, who had headed up the Fifth Corps at Chancellorsville, of his new command of the Army of the Potomac. Meade took off straight for the Pennsylvania line.

The Sixth Corps, under command of Maj. Gen. John Sedgwick, headed north to join the fray, acting as the army's rearguard. Forced marches of twenty-five to thirty-five miles a day exhausted the men, but the corps would arrive in time to serve as a reserve force for the battle.

On a log, four miles South of the State Line of Pennsylvania, near Germantown, Maryland July 1st, 1863.

My dear Wife:—

It is uncertain when you will get this, or when it will be mailed; but I hope you will not be kept waiting. If the satisfaction of receiving a letter is commensurate with the trouble, oftentimes, of writing it, they will always be welcome visitors, for, unlike home, where every convenience is at hand for writing, we are compelled to resort to all kinds of expedients to indict a few lines to anxious ones at home.[11]

Since leaving Fredericksburg, with the exception of the time spent at Stafford Court House, where we were employed most of the time in getting ourselves in light marching order—reducing trains, cutting down supplies of all kinds except bread and meat which was absolutely necessary to the subsistence of the troops, we have been on a regular forced march. Rising at two o'clock in the morning—long, long, before daylight expelled the darkness, and while yet the light of stars was in the sky, we were upon our way Northward, making from twenty-five to thirty

11. "Indict" meaning to write down.

miles travel daily, and encamping after the shades of night had shut out from view the surrounding landscape. From the best information we can receive; I am of the opinion that we are to fight at Harrisburg, Pa., or that location. After crossing into Maryland, at *Edward's Ferry*, our fare has greatly improved.[12] Chickens, eggs, milk, ham and vegetables of all kinds find their way upon our hitherto scanty board, and with increase of good things come also, what is much better—loyalty of the people. In some of the villages through which we pass the dear old flag is displayed, and the enthusiasm of the inhabitants knows no bounds. Handkerchiefs in the hands of beautiful women, waved with a hearty "god bless the boys in blue"—children with miniature emblems of our Nation's glory, following cheering—old men, with tearful eyes, and old ladies bearing in their loving arms refreshments for our weary soldiers, is in striking contrast with the hang dog, dejected hopeless faces of those we left behind. It really seems like getting home again as we remember the real, unaffected kindness of loyal Marylanders. My poor old heart has been full to overflowing, while in spite of every effort, the eye would moisten, as I have been the recipient of their bountiful hospitality. Thrift and prosperous wealth is written on all around us. As perceptible as the difference between Ohio and Kentucky—only separated by the Ohio river, is the difference between Virginia and Maryland. While both have been, and still are, to a great extent, under slave control, still Maryland taking a rational view of the question at issue, and by the prompt interference of the government to prevent its falling into the cauldron of secession, is comparatively a free and happy state.[13] Blessed by Nature in the productiveness of her soil—blessed in her institutions which are mild and human, compared with her sister slave states, and blessed by the honest industry of her sons, she stands forth a pattern of warm-hearted generosity, such as New-York or any other Northern State might feel proud to emulate. Never can I forget

12. Edward's Ferry, Md., was located about four miles east of Leesburg, Va., along the Potomac River and the Chesapeake and Ohio Canal. *Atlas*, plate 7.

13. Loyalists in Maryland had kept the border state in the Union since the beginning of the war, when secessionists tried various legislative mechanisms to vote for secession. Gov. Thomas Hicks prevented a secession attempt in 1861 by refusing to call the state legislature into special session to consider the question. When he could no longer prevent such a session, he moved the meeting place to the strongly Unionist city of Frederick, in western Maryland, and away from the secession stronghold of Annapolis. The attempt by pro-secessionists failed as the legislature voted it had no power to consider the question. See Janet L. Coryell, *Neither Heroine Nor Fool: Anna Ella Carroll of Maryland*, 47–49, 52–53.

how, weary, thirsting and faint from hot dusty marches, I have applied to her sons and daughters for relief, and never in vain. *Empty* I never turned from their door—however poor, a portion was mine, with a sincere welcome to it, the only regret being that there was not more. Then I say, God bless such a people, and keep from them the curse of the war which is hanging over them. They deserve and do get credit for the sympathy they extend to the army and their devotion to the cause of the Union. I hate to leave this beautiful country, for *beautiful* it is in every respect, and if I should ever see fit to leave my Northern home to find another among strangers, I know of no other spot to which I should turn with more delight than this. It cannot be that we shall remain inactive for long. Let us pray for the best.

Daniel.

The Battle of Gettysburg had been over for some time before Holt found the time to write his wife. Despite Holt's claims to glory for the Sixth Corps, only Newton's division was actively engaged in the battle, used to help chase Confederate general George E. Pickett off the field on the third day. Tremendously cheered by the Union victory, Holt expected the next battle to win the war, as the 121st pursued Lee's army into Maryland after the battle and stopped near Turner's Gap in the Blue Ridge Mountains.

> In line of battle about two miles
> West of Turner's Gap,
> [Maryland] July 9th, 1863.[14]

My dear Wife:—

I last wrote you, sitting on a log four miles South of the State line. I now write on a *drum head*—a very good place for such a purpose, but when I shall be able to send it off or when it will reach you I cannot guess. The mails have been very irregular of late, although we are so near home. I write under great weariness of body, but never in better spirits. At last I can say that "we have met the enemy and they are ours." The battle of the 1st, 2nd and 3rd July will ever be known as one of the hardest fought, most destructive of human life and most decided in its results of any on record. What the *name* of the battle will be I do not know, nor is it important, but inasmuch as it was fought near Gettysburg, Pa., I presume it will be known as the *"battle of*

14. This letter is probably misdated. See note 18 below.

Gettysburg. " Our regiment nor brigade was not in actual *fight,* although we came up just in time to save the day to our side. I say our Regiment. I mean in so saying, our division—our corps—the 6th. We had marched since the night before (starting at sundown and moving all night, until 3 o'clock next day when we took position in the front line of battle, relieving other corps which had been fighting and had expended their ammunition) *thirty-seven miles!!* a longer and quicker march than any yet on record. You recollect I told you that our corps brought up the rear, securing the main body from attacks of cavalry and light artillery which was hanging upon our advance, picking up stragglers and in every conceivable way annoying the moving colume. Well, after arriving upon or near the ground, and after half an hours rest in which we partook of such refreshments as our haversacks contained, (not having time to cook, or boil coffee) we were rushed over colume after colume as it lay in line of battle, until we took the place of, and relieved those who had been fighting so hard and so long. When the news of our arrival had reached our hard pressed and suffering boys, (and it was but a few minutes) such cheering as went forth from the mouths of our comrads in arms, both officers and men, as to fairly make the earth to tremble. Loud above clap of arms and roar of cannon rose that joyful shout until the echoing hill reverberated the glad tidings to the utmost limit of the line. Oh it *was* a joyful sound. Never until then did [I] know what enthusiastic intoxication was, and I venture to say, never in the life of the illustrious general who was opposing us, did such death knells fall upon his ear. The tide of battle which had [been] surging and driving for two days subsequently with strong prospects of disastrous results to ourselves, was in a moment turned—the God of battles made bare His arm—the hosts of disloyal banditti were driven back, and victory was ours. Oh who can tell or who can estimate the magnitude of that hour's contest! None but God, who knows all things, can tell what would have befallen our exhausted and famishing troops had not the old reliable sixth corps made its appearance just at that time. With desperate energy and determination Lee had forced his men time and again into the mouths of our belching cannons and as often been repulsed with awful slaughter,— a slaughter sufficient, it would seem, to satisfy the most insasiable appetite for blood, but again re-animating the broken and shattered lines of his retreating men, was leading them into empty guns and cannon, when General Sedgwick with the flower of the army, hurled back the lowering clouds of treason and planted the glorious flag of the Nation upon soil deserted and abandoned by our men a few hours previous.

This victory, so complete and perfect in itself, cost the lives of at least fifteen thousand of the best of our army, and as many more in wounded and missing: while the enemies loss, out of an estimated number of one hundred and twenty thousand, was at low estimates, from thirty to forty thousand, with the morale of their army perfectly broken, and they fleeing in the greatest trepidation towards their stronghold at Richmond.[15] Every house and every barn for a dozen miles around, is filled with dead, dying and wounded men, while the woods and roadsides are lined with discontented deserting beings, little, if any better than the brutes which are hauling their maimed and perpetually disabled brethren from the precincts of our power. There is no danger of their turning upon us. Thoroughly and effectually whipped and turned from the invasion of a free state, to a complete route, if we get them at all, it will be upon such ground as admits of no retreat—the only alternative being to fight. But while I thus encouringly write, believing that I shall soon see home, our work being done, I cannot but feel impressed that we have not yet done with them, however much they now suffer and are demoralized: The shattered, flying mass, will preserve a nucleus around which they will gather, and at some subsequent period will offer battle. Too momentous are the results of this rebellion to the hearts and purposes of the lights of *Southern Chivalry* to thus quietly witness the extinction of the brightest hopes of a misguided ambition. No, they will some day turn up in some quarter of the globe, but never, never, again upon free soil of the Nation.

The Potomac is too high for *fording*, and with boats destroyed and no immediate prospect of escape, I hope and expect that our work is only half done.[16] If they are pressed as we are able to press them, and as it is the desire of the men to do, you will hear of still greater achievements than the success at Gettysburg. Let us hope and pray that our

15. Holt's estimate of casualties was a bit high. The Union lost about 23,000 men killed, wounded, and missing; the Confederates about 28,000. The Sixth Corps, held in reserve until the afternoon of the third, lost only 23 officers and 321 enlisted men. McPherson, *Battle Cry,* 664–65; *OR,* vol. 27, 1:112.

16. Holt's reference is to the high rivers following the heavy rains that began July 4. The Union forces had destroyed Confederate-built pontoon bridges across the river. McPherson, *Battle Cry,* 666.

leaders so inspired will make more perfect a gloriously begun work. Everything is auspicious. Destruction marks their retreating footsteps. Fires, like those of burning cities, follow in their train. An eye witness— a citizen informed me that last night *eight acres* of baggage wagons were given to the flames in order to keep them from falling into our hands. But I have little time to write. I have said much more than when I sat down I imagined I should say. Long before this reaches you, and even before it was written, you have heard the glorious tidings. We are lying, for some inexplicable cause, inactive before a strong picket line of rebels, and may be lines of battle: but as to *lines of battle,* as some believe, I utterly scout the idea. I almost *know* that it is only a heavy rear guard to protect their army while the main force is stealing as softly and quietly away as possible.[17] Were it *my* way, I should carry this line at any rate, and if still in force before us, use them as we did three days ago.[18] As I am *not* boss, neither my tongue heard in counsel, I will be content to follow on as usual: but seems to me we are losing valuable time and advantage by thus delaying to follow up.

I have some interesting relics for the children picked up from the field and sacked houses, and hope to deliver them soon in person. Until then good bye

Daniel.

Lee withdrew to Williamsport, Maryland, and awaited the expected Union attack. When none came, he moved on, leaving behind a rear guard that the Union army ran into when they finally resumed the offensive on July 14. A skirmish at Falling Waters cost the Confederates close to five hundred men and two cannon, but Lee kept moving south. The Union army slowly followed, and Holt complained of Meade's failure to pursue the Confederates vigorously.

At a halt in Snicker's Gap,
near Snickerville, Virginia,
July 21, 1863.

My dear Wife:—

I write you from this point where we are lying for a short time to rest our weary bodies after an intensely hot march. We are slowly wending

---

17. "Scout" meaning ridicule. Holt's perception is accurate; Lee withdrew and awaited a Union attack. Ibid., 666–67.

18. This phrase may mean that Holt misdated his letter as July 9 instead of July 6.

our way Southward, our destination being Warrenton, so I understand. In my last I wrote as I felt—hopeful and full of enthusiasm and with a mixture of uneasiness because I thought I saw a lack of energy in pushing forward to completion a work but half accomplished. [Rueing?] the persistant determination of rebels to accomplish the downfall of the Government, and their almost superhuman efforts to bolster up and support their cause, I could not but feel, and so expressed my feelings, that we were letting Lee and his legions escape when it might have been different. You recollect that I said, in my last, while the army was lying before what appeared to be, the entire rebel force behind strong fortifications, that it was my impression that it was only a strong rear guard protecting the retreat of the main army. My suspicions were correct in every particular and the result has been just as I feared it would be—an escape of an army which we ought to have almost totally destroyed and annihilated. One morning as the light gave our boys the first faint outlines of the enemies works in front, we were—*surprised?* to find that no guns pointed threateningly towards us, nor did any sentinel watch the movements of the Yankees who a day or two previously had given them such decided evidences of their power to punish. A recognizance was made, and those bristleing lines of bayonets with the hands which held them, were gone, as were everything of a hostile character. At Falling Waters[19] we had quite an engagement with them, resulting in the capture of several hundred prisoners with quite a number of guns. At this point we ought to have made complete, their destruction; but as at Antietam they were permitted quietly to decamp and take their own time to partially re-organize their army, so that something like order might be preserved in their retreat. At Funkstown[20] they engaged us for three days in picket duels until they had perfected a crossing by means of boats *constructed* on the spot and wading, or rather *swimming* the river. Here great numbers of sheep, swine and cattle were drowned, their carcases floating down the stream, lodging upon the banks and every obstruction which interposed upon their downward passage. On the 16th we arrived within two miles of *Berlin,* the point of our former crossing into Maryland, where after a tedious delay in getting a bridge laid across the river, we crossed again

19. Falling Waters, Va., is in present-day West Virginia.
20. Funkstown, Md., is ten miles south of the Pennsylvania border on Antietam Creek.

upon the Sacred Soil of the Old Dominion. As we passed our fighting ground on the 15th (Crampton's Gap) old associations were revived and I could not but feel a deep sadness as I reflected that here just ten months ago, day before we reached it, our regiment presented the appearance of a brigade, so full was its numbers and so healthy its men; but now, with less than four hundred, (all told who were present) and many of these nearly ready to fall out on accunt of sickness, it took but a short calculation to reckon how long at this rate it would be that our organization as a regiment would be continued. Little or no change had taken place since we left the bloody field, except that vegetation somewhat obscured the graves of sleeping friend and foe and solemn stillness reigned alike o'er all. We passed the defile with mournful hearts, not knowing when, in the order of God's providence, we might be as quietly filling a lonely grave upon the shores of the Potomac.

After crossing the river at Berlin on the 17th we slowly continued our march until we are resting at Snicker's Gap. I have thus, though in a roundabout, and imperfect manner brought you with me from Gettysburg here. Many portions of Maryland are of surpassing loveliness. Emmitsburg,[21] situated in a perfect paradise of beauty, sent out her Sisters of Charity in great numbers to administer to the comfort and wants of the wounded and dying; while the Catholic Priests mixed freely up with both loyal and disloyal consoling and granting absolution. All was done within their power to smooth the hard pillow of dying humanity. No man, how ever strong his prejudices, should detract from the circumspect holiness of these voluntary outcasts of the domestic hearth. With a duty to perform, they sought the couch of suffering and lighted up the dark passage to the tomb.

Since our Gettysburg affair, and during our stay there, I was detailed to Division Hospital, leaving Dr. Slocum in charge of the regiment. A dozen or fifteen surgeons thus keep together and attend to all who are sent to the rear. This is often an Herculean task. If our division suffers greatly the labor is in proportion to the loss. Operations are here performed, the sick cared for, and ultimately all are sent to General Hospital where greater comfort and better nursing is secured.[22] Riding

21. Emmitsburg, just south of the Pennsylvania line, is some ten miles southwest of Gettysburg.

22. General hospitals were located in Fredericksburg and Washington; by the end of July, a tent hospital was open in Gettysburg. Called Letterman Hospital or Camp Letterman, it was used for the wounded who remained at Gettysburg. Gillett, 213.

in the rear of their division, it is their duty to look out suitable places in which to establish field hospitals in the event of an engagement—superintend the Ambulance train, direct its movements and take care of its occupants. Thus you see that I have had time more leisurely to observe the effects of the battle than if with my own regiment. Notwithstanding the *preference* given, I had much rather be with my own men for the reason that when an action is over and you have sent your wounded away provided for, it is the end of the matter; whereas in a Division Hospital your work has only just begun. Here amputations and operations of every kind with subsequent treatment is to be given—the very *worst* part of the business. If there is one thing more disagreeable or more dirty than another, it is that of dressing sloughing, stinking gun shot wounds.

I have thus, unintentionally spun out a long, imperfect and half-clad letter, under a thousand interruptions and most happy shall I be when it gets off. I am pleased to have Willie write in his printing kind of way; I think he improves very fast; and so too, you say that Bella is making a beginning.[23] She is very young for that I should think, but if I were in your place I should not put her to much of a task for what she gains before six years of age, she will in my opinion loose before she is twelve. When we come to another halt sufficiently long to say a few words to you, I will let you know where we are and how we are getting along.

> Daniel.

> Camp in field of the 121st Reg.
> N.Y.V. White Plains, Virginia
> July 24, 1863.

My dear Wife:—

Here, at this point, on the 9th day of November, 1862, I passed a most uncomfortable day and night. Snow fell, the first of the season, upon the mountain tops, and in the Valley, where we are now lying, before evening set in, eight inches covered the ground, and all disappeared in two days time! I well recollect how cold, wet and uncomfortable we all were and also have a vivid recollection how Huckans failed to steal a turkey belonging to the Surgeons of the 5th Maine. He had killed (or rather *attempted* to kill) the old gobbler by cutting his head off, when *lo!*

23. Bella refers to Holt's youngest daughter, Isabel, born Sept. 3, 1860, and the person who preserved her father's remarkable letterbook. Willard and Walker, 289.

and *behold!!* he opened his mouth and out came a sound—a dismal sound, sufficiently loud to reach the ears of the doctor's cook who was at that very moment looking for the strayed bird, and then a scene ensued. The fellow was going to *whip* Huckans who stoutly declared that he *would not* be whipped for such a small offense as that, whereupon a spirited debate ensued which ended in the cook of the 5th Maine carrying off the fowl which *ought* to have graced the board of the 121st doctor's. This was galling but had to be endured, especially as their claim was prior to ours, but in view of original *tittle,* we had *possession* which being *nine* points in law, ought to have been ours.

We may remain here for a few days. This I infer from the fact that this morning we were ordered to make ourselves as comfortable as possible by permanently pitching tents, &c. This means to look around a little for something to appease the appetite and wash up. We have improved [upon] the opportunity as best we could and have just sent four men off to pick a bucket of blackberries of which there are hundreds of bushels growing upon our old encampments. They are mostly of the *low* or *running* kind—very large and juicy, but not so sweet or pleasant a flavor as those growing with us at home; still with sugar and milk (if we are so fortunate as to get the latter) they make a dish worthy of a place upon the table of an epicure. Large quantities of excellent wine, I am informed, is made of the juice of them, and I see no reason why its manufacture should not be profitable. All the real expense out is for sugar, which at the present high prices, and scarcity of that commodity, I should think would have a tendency to lessen its manufacture. And then too, *Yankees* are fond of a good article, and are not backward in making known their partiality for it; which, I am pleased to record of the good heart of our Southern sisters, is seldom refused to our thirsty boys, when accompanied with an intimation of thirst, is evinced a willingness (to save their dear feet a weary step) to help themselves to it. Almost *always,* it is pleasant to remark, we are saved the trouble of getting it ourselves, but the hand of a house servant is ready to pour the sparkling fluid out for you. During the time of cherries (which is now over) we had a rich repast. I never shall forget the pies and puddings which Huckans, in the greatness of his heart and boundless sympathy for my stomach, made for me. Like times of old, when you and I were young I have sat for hours beneath the wide spreading branches of this noble Southern tree, and filled and refilled an unsatisfied appetite, until *want of capacity* fairly made me desist from the epicurian feast. Oh how rich and luscious to the taste and how perfectly compatable to health and vigor is their eating! Even now my mouth waters as I think of those great juicy clusters as they reddened the tree invitingly urgeing you to partake of their richness. Never, until I entered the army and came South, did I behold such spontaneous abundance of fruit and flowers. On every hand, grapes, berries and fruits of every kind offer their tempting juices to palliate the thirst and stimulate a weary body to further exertion. These cherries grow wild as well as cultivated. They are like the large red and black ox hearts and fully as good. The trees, large as our Balm of Gilliads[24] and bearing bushels on bushels, line the edges of woodland, fringe the margin of streams, and in rows, as our maples, afford shade to highways and roadsides. It is really too bad to witness their destruction by our men in attempts to possess their fruit. Great branches strew the way, and in many cases the entire tree is destroyed by cutting off every twig which bears or contains a single ripe cherry. This ought not to be. If we come along another year we shall sadly miss their shade and fruit. To-day, for the first time I had a dish of *new* potatoes, obtained cheap *for the digging.* Being *always* in the rear of Cavalry and a heavy advanced guard, we have but little chance to obtain much, even though it were abundant. Not until we come to a halt as now, and are ordered to make ourselves comfortable, (which we fully know the meaning of) do we get enough to pay for the trouble of foraging. But when we *do* set out we never fail of bringing in *something* if nothing more than a box of honey, a turkey, pig, sheep, chicken, duck, goose, calf or something which will change the programme from pork and hard tack to more sumptuous living. Night before last, our camp resembled the Fifth Street Market in Cincinnati after market hours. Every possible evidence of successful foraging exhibited itself. Here a spatter of feathers—there a sheep pelt—here again, honey boxes minus the melifluous contents—dead bees—canteens of milk, pig's heads and calf's innards formed a curious medley, while adown the garments of our boys ran in lines of *red* and crimson, the indubitable evidence of a sanguinary conflict with the living property of an outraged Confederacy.

Methinks I hear you ask if all this was compatable with, and strictly in accordance to the laws of health? Well, if you were only to be with me

---

24. "Ox heart" meaning large, heart-shaped cherry; "Balm of Gilliads" (Gileads) meaning American balsam fir tree.

one hour next morning at sick call, you would not ask the question. One man has diarrhoea—oh *such* a diarrhoea—another colic, and *such* pains no mortal man *ever* felt or knew. "What could produce it, doctor? I have been careful of what I eat—nothing but a little fresh pork, honey, new potatoes, *ripe peaches* and a very little apple butter!—nothing which could produce this awful pain in the region of the epigastrium. Oh dear, I'm almost dead, give me a camphor and opium pill, and mark me sick to-day." Of course, I do so, and to divers others also.[25] Poor Ed Cox, who is now attached to the Hospital squad, eat a quarter of a small sized hog and came near dying, according to his own account. I gave him a dose of four ounces of commissary and he revived.[26] We have some laughable as well as painful incidents connected with our life here in Dixie, not the least of which are some of those resulting from such scenes as I have already described.

B[ut?] I will not weary you with details in which you have no special interest and will close by saying good bye.

Daniel.

Having failed to catch Lee in the pursuit after Gettysburg, Meade spent the rest of July rebuilding the army, refraining from attacking Lee in a position of the Confederate general's choosing. While Holt was happy with the abundant supply of provisions, as indicated in the previous letter, he was disappointed by Meade's inaction.

Camp of the 121st Reg.
N.Y. Volunteers
Warrenton, Virginia
July 31st, 186[3].

My dear Wife:—

We have been here since the 25th, doing nothing and in no manner whatever making ourselves useful to our country or to any body. I only write to inform you of our change of location. The same old stories of camp life and the same routine of duty is gone through with. When, if ever, I can say anything which will be interesting, I will do so. To-day being Brigade Inspection, I must, of course appear with all the rest "armed and equipped as the law directs," for military review and

25. "Divers" meaning various. Camphor is a stimulant.
26. Holt's reference to "commissary" is unclear but may refer to commissary whiskey.

inspection. Cox is brushing up my clothes, blacking boots and polishing sword &c., &c.—all for nothing. The drum taps and I must follow on. Good bye.

Daniel.

Bushwhackers under the nominal command of John Singleton Mosby were a constant threat in middle Virginia. Mosby's Rangers operated so successfully in the areas around Leesburg, Front Royal, and Manassas that the region became known as "Mosby's Confederacy." His eight hundred partisans, operating in small groups of twenty to thirty, disrupted communications, stole Union supplies (badly needed by the Confederacy as the effect of the Union blockade began to tell), and harassed Union troops constantly between 1863 and the end of the war.

Camp of the 121st Reg.
N.Y. Volunteers
New Baltimore [Virginia],
August 2nd, 1863.

My dear Wife:—

The last time I wrote you was from Warrenton. I now address you from New Baltimore, distant from Warrenton four miles. Here, last September, we lay for a week, and here "little Mac" had to step aside and make room for Burnside; and never, I venture to say, did the sides of any poor, disgraced little mortal *burn* more deeply and more effectually than did our defunct hero's at this time, to see himself so unceremoniously ousted from a position which he so illy filled and so ignobly bore both to his country and/himself.

The 2nd Brigade is here alone, forming the extreme left of the army, four miles distant from any help in case of attack and it is *rumored* that we are to remain here as long as the Army is lying in its present inactive quarters near Warrenton. It is not for me to *know*, and sometimes I think I do not *care* what we are doing so far from any danger except it is to have time to weep and mourn over our folly in not annihilataling Lee's army while in our power at Gettysburg. If so, for *one* I have fairly repented and long for another opportunity to redeem a soiled and tarnished honor. Thoroughfare Gap, three miles distant is an objective point with the Army, and perhaps it is both to guard its passage and prevent a flank movement that we are here. On every side we are environed by Mosby's roving bands of guarillas who come suddenly down upon our men when found outside of camp, either killing or carrying them off captive. One instance will illustrate the devil daring of these fellows and the impudence of secesh women who are their particular friends and abettors. On our arrival at Warrenton a lady applied to Colonel Upton for a *guard* to protect herself and property from destruction by our troops. It was granted; and his aid, a young man of pre-possessing appearance and agreeable mien proceeded to the house, not more than half a mile from the encampment, with a guard, when both aid and guard were seized by a band of these bushwackers and carried off. The *lady* (?) knew of their being there and laid the plot for their capture.[27] After securing her object she returned to camp, blandly informed Colonel Upton that those who he had sent to her relief had been captured and asked for *another*. It would have been in perfect keeping with former preceedents had one been granted, but strange to say, it was, for the first time in the history of the regiment *denied! I have not met a loyal man in Virginia since coming into it for the last time.* All are tinctured with secession except the more intelligent and refined. I mean, of course, those real speceimens of godly manliness and sobriety—the Negroes: and even some of these are foolish enough to imbibe the notions of their less sensible and refined brethren, the white population of Virginia.[28] When you enter a house here, you do not see the lord of the mansion, but about eight or ten females of all ages and colors sitting upon the piaza grinning at you like a set of dead monkeys; and if perchance your enquiries should extend to husbands, sons or fathers, you are cooly told that they are in the Confederate Army, or better still, that the cruel Yankees have killed them. Notwithstanding their evident hatred of the d——d Yanks, they are without exception, from the very highest F. F. VS to the very lowest VF's, ready to trade with you:[29] a pound

27. Women who served the Confederacy as spies have had a long and romanticized history, but no general study of their work yet exists. The most famous spies were undoubtedly Belle Boyd, who served Stonewall Jackson in the Shenandoah, and Rose O'Neal Greenhow, a prominent Washingtonian. See Belle Boyd, *Belle Boyd in Camp and Prison*, and Ishbel Ross, *Rebel Rose*.

28. Stories of blacks who actively supported the Confederacy remain largely anecdotal. Most blacks took full advantage of Union troops moving into their geographic proximity to leave their owners. Early in the war, Confederate officers did take black slaves with them to act as their personal servants, but as the war dragged on and escape from slavery into Union lines became more common, slaves were kept farther south and, in some instances, transferred to more remote locations to prevent their escape. See John Hope Franklin and Alfred A. Moss, Jr., *From Slavery to Freedom: A History of Negro Americans*, 191–95.

29. "FFVs" meaning First Families of Virginia; "VFs" meaning Virginia families. Both terms refer to the upper classes in the social caste of Virginia aristocracy.

of sugar or salt will purchase (in a great many instances) all they can get or accommodate you with. At Warrenton, aristocratic a place as it is, where previous to the war you would imagine yourself in the very lap of luxury, our men freely enter the best homes and open a trade for anything they possess if you only bring such articles as are daily dispensed to the lowest soldier in the ranks of the Union Army. A perfect panic prevails among all classes to become the possessor of some despised soldiers pocket knife, comb, canteen, or anything which he may happen to have to dispose of. The blockade has effectually closed the door upon the trade of these inland towns, and except articles of home manufacture (and these are few and far between) they are as poorly off as any people can be. It is hard to think that *honor* should be compromised for pork and molasses, sugar and coffee and such like commodities in daily use among our men, but such is no doubt the case, as many well authenticated testimonies verify. Here in one of the most productive portions of the United States where wheat forms the staple, flour is worth in greenbacks or gold, fifty dollars a barrel, and in Confederate bonds, almost its weight. Hundreds of families with abundant means are destitute of it, and have to eat horse feed,—corn for a living. The fact is that *wheat flour* is not to be had, except through our brigade commissaries, and that in very limited quantities. As we move along, we take their grainary crops to feed our horses and fill up holes in roads for wagons to pass over, and in a thousand ways use up the food of the people. It *must* tell soon in almost a famine if they do not stop this insane opposition to rightful powers. Too keenly are they made to feel what befell an people upon the invasion of Pennsylvania, where every horse, mule, cow, sheep or hog was driven off, and grain indiscriminately destroyed. Surely, the avenger is upon their track.

It was my intention, and still is, to give you a more minute and detailed account of our march from Fredericksburg to Gettysburg, and from there to this point. It was one of intense interest to *us* and if I am capable of truthfully giving it, will be somewhat interesting to you. Until I have time and inclination to do so, I remain as ever your loving

Daniel.

As the war dragged on, desertions began to increase. Firing squads became a necessary evil for both Union and Confederate armies. Although Lincoln commuted a number of death sentences, the value of execution as a deterrent was clear. Witnessing a military execution shook the hearts of even the hardest veterans. Holt declined to mention the soldier's name in this letter home, but the

Herkimer County Journal *printed his name, Thomas Jewett, and claimed that he had deserted at the Battle of "Fredericksburg" (Chancellorsville).*

Camp of the 121st Reg N.Y. Vols
New Baltimore, Aug. 15, 1863

My dear Wife:—

I have just this moment arrived from witnessing the execution of a soldier of the 5th Maine regiment for desertion.[30] He was shot according to orders, after an examination and trial by court Martial. This was his *third* offence—once while a soldier of England, and *twice* since joining his present command. The penalty was dreadful and so also was the crime. How often have I prayed that I may never witness such a scene with one of my own sons, nor hear of disgrace attaching to their names by any unsoldierly conduct; and I believe I never shall. I feel that in them I may safely trust their own as well as my reputation.

You have often read of and seen illustrations of military executions; and they are true to life. Enclosed within a hollow square (except upon one side left open for the culprit and attendants) the poor fellow, with the Chaplain and shooting party pass slowly around, drawn by four horses in an army wagon. The prisoner seated upon his coffin, while different bands composing the division strike up a dirge as he slowly moves along, until at length arriving at the fatal spot, the vehicle stops, he is helped to dismount—the coffin is taken out and placed upon the ground while he sits upon it listening to the reading of the findings of the court and death warrant; a prayer by the Chaplain, blinding the eyes and upon a signal given, eight bullets pierce the heart and the spirit goes to meet its God. All is over, and we slowly wheel into line and go to our respective quarters. It is a sad sight, and I think I shall never again witness such an one if I can help it. Unlike a death in battle, when all is excitement and you are looking for it, here every preparation is made and all the steadiness of decorum marks the whole transaction.

Since coming in we have had orders to be ready to move at a moment's notice, which may mean something or nothing. At any rate we have had no orders to send off or to dispose of the sick, and until such comes, we attach but little importance to such commands. I have

30. Thomas Jewett, an English laborer who deserted his regiment at Salem Church, was tried and sentenced to death. An account of his death by the Rev. John R. Adams, Chaplain of the 5th Maine, can be found in Robert I. Alotta, *Civil War Justice: Union Army Executions under Lincoln*, 75–76; see also *Herkimer County Journal*, Aug. 27, 1863, 2.

learned one thing and that is not to *fret* when orders come, because not oftener than once in half a dozen times when we are ordered to be *ready* do we really *go.*

Last [night] Seargent Jones of Company *I* died in our regimental hospital.[31] He performed his duty well while with us, and I have no doubt his spirit is happy now, as he evinced in life a regard for God's word, living in peace with all around him. If we move as some suppose we may, I will let you know. Until then no more from

Daniel.

Camp of the 121st Reg. N.Y. Vols.
near New Baltimore,
August 20, 1863.

My dear Wife:—

Since last writing you, I have been *promoted!!* from a simple Assistant Surgeon to a real live kicking Brigadier!!![32] The commission has not yet arrived, but no doubt will, as good things *always* come slow. You may perhaps feel anxious to know when such a change came over the spirit of my dream. I will tell you. It was an unexpected honor and came upon me with stunning effect. On the 12th the 121st took into its head to have a little sport in hunting up guerillas, and upon the morning of the eventful day (to me) started at early dawn and travelled until we reached White Plains. Here we arrived about noon and rested until sundown when it [the regiment] separated into two parts, one of which was under the command of Lieut Col. Olcott,[33] and the other under Colonel Upton. The part under Colonel Upton took to the right in the direction of Middleborough while that under command of Lieut. Col. Olcott took an opposite course to Salem.

As I have already stated, the object of the raid was to secure the person of Mosby if possible (who we had information was at the time of our departure, in our immediate vicinity, and who would that night be

31. Levi S. Jones enlisted July 23, 1862, at Winfield, N.Y., and was mustered in as a first sergeant with Co. B of the 121st on Aug. 23. He died at New Baltimore on Aug. 13, 1863, of a hemorrhage of the bowels. *Annual Report,* 104.

32. Holt's comment regarding his promotion is not to be taken seriously, as his story reveals.

33. Egbert Olcott attended law school in Albany, N.Y., before the war. He helped raise troops early in the war, and on Aug. 23, 1862, accepted a commission as major in the 121st. He was promoted to lieutenant-colonel on Apr. 10, 1863. Phisterer, 3436; Pension and Service Records.

at Middleborough with a small part of his murderous gang and a number of officers). The distance from White Plains to this place (Middleborough) is nine miles—a short march by daylight, but in pitchy darkness, quite another affair. Stopping at suspicious houses on the way, we secured quite a number of horses and some men, (most of whom were subsequently *released upon proof of their loyalty*, as also the restoration of property taken) among the men, an *intelligent contraband* was secured who gave a great amount of valuable information as to the real sentiments of the people of the district and the usual stopping places and lurking dens of the guerillas. An incessant march of seven hours, over mountains, mountain streams and awfully muddy roads, brought us at three o'clock to the precincts of the town. Here we rested for two hours. When the first gray streaks betokened approaching light, we deployed and surrounded the town, a portion of the regiment and a squadron of Cavalry entering it by the highway. So quietly and so effectively was the town surrounded, that not even the barking of a dog gave notice of our approach. The first intimation the bewildered inhabitants had of the uncomfortable proximity of their dreaded neighbors in blue was one unceremoneous invitation for them to arise and let the men search for concealed rebels and arms, after which to cook breakfast and feed their visitors who had taken so much pains to make them an early call.

Well, our search for Mosby resulted as many heretofore had resulted—in a total failure. Instead of lodging at the hotel as we were informed he intended to do, we found to our disgust and mortification that he had cooly witnessed our approach and search of the village about a mile distant. Our scrutinizing zeal in efforts to capture the father of the gang resulted, after all, in something grand—the *bona fide* capture of an out and out reb man, and *two women!!*[34] After having satisfied ourselves that there were no others in town, and well secured what stray horses and mules the place afforded, we started about noon for the stronghold of the gang. This, of course, was in the mountains, and thither we wended our way, meeting with no special accidents and firing no guns. However, we were frequently close upon the track of the runaway and once came very near capturing him. Our cavalry

34. Women enthusiastically joined in Mosby's effort to defeat the Union. One nineteen-year-old, Antonia Ford, wound up in Old Capitol Prison for months on suspicion of helping the raiders. McPherson, *Battle Cry*, 737–38; Kevin H. Siepel, *Rebel: The Life and Times of John Singleton Mosby*, 75–76, 151.

approached a house from one direction while the infantry advanced from another. In this house he had, not ten minutes previously, been regaling himself with a bowl of milk, not thinking we were so near. On this occasion, as on a great many others, he owed his escape to the vigilance of woman. The whole country had been aroused and the alarm given that we were on his trail, and as a consequence we lost our bird from this fact. Knowing the country as well as I know the rooms of my house, and having horses fleet as the best in the army, if we secured this notorious murderer, it would have to be through strategy, not absolute open-handed fair play. So when the woman saw us approaching who was watching on a hill top a short distance from the house, she gave the alarm by waving a handkerchief, and the gallant Colonel jumped into his saddle and in ten minutes was far away upon the mountain road. We rode up just in time to see the *bowl* not quite empty of its lacteal contents,[35] out of which he had eaten, but not in time to see the veritable Mosby himself.

Following on as rapidly as possible, we came upon a deserted camp in which we got about a dozen first rate horses and captured two men. Getting farther and farther into the Lion's den we secured more horses and men, but not enough to compensate for the danger to which we were constantly exposed. Our force, all told, did not consist of more than fifty men, Infantry and Cavalry, and Mosby could, at almost a moment's notice raise the whole country in arms against us. Another motive prompted us to retrace our steps, and this was that night was approaching and we *on the wrong side of the mountain!* Reluctantly we turned our weary steps again towards White Plains which we reached about ten o'clock, thoroughly tired out and satisfied with our day's work. Here we encamped for the night and here I slept as upon the previous occasion at the house of my dear friend, Mrs. Murrey, for whom I shall always entertain feelings of respect from the fact that she acted the part of the Good Samaritan in every respect.[36] She administered to my wants by cooking the best she had—giving a bed—a *good* one, too on which to lay my tired body, (the first I had enjoyed in a long year) and upon parting cordially invited me to call again, which of course I *shall* do if I ever happen in that part of the

35. "Lacteal" meaning consisting of milk.
36. No information can be found regarding Mrs. Murrey. She may have been an old family friend.

country again. Well satisfied with the general result of our raid thus far, and waiting to hear from Lieut. Col. Olcott who had not reported, our men engaged in all kinds of boyish sports such as only soldiers let loose from all restraint and duty, know how to enjoy. *Sham fights*—taking rebel forts and fortifications—getting killed—being wounded, and *bringing the wounded to the Surgeon for treatment,* running rebs out of captured rifle pits, loading and firing cannon, taking of batteries and a thousand things to amuse and keep up the spirits were entered into with a zest worthy of the good hearts which prompted them.—After playing all the forenoon to the utmost extent of their ability, they started back about noon for our encampment at New Baltimore letting Col. Olcott take care of himself. At night we reached camp in all manner of ways and times—*every man riding a horse;* our regiment looked the strangest you can imagine. Mounted on steeds without saddle, bridle or halter, the boys made use of *bark* for halters and used their blankets for saddles. From the thoroughbred Virginia racer to the broken down, sprained, ringboned, glandered plug,[37] our boys looked like gurillas indeed, beating Mosby himself. Shortly after our arrival in camp, Col. Olcott hove in sight similarly armed and equipped. His operations had been quite as successful as ours. In all we were better off by about sixty or seventy horses and mules, and any quantity of *apple butter,* honey, &c.

I had almost forgotten to tell you how I became a Brigadier. It was because of eminent qualifications exhibited on that occasion in leading the men, by command of Col. Upton, *out of danger* when we supposed Mosby might gobble us up. Instead of the *rear,* as usual, I rode in *advance* and thus secured the high commission.[38] It was a simple transaction, full of daring energy and marked an event in life long, long to be remembered.

I have briefly recited the incident which resulted on our raid of the 12th inst. and said nothing of the order to be ready to move at *five minutes* notice. So little does this effect us having had so many such calls of late, that I attach but little importance to them. So far as *getting ready* is

37. "Ringboned" meaning with a deposit of bony matter on the pastern of a horse (the pastern is above the hoof, below the fetlock on a horse's leg); "glandered" meaning suffering from glanders, a contagious disease characterized by swollen mucous membranes and enlarged glands of the lower jaw.

38. In other words, Holt led the retreat from Mosby, thus taking charge as a brigadier would.

concerned, we are so, if it is necessary to move. In fifteen minutes I could have my house upon my horse, the sick attended to, and everything in marching order. It does not take long to *get ready* and *move* when once we set ourselves about it. Unlike a journey at home, where days and weeks are necessary to *prepare* for a start, all we have to do here is to roll up your blanket, pack your haversack with hard tack and pork, put your extra shirt and pair of socks in your knapsack, shoulder arms and off. Truly a very simple operation and very quickly performed.

On dress parade to-day the sentences of two men were read off for desertion. The finding of the court was *guilty* of the charges and specifications, and the sentence resulting that the letter *"D"* two inches in length should be indelibly marked upon the back of the right hand, that all pay which may now be due or may hereafter become due, shall be forfeited, that they should serve out the balance of their enlistment (2 years) upon the public works with a chain upon their legs to which an iron ball weighing twenty pounds should be fastened, and that the elective franchise be forever denied them:—that no office of trust or emolument should ever be given them. This is a hard sentence, but just after all. I have sometimes thought *death* preferable, but no man can give a good cause for desertion, and if it were not severely punished, no security for the army would exist.

Dr. Houghtaling has tendered his *unconditional resignation* and it has been accepted. So he will be off in a day or two. Of all *timid* men I ever saw, he was the most so. At Salem Church where he ought to have given me aid and assistance, he fled in a most shameful manner, insomuch as to call down upon him the bitterest curses of the men who saw him flee in such disgusting haste. Never has he been where *duty* called when an action was pending, but was always in the rear far out of danger with sneaks, dead beats, bummers and cowards. I pity his constitutional cowardice, for I think he suffers as greatly as those who are wounded by the leaden messenger. In *resigning* he has saved a dishonorable dismissal from the service, thus saving himself and friends the stigma attaching to a deserter. I pity any man, as I have said, thus constituted, but none, better than Dr. Houghtaling knew his duty, and none, worse than he performed it. If anything transpires different from what now appears, I will let you know.

Daniel.

While the Union forces in the East did little beyond rebuilding their forces and watching Lee, Confederate and Union forces in the western theater were on the move. Gen. William S. Rosecrans, commanding the Army of the Cumberland, maneuvered Confederate general Braxton Bragg out of middle Tennessee in late June and early July. He then moved on to Chattanooga in late August and forced Bragg out of the city by threatening his communications. Early information to the East was that Rosecrans was badly beaten—an inaccurate account.

> Camp of the 121st Reg. N.Y. Vols
> lying at New Baltimore,
> August 25, 1863.

My dear Wife:—

I suppose you will expect a letter even though I have nothing to say. Were it not for an occasional raid or scare by having a gang of Mosby's men enter camp without giving the countersign, and kicking up a general [mess?], life would pass heavily enough. Yesterday was noted for two events—one an order to strike tents *immediately* and hold ourselves in readiness to move, at five moments' notice: the other by detailing a squad of twenty men who accompanied me with an ambulance to White Plains to bring in a sick cavalryman who had been left by the rebs to take care of himself as best he might. We met with no opposition to our adventure although a camp of the enemy was within a mile or two of the house where our man was lying. On the way we encountered rebel videtts who treated us very civilly when they ascertained the cause of our presence in their country,[39] and kindly offered any assistance in their power to get the poor fellow into a place where he could receive regular treatment. These men, after all, have a heart *sometimes* when they are so inclined, and know as well as we what constitutes a real man, strange as it may appear. To us, who know them best, they are more to be trusted than Northern copperheads and make better citizens.

A gloom was spread over the camp this morning by the news that we had sustained defeat and heavy loss of life at Chattanooga. General Rosecrans was reported to be terribly whipped.—General Kilpatrick, our pet general, also, it is said, got into one of his dare devil scrapes and lost fifteen hundred of his men in killed, while he with the balance

39. "Videtts" (videttes) meaning mounted sentinels posted in advance of an army.

of his command had to get away in any kind of flight which presented.[40] This news was received, so it is said, at Corps Head Quarters, night before last, by telegraph from Washington. I am inclined to think that it is *not* true or that it is greatly exagerated, for Kilpatrick returned to Culpepper last evening, having in charge some one hundred and fifty prisoners, and fifteen ambulances filled with wounded. This does not look very much like precipitous flight or being very badly whipped, and so I hope it will turn out with Rosecrans at Chattanooga. I fear however, that we shall not achieve very important victories until our ranks are filled—not with the [illegible] of poor houses and low dens in cities, but by intelligent yeomanry of the country. What we need more than anything else is—*men* not *money! Money* cannot fight—money cannot shoot a gun, and money does not appear to procure *substitutes!* If it did, our thinned ranks would soon be filled and we could present to our foes such a front as to effectually silence every gun and put an end to unnecessary carnage. As it is, the Conscription Act has brought back a few deserters, and once in a very great while, supplied a new man.[41] However, with all this, we are no more than able to keep our army at its present fighting numerical strength:—Deaths, disabilities and other causes decrease our ratio so fast as the act fills it. If we are defeated it is because the country has so decreed it: not because we less heartily enter into battle, or less heartily hate secession and traitors, but because we are dying for want of support from home.

But you know my feelings and my mind, and it is unnecessary to say more on this score. I have not in one jot or tittle ignored a principle or in the smallest degree become less enthusiastic in a desire to see traitors punished. I feel that if *any* thing is to be done, it ought to be done at once, while the power of the rebellion is so nearly exhausted, and foreign intervention so far off.—Now while everything is auspicious the blow, heavy and crushing, ought to fall. It can be made *fatal* now, but if left to rescusitate until Spring; thus giving them a chance to fully reorganize and equip their army, we may be troubled for years to come:

40. Chattanooga would in fact be a Union victory. On Aug. 16, Maj. Gen. William S. Rosecrans had begun operations against the Confederates led by Braxton Bragg and would occupy the city without a battle on Sept. 6. Kilpatrick had been detached to harass Lee during his retreat into Virginia but had not accomplished much beyond capturing some supplies. McPherson, *Battle Cry,* 670; *B&L,* 4:83.

41. The Draft Act, signed by Lincoln on Mar. 3, 1863, required complicated and time-consuming methods of determining who was eligible for conscription. The first names were not drawn until July 11. Nevins, *Organized War,* 119–21.

and we at last be compelled to recognize a rotten, stinking confederacy with Slavery as its chief corner stone. Had I the voice of Gabriel and the power of the Infinite, I would, it seems to me, use such faculties in raising the North to a full and perfect consciousness of its condition. Instead of quietly slumbering upon the summit of a smouldering volcano, which at any moment might swallow up its unconscious sleepers, I would ring in the ears the thunders of Sinai and tell them to arouse from their lethargy and strike for freedom. Never since the world began have questions of so vast magnitude presented themselves for settlement as now; and never, so it appears, was a Nation so profoundly slumbering over its own destruction. Oh could you see it as I see it, and could all feel as I feel, not a [month?] would roll its [round?] into eternity before the hostile fields of the South would be covered so thickly with blue uniforms on the bodies of loyal men, that not another drop of patriot blood would moisten the thirsty soil of an enslaved people. God grant our Senators wisdom and our officers pureness of spirit. Then will the people mighty in powers and strong in battle gird on the armor and achieve the victory. Hoping to hear from you I remain as ever your

Daniel.

FIVE

We left Lee to undisturbed enjoyment of his shelter

October 2, 1863 – March 5, 1864

T*he waiting and watching and rebuilding by the armies in the struggle continued throughout the late summer of 1863. Both sides continued to shift their units about, hoping to find weak points in each other's dispositions, but neither commander was willing to attack the other in a prepared position. While clearly competent, Meade continued to show himself to be overly cautious. Lee, on the other hand, was simply too weak to attack, especially after the detachment of Gen. James Longstreet's corps to join Braxton Bragg in Tennessee. Bragg's success at Chickamauga on September 19–20 necessitated the detachment of the Eleventh and Twelfth corps from the Army of the Potomac to help protect Chattanooga, further reducing Meade's willingness to launch an offensive. Meanwhile, the men marched, countermarched, and waited.*

> Camp of the 121st Reg. N.Y.
> Volunteers, Culpeper [Virginia],
> October 2nd, 1863.

My dear Wife:—

At length, after marching and countermarching, changing camp five times in as many days, we are brought up at this point, with the understanding that we have no abiding city, and that in all probability we shall move again in a day or two. I understand it is the intention to get nearer *"Uncle John"* as Gen. Sedgwick is familiarly called by officers and men. We had worked hard, as is our custom upon entering a new encampment, in getting our houses in order—setting out shade trees—(pine bushes,) around our tents and policing the grounds in a naturally beautiful grove of chestnuts, and after getting everything in good order were compelled to leave. The reason for thus abandoning this pleasant spot, is that the third division of our corps broke camp last night at midnight and have gone, I understand, to guard the railroad a few miles below Culpeper, and we are to take its place. We have been expecting orders to move, every day, but none has yet come. Great uncertainty exists in our Corps as to its ultimate destination and as to what disposition will be made of this reliable body of men. Of course the old plan (projected perhaps by our own newsmongers) of going South is again the chief talk, but *I* think it more likely that *here* the final winding up will take place, and here we shall be in at the death. Time will tell, however, and when that time comes I will let you know.

Daniel.

Once Lee learned of the departure of the Union Eleventh and Twelfth corps for Chattanooga, he began to make plans to turn Meade's right and race him to Washington, hoping to be able to attack the Union army on the march and defeat it in detail. Meade, however, was able to withdraw in good order, giving A. P. Hill's corps a bloody nose at Bristoe Station and then concentrating around Centreville. This left Lee with little option except to retreat, and he made his way back to his original positions, with Meade following at a respectful distance. Lee's movement had begun on October 7, but Holt, writing two days later, was unaware of this, and devotes his letter of October 9 to activities on the picket line and disciplinary problems in camp. In the subsequent letter, written after the maneuvering was over, Holt expresses pride in his army's success in outmarching the Army of Northern Virginia and frustrating Lee's designs.

Picketing on the Rapidan
at Raccoon Ford
October 9, 1863

My dear Wife:—

We came here on the 5th taking in Culpeper on our way, and are now upon the extreme front of the line. We found and relieved the Second Corps which had been here for a long time, and right glad did the poor fellows seem to be to get away. Independent of the unpleasantness of being shot at every time you show your head on picket line, they have been lying in mud and water, so thoroughly soaked as to be perfectly *water proof*. Our corps with the First now occupy the ground, and ordinarily with such a heavy force in front, would indicate a battle, but none is anticipated:—each party apparently being willing to let each other alone for the present. Our lines are so close to those of the rebels that we can hear orders given to relief parties as they throw up rifle pits within easy musket range. When we first came here (or rather previous to our coming) no sentinel was safe upon his post because of the beastly, murderous practice of shooting at men on duty. With our boys we sent a regiment of sharp shooters with telescopic guns, capable of killing a man at half a mile, and in their hands a perfectly sure thing of hitting whatever they shot at.[1] Only three days elapsed before a party, under protection of flag of truce, came into camp and requested that *no more firing should be kept up while men were doing duty on picket!* We had taught them a wholesome lesson—one never to be forgotten, for everytime a sharp shooter discharged his gun (and that was *very* often, as our lines were within hailing distance) up popped a reb in air,—and *dead* upon the ground he fell, to be dragged off by his comrades or more frequently left until night and thus removed under cover of the darkness. I say we taught them a lesson, and so we did, for now our men and theirs freely meet, exchange papers, trade coffee and sugar for tobacco, and fraternize in the most pleasant manner imaginable. Yesterday I went within a few rods of their works (a thing which would have cost me my life three days ago) and saw them busily at work throwing up rifle pits and building a four gun fort, upon the mantle of which their flag was defiantly flying—saw parties relieve those in the trenches—heard the order to *"limber up"*[2] and witnessed the guns going off at railroad speed down the road. What this meant—so sudden and apparently without cause, induced me to venture a little nearer, when I discovered that my presence was not agreeable and was politely requested to retire within our own lines, which I can assure you I was not long in doing. The sight of *shoulder straps* leisurely inspecting their works with a glass in hand, was calculated to excite their wrath, and I now wonder *why* they did not add one more to the murders committed on that very spot. I think if I ever wish to inspect rebel works again in daytime, in advance of our most extended lines, I shall do so in a soldier's blouse or an army overcoat which conceals your rank.

1. Telescopic sights for guns, first patented in 1854, were usually individually owned; they were not standard issue. John James Field, *Abridgements of the Patent Specifications Relating to Firearms and Other Weapons, Ammunition, and Accoutrements, 1588–1858*, 156; Jack Coggins, *Arms and Equipment of the Civil War*, 36.

2. "Limber up" meaning to attach a limber (the two-wheeled, detachable front part of a gun carriage that supports the ammunition chest) before moving off.

On the first night of our arrival, about midnight, as I lay in my tent, I was awakened by the report of a gun close at hand, and an exclamation of *"Oh!!"* In the morning I found out that a Captain of a Massachusetts Regiment had been shot by one of his men, killing him instantly. Upon inquiry I found out that he was a regular tyrant and universally disliked in his regiment. Both officers and men participated in the dislike and very little investigation into the affair took place—no one feeling like taking upon himself the trouble of sifting out the affair:—At home, such a tragedy would excite general consternation, and hundreds would be upon the track to discover the perpetrator of the crime: but here, after the first slight shock of cooly calling an officer out of his tent (as in this case) and then shooting him is over, no more attention is given it, and the command moves on as before.[3]

To-day I witnessed another military execution. The poor fellow was a private by the name of *Connelly*, belonging to the 4th Jersey Volunteers.[4] He was a deserter and filled a deserter's grave—little mourned to appearances here, but perhaps occupied a seat in a mother's, wife's or sisters heart as firmly as the best soldier's in the service. He was a simple, inoffensive looking young man of about twenty or twenty-one years, and unlike the one who was shot at Warrenton, of which I have already told you, appeared to be deeply depressed in spirits. With head hanging upon his breast as slowly the wagon passed bands playing dirges, never looking up until halted upon the spot which marked his grave, he received his doom in silent communings with his God. I never want to see *another* such sight, and hate to think of it. So different from any other death and so little sympathy generally shown a poor mortal who we know is within a few moments to appear before that tribunal of Heavenly justice, that I for one wish to close my eyes and heart upon all such scenes.

I paid a visit to Charley Hamlin day-before-yesterday. He was well, and sends his respects. This corps will leave to-day. Good night dear wife. God bless you.

Daniel.

---

3. Assaults on officers were punishable by hard labor, loss of pay, or the attachment of a ball and chain and time in the guardhouse. It is difficult to ascertain exactly how many officers were killed by their own men, but it seems the number was small and decreased as the war went on. Billings, 156–61.

4. Pvt. Joseph Connelly, Co. H, 4th N.J. Infantry, was executed Oct. 9, 1863, for desertion. Alotta, 196–97.

Camp in Field at
Fairfax Court House,
October 17th, 1863.

My dear Wife:—

It would take a "Philadelphia Lawyer"[5] to keep the record of our journeyings since I last wrote you while picketing on the Rapidan. It was not our *good?* fortune to long remain in that pleasant spot of marsh and mud, but Mr. Lee saw fit to change the programme for us, and so we have been "dancing the juber" ever since.[6] But I will not proceed immediately to recount the incidents of the march from that delectable region to these heavenly plains, but carry you back again to our exodus from New Baltimore to the waters of that classic stream—the beautiful Rapidan. I have never yet done so, and for fear that *"the word will be forever lost,"* I will proceed to state that after diverse orders and countermanding of orders, we were at length upon the road on the 14th. It was evening before we broke camp, but the roads being good most of the way, and the evening pleasant, we reached Warrenton, four miles distant, in a short time, and spreading our blankets consigned our weary limbs to rest upon the bare ground, and slept peacefully until the morning. Here we remained until night, the rest of the Corps having preceeded us. As I have previously told you our brigade was detached from the main body and stationed upon the extreme left four miles from any support whatever. This will account for our being so far in the rear.

At sunset, after remaining in town all day to the disgust of those who were anxious to join our division again, we started on a night tramp to White Sulphur Springs, which point we reached about 11 o'clock, the distance traveled being about twelve miles. The country through which we passed was perfectly open, filled with garillas and the best adapted for surprize and ambuscades of any in that section. Will you think me cowardly when I tell you that I traveled that night in as much bodily fear as I ever rode a twelve miles in my life? It was so, coward or no coward,

5. "Philadelphia Lawyer" meaning a very shrewd lawyer; an expression from the eighteenth century indicating a situation as confusing as legal technicalities are to the layperson. Mitford E. Mathers, ed., *A Dictionary of Americanisms on Historical Principles,* 1230.

6. "Dancing the juber" meaning a dance called the "juba," a popular, rollicking dance, where the dancers clapped their hands and stomped their feet, dancing in a jig-like way. John Russell Bartlett, *Dictionary of Americanisms: A Glossary of Words and Phrases Usually Regarded as Peculiar to the United States,* 222.

and I know of others who partook of the same emotion, and I think justly, too, when I tell you that our regiment *alone* accomplished the deed. Why *we* should be left all day in the very teeth of a vastly superior force of enemies, and *at night* setting off upon such a hazardous march to overtake our division, I never could guess, unless it was to gratify a spite against the "two hundred dollar sons of b——s" as *bully* Brooks called us as when he sent us into the fight at Salem Church.[7] All will agree with me in saying that this night the most strange *sounds* and sights were seen of any we ever traveled. About midway between the two points (Warrenton & White Sulphur Springs) we were halted, formed into line, loaded guns as quickly as could be done and stood waiting for some time expecting a volley from an unseen force, which we imagined lay concealed in the woods through which we were passing. Upon the right and left signal lights and guns were let off, and for what reason I never knew. When within about three miles of the Springs, we came within the lines of our cavalry videttes, and then and not until then did we feel secure and draw a long breath. No doubt you will think I have consumed much space in telling how foolishly alarmed I was, but I venture to say that even *you* with all your known disbilief of hobgoblins, would have preferred being at home than there.

These Springs, once a famous resort for invalids and persons of ease are very large and the water excellent. The buildings were destroyed last year by order of General Sigel for what reason I do not know.[8] They were beautiful and very costly, and even now their is to be seen in the blackened ruined walls, of five stories in height, the remains of architectural perfection in design and finish. Previous to the rebellion, few if any resorts could compare with the grounds and pleasant surroundings of the establishment. A large hotel and a few cottages of attendents still remain; to be occupied by men and horses; but what remains of this once magnificient structure is only calculated to fill the mind with sadness at the desolating destruction of war. Resting here over night, we next morning continued our march crossing the North

7. Gen. William Thomas Harbaugh Brooks commanded a division of the Sixth Corps at Salem Church. His reference to the "two-hundred-dollar sons of bitches" refers to the bonus money paid enlistees, thought not to be quite as good a soldier by those men who had volunteered without any monetary inducements. Ezra J. Warner, *Generals in Blue: Lives of the Union Commanders*, 47.

8. Franz Sigel's corps was operating in the area around White Sulphur Springs in August 1862 before withdrawing toward Manassas, Va., in the maneuvers leading up to Second Bull Run. *B&L*, 2:463.

branch of the river Rappahannock, and Hazel Rivers. Eighteen miles of as rough going and muddy roads as ever lay exposed to the elements brought us to that spot so long desired and so little appreciated—our own Corps and Division. How heavy trains ever get over such roads is a mystery to me. A continual succession of holes large enough to engulph an ordinary sized Brigade—up one mountain steep and down another—through fields and heavy forests, all, all alike present barriers impassible to the eye, but to the persevering energy of human effort at last overcome until at last, one and all stand upon ground too danger-ous to occupy, and we are forced to withdraw to a more respectable distance. We have at last come to a halt, General Lee challenging our boys and they *"not having the pass word."* Our whole army is here and *some* move will very soon take place. Let us wait and watch. Just at this very moment as I write, heavy canonading is going on in front and I have no doubt an engagement between some portions of the two armies is now going on.[9] I expect every moment to hear the order to advance, and perhaps before this letter closes I shall have to say that we are up and off.

Heartily glad as I am to be with our corps again, it has cost an effort to do so. Imagine yourself so sleepy and worn out that you fall into the hands of Morpheus as soon as you stop running,[10] and lying down to rest to be thoroughly soaked through from falling rain, and feeling *something crawling o'er you,* you arise to find yourself lying upon a nest of red ants and these industrious little bodies swarming by thousands over your naked body, and still more to feel a great damp substance making tracks for *head quarters* and upon investigation finding such company to be a great white grub two inches in length and as thick as your thumb, what would *you* do under such circumstances? I don't know, surely, but if *I* was not *riled* and thought *hang it!* I should greatly wonder. So it is— so much for the luxury of camp life.—Added to these little torments, suppose diarrhoea should keep you going, horses get to kicking and the guard having to be called to still them; mules setting up such an in-fernal chorus as only mules can do, and you have a perfect and truthful picture of the night I spent at Sulphur Springs. I hardly know whether I should prefer another such a night as this or take the one at New

9. It is not clear to what Holt is referring. At this point in October, Lee had begun to pull away from Manassas and was fighting minor skirmishes as he withdrew. E. B. and Barbara Long, *The Civil War: Day by Day,* 423–24; *B&L,* 4:83–85.

10. "Morpheus" meaning the god of dreams and sleep.

Baltimore when Mosby came down upon us, carrying off our brigade flag, *wounding a base drum very* badly; knocking over a dutch musician and finally decamping after thoroughly scaring every man half out of his skin. I say I do not know *which* I should prefer, but am of the opinion the latter would be preferable. What do you say?

Living at Raccoon Ford on the Rapidan proved the beginning of a series of marches little anticipated by our troops a week previous to arriving here. *Why* we had not a general engagement I do not pretend to say. Perhaps neither party was in mood or readiness for it. The facts are all we know. For reasons best known to Confederate Generals, we ascertained one very fine day, that a few scattering sentinels were all who confronted us in place of heavy lines of battle. Lee had suddenly left, (as afterward proved) for *Washington!*[11] Not long were we inactive. In half an hour nothing but camp refuse, tent poles and debris of every description marked the spot where tens of thousands of the best blood of the Republic was waiting to decide a contest already too protracted and prove to the watching eyes at home, their willingness to redeem the honor and integrity of the Nation. A rapid flight—almost a double quick, brought us near sunset to Rappahannock Station, on the Orange and Alexandria Rail Road, when we were allowed to refresh ourselves, feed horses &c. during which time the high and costly Rail Road bridge was destroyed together with station house, &c. The order for *"falling in"* came at length like a death knell to our unwilling ears, and we started—*not* in the direction which we had been going, but upon the back track as fast as legs of men and horses could carry us until reaching Brandy Station, six miles from Rappahannock, we as suddenly came to a halt and prepared to encamp for the night. Tired as any one need be after such a day's forcing, we made a large beautiful fire—such a one, as I now think of as the most comfortable I ever saw, and spread our blankets for a night's rest.—Here also we destroyed what of Rail Road track and buildings we could about the Station. When again the bugle sounded its *t-w-a-t!! t-w-a-t!!! t-w-a-t!!!* and again we were on a move *back again* to Rappahannock Station which we reached about midnight dragging along the weariest bodies you ever saw. On this march I sprained my ankle horribly, walking over the uneven ground, in many cases, and for hundreds of yards from six

11. Holt's confusion regarding Lee's movements here probably reflects that of the Union command.

inches to a foot under water. I had let a soldier ride my mare for fear I should fall asleep and be run over by batteries which crowded and jostled on every side. At last, after a forced march of at least thirty miles over roads as bad as you ever saw, we finally sank to rest and slept sweetly until daybreak next morning.

Starting again as soon as we could boil coffee and cook our breakfast, we continued to force our way as though the fate of the world depended upon our getting to Washington ahead of our adversary. And indeed this *was* the case, as we afterwards found out. Stretched out, as far as the eye could reach on the extended plain before us, the whole army, with its train of supplies, ammunition, baggage, &c.— there long lines of ambulances, endless batteries, with squadron upon squadron of cavalry, all mixed up with and moving together with heavy lines of Infantry marching by companies, formed the most imposing sight the eye of man ever rested upon. Never until now, did I see such a vast concourse of living, moving, matter. As if the universe had yielded up her countless millions, and the cattle upon a thousand hills had been brought forward to give life and add spirit to the moving panorama before us—*such* a sight seldom falls to the lot of man to witness. It takes just such a sight as this to really impress a person with the vastness of the work which we are engaged in, and thank God, able to carry forward to successful termination. I often thought of you and the good friends at home while I looked upon this inspiring scene, and felt willing to undergo almost any discomfit if you could have seen it. Nothing more grand or imposing can be conceived than such a sight as this. Only once in a great while can you get a glimpse of the life which is transpiring about you—only once in an age have presented, as now, a bird's eye view of the country upon whose face is moving these innumerable caravans of animate existence:—

Onward, Catlett's Station, Manassas Junction, over Bull Run battle field to Centerville—fleeing as from the presence of offended Deity our Army wends its way. Day and night, alike, until safely within the fortified grounds where both armies in turn have defied each other, did we strive one with the other to be the first to enter: and here in advance of Lee about twelve hours, did we offer him battle which in his wisdom he saw fit to decline accepting. It was difficult to see the reason of such eccentric actions, but one thing we all do know, and that is that Meade has outgeneraled Lee in his contemplated attack upon the Capital of the Nation. For three days we have waited for Messrs. Lee,

Longstreet & Co. to pay us a visit; but not even the friendly greetings of a few stray shells into our camp has given us notice of his whereabouts. Just now a reconnoisance in force is sent out with a view of ascertaining his exact position. No doubt we shall find out all about it before night. They cannot be far off, as we have had every day more or less friendly interchange of compliments with him. At Catlett's we came near losing our whole supply train by its being, by some inexplicable reason out of its place. As it was, only a few wagons were destroyed, but the excitement of the attack, with its boldness, served to make us more wary in the future. It seemed impossible to march more closely and in better order, but notwithstanding the precaution taken to prevent surprize, we have been almost caught napping.

Well, it appears we were *not* to fight at Centerville or Bull Run. We had not been flanked—Washington still stood the pride of American genius—we had done a gallant deed in out-marching, out-generaling and out-witting the proudest son of Southern Chivalry, and now we were ready to complete the *grand rounds* which began at Raccoon Ford on the Rapidan and ended at Fairfax Court House. Most of the time had been spent in marching with daily expectation of a fight, but independent of the frustration of designs against our Capital, and the morale infused into the army, we might about as well have remained in quiet upon the banks of the Stream where we confronted the hosts of treason.

Leisurely taking the back track, Lee found his way to Rapidan, while we settled down again near Warrenton. I have spun out an *awful long letter* the real pith of which could be written on half a page, but you must excuse it. I will do *better* next time.

Daniel.

Camp of the 121st Reg. N.Y.
Vols. Warrenton, Virginia
October 26, 1863.

My dear Wife:—

It is, I believe, somewhat over a week since I wrote you, and *two* since I received your last.—The reason for my not writing before is, that we have changed camp not less than *four* times during the week past and the weather has been so uncomfortably cold, with rain and frost, that I have been pretty nearly frozen to death. I have no fires as the Colonel and his mess have at which to sit and keep comfortable, but have to sit and shiver with overcoat on in tent, feeling very little like saying a word to anyone, trying to while away the time as best I can. As it is, I have *nothing special to say;* but I know that unless I write pretty regularly you will feel uneasy and be running to Mrs. Huckans to learn if I am dead or alive—Tom keeping her so well posted on all such matters.

I do not know but I shall have to resort to *"Poetry"* as you say, to fill up: but I think I will tell you how nearly I came [to] going *crazy* the other day. Well, if not perfectly *crazy* I was *wholly mad!* When we left Bull Run[12] our baggage wagons were behind and in their endeavors to escape shelling and other unpleasant incidents, overset and spilled out their contents; so that when we finally brought up here, I was minus my trunk and everything I had in the world except what was upon my back. If I preserved an equilibrium then, it is a wonder—a greater one if I *did not give the Quarter Master and* all others concerned, about as good as I was capable of giving for *neglect of duty* &c. My clothes, (all I had) Album, relics of all kinds, sash, trinkets for the children, *love letters*—all, all were gone without hope of resurrection, and here I stood cold, shivering, desponding—*mad!!* Who would not be? In this unenviable state of mind and body, nothing going right—all going wrong, I received a note from the Adjutant of the 95th Pa. Vols. asking me to stop over to his quarters for a few moments. I responded to the call, when *lo!* the first object that met my eyeys was the identical lost trunk safe and sound! For this purpose (of delivering it to me) did he send for me. It appears that one of their men seeing it upon the ground, picked it up and put it into their regimental wagon, thus saving all I possessed. Do you think I could hold out mad any longer? *I* could not. Perhaps some one else could, but I had had my fill, and after giving the good boy almost all the money I had with a promise of more after pay day, I shouldered the precious package and retired. *I feel much better now!* and for fear I shall feel worse before long, I will close, wishing you all kinds of happiness.

Daniel.

Meade's inactivity following Gettysburg and his unsuccessful attempts to carry on a decisive engagement with Lee in Virginia produced a great deal of criticism.

12. "Bull Run" refers to the position near Centreville, Va., which the Union army occupied during the maneuvering after Gettysburg. *B&L,* 4:83–85.

Holt was displeased but felt that Meade should not be replaced. Having seen the effects of four changes of command in the preceding year, he did not relish the prospect of a fifth.

He also found time to send a note to General Lee, thanking him for the kindness shown to him while a prisoner six months previously.

Camp of the 121st Reg. N.Y. Vols.
at Warrenton, Va. Nov. 7th, 1863

My dear Wife:—

We are beginning to feel really comfortable at the thought of making these quarters permanent ones for the winter. The Regiment with the Brigade, lies about a mile South of Warrenton, on a low ridge of small pines thickly set, with timber sufficient for all purposes, within two miles. After policing the grounds around Head Quarters and erecting comfortable log huts, the condition of affairs appears the pleasantest contrast imaginable to that of a week or two ago, when we were changing encampments and making improvements every day, only to be abandoned for others to take up and finish. I contemplate good times soon, as we have made arrangements with a family in the City [13] to supply us with light biscuits, fresh butter and honey, in exchange for which we are to supply them with coffee and sugar. This is a good arrangement for us as these articles cost us a mere trifle in comparison with their prices, and we receive for them the same as it would cost them if purchased in one of their stores. This family has also supplied us with a parlor stove which now graces our little home among the pines. So unlike old arrangements is it, that we begin to feel that we *are* somebody after all.—We can now invite a friend into the *parlor* (as our sleeping apartment is separated from kitchen, dining room and drawing room by a couple pieces of shelter tent) and take a social chat with pipes, *wine*, &c. I am afraid it is *a little too good* to be permanet, but we have concluded to enjoy it to our utmost capacity as long as it lasts, and if compelled to relinquish it, try next time to *improve* upon our experience. After a year's hard knocking over the country, and mixing up with "every sort and condition of men" we are better able to make use of and appropriate the blessings which surround us. I can see no reason for leaving this spot. (as we have a

13. The "city" is the county seat of Warrenton, about forty miles west of Washington, D.C.

rail road to bring supplies from Washington and are within supporting distance of the defences about the Capital) unless it is to go
further South. By going *South* I do not mean Texas, Charleston or any
other *far* Southern part of the Union, but perhaps near our old
encampment of last winter—Fredericksburg. This, [Warrenton] in my
estimation is a more advantageous position for our army to occupy
than this [Fredericksburg]—being more directly in the line of
Washington—nearer rebel lines, and if raids are to be made, saving
two or three days hard marching and being nearer help if we get into
difficulty. All these are things worthy of thought and will no doubt influence the decision of Gen. Meade. I am very sorry to say that
General Meade has lost the confidence of the army to a great extent,
and I think justly so, but I would not for the world have it said so,
coming from an officer under him. You know how such reports go
when once in circulation. *"A voice from the Army of the Potomac"* rings
through the land like the swelling cadence of a hurricane, and a word
spoken, even by the most obscure and humble member of that great
family, has more effect sometimes for weal and for wo[e] than all the
preaching of elegant enthusiasm at home.[14] I would say nothing to
create distrust for I feel that we have had enough of change already,
and far too much for the good of the Nation. Better to hold on to a
fair man, than to change for an untried one. This has been the death
of us in more senses than one.

New-York by her political expression has spoken in louder and more
fearful tones to the Southern Confederacy than all the cannon of the
Universe pouring death and destruction into [them]. The Army is in a
perfect frenzy of delight over the joyful news.[15] The whole North,
judging from the popular vote, just given, is ablaze with patriotic fire,
and now, if she will only send her *sons* instead of *votes,* we will soon lick
up the last drop of rebellion and your weary old husband will forever
bid good bye to hard tack, salt horse[16] and rusty bacon and seek an
asylum from such warlike scenes as these in the sacred circle of *home!*

14. "For weal and for wo[e]" meaning for better or for worse.
15. New York's legislative elections were held in 1863. Republicans won despite
Union difficulties in the field, in large part because the campaign stressed Unionism and
abolition conjoined as the war cause, thus appealing to both those who supported the
Union above all and those who wanted abolition of slavery regardless of cost. Republican
party candidates won two-thirds of the New York districts. McPherson, *Battle Cry,* 687.
16. "Salt horse" is a derogatory term for salt pork, a staple of the soldiers' diets. James
I. Robertson, Jr., *Soldiers Blue and Gray,* 15.

I found an opportunity to-day, through our friend, Mr. *Fink*, to convey to General Lee a note thanking him for the kindness shown me while a prisoner in his hands. It was an opportunity, which seldom presents itself, and one which I had for a long time been looking for without success. I think no one would blame me for this "holding correspondence with an enemy with whom we are at war" if they only knew the circumstances of the case. At any rate, I have written it and feel glad of being able to express what I feel—real satisfaction of the result of my captivity and gratitude to General Lee for thus letting me off while thousands were finding their ways to prison houses to linger along and die at last eaten up by vermin and reduced to skeletons by hunger. How could I but feel a sense of unalloyed kindness toward such a man whose word is law and who as easily might have caused my death?

Daniel.

On the very day Holt was writing the preceding letter complaining about in-activity, Mosby once more stirred things up by attacking the army's supply trains. This news was quickly overshadowed by a successful Union attack on the Confederate redoubts near Rappahannock Station. The attacking force consisted of Upton's brigade and that of Col. Peter Ellmaker, under the overall direction of Brig. Gen. David Allen Russell, temporarily commanding the division. The 121st played a conspicuous role in the action, helping to capture the better part of two Confederate brigades at remarkably little cost to themselves.

Camp of the 121st Reg. N.Y. Vols
near Brandy Station [Virginia]
Nov. 9, 1863—

My dear Wife:—

You no doubt are somewhat surprized to hear from me so soon, and still more by receiving this written at *"Brandy Station."* After the joyful strain of the one of the 7th (the very day we left Warrenton) and the confident expressions of remaining for the winter, *I* as well as you, was taken back at being ordered to "strike tents" and march *immediately*. We had heard the night before that we were to leave in the morning, but inasmuch as it was not *official* (the sick not even being provided for) and as such rumors are *daily* in circulation, I did not deem it of sufficient importance to even tell you of it, and it *must* indeed have been of no importance in our minds, for I tell you *everything* I think of, real or unreal.

The morning of the 7th was ushered in by an announcement that Mosby had made us a visit and carried off about one hundred and fifty horses and mules, set fire to the wagons, and captured several teamsters. This little item occurring as it did, in our very midst, just at the break of day and after the promulgation[17] to "move on in the morning," rather disarranged the calculations. Instead of having *four* horses to draw our hospital wagon as usual, only *one* could be found, and three instead of four on our baggage. So throughout the division our ever trusty friend Mosby relieved us of trouble in looking after them.—Surely we were in a bad fix; but in a short time almost all the horses were recovered, and we were on our way Southward. So complete was the surprise and so perfect the arrangements, that before our men were aware of it, (they sleeping *in* the wagons and under them) that the camp was entered by what was supposed *our own cavalry* (they wearing our uniform) and *every horse* in the brigade was cut loose before a tenth part of the teamsters knew of the business going on.

At 2 o'clock P.M. we arrived at Rappahannock Station, where we halted, formed in line of battle, deployed skirmishers and in about half an hour were engaged in driving in rebel pickets.[18] After thoroughly exploring the ground and ascertaining as correctly as possible under the circumstances, the strength of the force opposing us, about an hour before sunset we took up our line of march directly for the defences about half or three-fourths of a mile in front. As soon as we emerged from the timber which concealed us from sight, and aided in perfecting plans for the reduction of the forts and rifle pits which were swarming with graybacks, a furious shelling commenced, to which we replied in as spirited and effectual a manner as two or three batteries of light three inch Parrots could do. Very slight loss was sustained, I presume, on either side, during the short interval between leaving our position in the wood and the time of getting behind a long ridge running parallel to their works about a fourth of a mile from them. Under cover of this friendly hill, we remained for some time, until a

17. "Promulgation" meaning order or command.
18. At this stage in the campaign, Sedgwick was in command of the right wing of the army, consisting of the Fifth and Sixth corps. Maj. Gen. Horatio Wright, the senior division commander, replaced him at the head of the Sixth Corps, and Brig. Gen. David Allen Russell replaced Wright in command of the first division of the corps. Upton, meanwhile, had taken command of the brigade containing the 121st, replacing Bartlett, who had been assigned to divisional command in the Fifth Corps. *OR,* vol. 29, 1:222, 559.

definite understanding as to the attack was discussed—the regiments making the attack—the supports—reserves, &c., &c. After settling the questions, as I have already said, the 5th Maine, in line with the 121st Reg. N.Y. started off on double quick, leaving the rest of the Brigade to support if necessary. It had now become so dark that the defences of the Rebels could no longer be seen, although but a few rods intervened between friend and foe. Only by extended lines of fire could we know where to direct our steps and this must not be long delayed. General Upton, who led this gallant little party[19] here battled the line and addressed it with all the coolness imaginable informing the men, in a loud voice (so loud as to be perfectly heard by every Rebel in front of us,) that *four* heavy lines were supporting us; that *die* probably many of us soon would, but it was a good and glorious cause, and that *he* was there to share their fate, and thus by his own dauntless bearing and cheerful words of patriotism, infused a spirit in the hearts, and nerved the arms of his men sufficient to insure success to any enterprise. Perhaps you will better understand the situation when I tell you that *not one* line within *supporting distance* was in reserve to render help if necessary. After taking off knapsacks and stacking them in a pile, with a sufficient guard over them, and receiving orders to carry the works at the point of the bayonet, the last word was given and with the alacrity of school boys and determination firm as a rock, our boys scaled the almost perpendicular walls of the fort and ran like mad men along the low lines of embankments caused by earth thrown up from the pit below. One long line of fire—the sharp deadly report of musketry—belching of cannon, the wild shriek of dying men mingled with cheer after cheer of the assailants, as with bayonets fixed they broke down and carried away all opposition; and those works, together with the men who defended them, fell into our hands. Until the very moment of scaling those works, Dr. Slocum and myself were with the troops, and I must say, for *once* at any rate, I felt it uncomfortable to be crawling into the very mouths of those guns which were throwing forth iron death into our little line. Not finding it on my card of instructions to storm a fort without gun or any other article of offensive warfare, I concluded to remain *outside* while others reaped more glory, perhaps by going in. Our loss as a regiment was *very* small—in all amounting to

19. Upton did not make general until May 12, 1864; he was still colonel during this raid. Holt, in copying his original letters into his letterbook, no doubt made this slip then.

only *four!* killed, twenty-three (23) wounded and one missing, while we secured and had awarded to us by General Meade, 3 Colonels, 2 Majors, 17 Captains, 27 Lieutenants, 651 Privates and *four* stand of colors.[20] The 5th Maine was successful as ourselves and perhaps a little more so; for *they* had awarded to them *five* rebel flags against *four* to us.—Thus in this little encountre, we made short work of at least *two thousand* prisoners beside a large number of killed—the number exactly, I never knew, but the *ditches were full of them,* and all we had to do next morning was to *turn the pit* and they were buried.[21] It was some satisfaction, even though it came through death and blood, to thus pay back a little of the drubbing which we so unceremoniously had to receive upon previous fields.

It is truly amazing for me to think *how few* of us were not killed or wounded in this affair. Not because they were silent, for an incessant fire was kept upon us, not because we were too far off, for we could hear officers give the word to their men—not because of their *love* to us, for we have had too many counter assurances from that; but because we were *too close;* the balls passing over our heads, instead of falling short. Had they come three or four feet lower I am afraid I should not be able to render so good an account as I now do. All the men we had killed had been *hit in the head*—and in *front* at that. It would be worth seeing could you look upon the field next morning. Such sights of guns, knapsacks, &c., &c., as covered the ground, and such heaps as they made after being collected and stacked together was truly refreshing to behold. I have a dress sword captured from an officer by one of our men, which I intend if possible, to get home.

Quite a serious calamity befel me here upon that night; and it was no less than the loss of my overcoat and pocket case of instruments. I had been dressing the wounds of those who were hurt and brought to the rear, when wishing greater freedom of my arms than could be had in such cumbersome folds, I took it off and laid it upon the ground beside me. An ambulance just then arriving, I saw to having it filled, and when

20. "Stand of colors" meaning the flags carried by regiments. Each regiment carried its own flag into battle.

21. The Confederates counted 6 killed, 39 wounded, and over 1,600 captured or missing. Several hundred of the latter were presumed either to have been dead or wounded, left behind Union lines after the battle, or to have deserted. The fact that the Union reports list only 1,300 prisoners, combined with Holt's observation of large numbers of Confederate dead, indicates that as many as 300 Confederates may have been killed in the action. *OR,* vol. 29, 1:616–24.

it started back, some good soldier appropriated it to his own use. The night was a *cold* one, with keen freezing air from the North and no wood to build a fire. Under such circumstances it was hard to part with so good a friend, but I hope the poor wounded fellow who has appropriated it will enjoy many a happy hour within its warm embrace. I shall have to buy or pick up another right off for I cannot stand these cold days and nights without even an overcoat to keep me warm.

Next morning, we followed up, did not succeed in bagging any more. The visit was an unexpected one to them as it was unexpected to us. I mean *soldiers* of the army. Not one could guess the object of our leaving Warrenton that morning—not one supposed that before night we should be fighting one of the most brilliant battles of the war—brilliant, on account of its suddenness and complete success, and brilliant on account of completely breaking up their winter quarters in this direction. Log huts, far superior to ours in construction and capacity had been erected, stables for horses, and sheds for wagons—in fact they were beginning to feel like permanent house keepers, when we, *sans ceremonia* entered their borders and compelled retreat![22] It was a sad thing, thus to send them out upon so cold a night, after taking away their houses, blankets, tents and victuals, and next day still holding over them the threatening rod of vengeance pursuing like avenging angels, but we could not but recollect Bull Run where many a Yankee made better time to the rear than they, and concluded to *go it* even though the pill was a bitter one to them. The poor fellows lost their miserable eleven dollars a month in *confederate bonds* for their services which had *not* been paid, but which would have been next day, as the Paymaster was on hand for that purpose, and clothing which lay packed in great abundance in their shanties ready to be issued, but which like all the rest fell into our hands for *what* purpose Heaven only knows. Some of the clothing of officers, direct from England, manufactured there for the Sons of Chivalry, was *first rate,* and *I* should have liked, as some of our boys did, to have got a nice overcoat to replace the one I lost, but this fell not to my lot.

General Meade has bestowed upon us a deserved and well merited compliment for achieving such a result with so trifling a loss of life and property. We feel well over it, as it is the *first* time we appear to have been appreciated. Heretofore, the tide has been uniformly against us, but *now* the tables are turned, thank fortune.

22. *"Sans ceremonia"* meaning without ceremony.

If compelled to fight Lee behind his works on the Rapidan, we shall have the warmest work we ever got into. No labor or skill has been unemployed in perfecting a series of defences and fortifications such as to defy any armed force which may be brought against them. We have been where we had a slight foretaste of what awaited us if we persisted in making their acquaintance unasked. I hope we shall *now* really settle down for the winter, as the weather is growing too cold for active duty, and the state of the roads forbids rapid marching. I have nothing of personal moment to relate and therefore bid you good night. It seems a long time since I saw you last but the time is not far distant, I trust when we shall meet again,

Daniel.

After the reverse at the Rappahannock redoubts on November 7, Lee withdrew to a strong position behind Mine Run. Meade pursued cautiously and, after a half-hearted attempt to turn the Confederate position in late November, pulled back and settled into winter quarters, much to the relief of Holt and the soldiers on both sides.

Camp of the 121st Reg. N.Y. Vols.
at Welford's Ferry on
Hazel River, Va.
December 4, 1863

My dear Wife:

Very great events have transpired since my last writing. It is unnecessary to say how uncomfortably situated we were for a month or more upon these muddy, slippery grounds, without sufficient covering either in tents or blankts, and with such beds as could best be made upon frozen ground upon which a few bushes or a little hay or straw had been strewn. Too often have you have been told it to soon forget it. You hear about men becoming *toughened* to it:—so they do, to considerable of an extent, but it is done at the expense of health in nine cases out of ten. Were it designed that man should endure all the rigors of a Northern Winter without covering sufficient to ensure a proper degree of warmth, God would have given us *scales* and *coats of hair and fur* such as cover the horse and beaver, and envelope like a blanket the thick hide of an elephant or rhinoceras: but instead not a living thing upon the face of the earth has a less protected natural body than man. For a while we can be brought to bear extreme low and high degrees of temperature and have the power of throwing off attacks of disease, which if inflicted upon more sensitive persons would surely produce death; but not *long* even upon the most thoroughly trained subject can the elements be brought to bear in vain. Nature true to herself at last must give out and then both alike are brought to grief.

We had received repeated intimations that we were to move, ever since we had been ordered here, but inasmuch as day after day passed, still finding us occupying the same soil, we came at last to think we should *not* make further advances this year; but contrary to expectation we were ordered out at daybreak on the [date missing] and continued to move all day until we came into the vicinity of what is known as *"Robinson's Tavern,"* near Mine Run.[23] The march was a cold and cheerless one in the extreme, men and animals alike partaking of the gloomy aspect of surroundings. The entire army moving at once, betokened something to do, and this upon such days and nights when ice formed upon and over everything which contained moisture, was regarded by our veteran troops as equivalent to defeat or *running.*—You may, therefore imagine our feelings as we onward tread our way over frozen hubs and ice covered streams; not a word of comfort spoken by a single mother's son, and not even a *song* (those sure and pleasant evidences that we were still alive and ready to execute orders) escaped the purple lips of a half frozen face, but sullen silence, broken once in a while by an oath as some poor fellow fell headlong into a frozen pool or sluggish stream of water, from whence he emerged dripping with ice and frozen mud, these were all the incidents which marked that day's marching. Added to this, the still greater suffering of not being permitted to light a fire at which you might warm your freezing feet and hands, nor even to boil our coffee—a beverage the most highly prized of anything which a soldier can enjoy, and you have still another lack in that day's service. I do not know *why* we were thus punished—for *punishment* it surely was. Our advance had been proclaimed from the time of breaking camp and every rebel knew as well or better than we, that the object of the move was to offer battle on the day succeeding. However, it was promulgated that *"no fires be made, not even for boiling coffee."* Many of us had but an overcoat—the baggage being in the rear—not a tent—not a mouthful of anything except what our pockets

23. Holt was referring here to Robertson's Tavern, about one mile east of Mine Run, the small creek halfway between Chancellorsville and Rapidan Station. *Atlas,* plate 44-3.

contained, and we were expected to fight a battle in the morning decisive either one way or the other.

Of all *hard looking* places, that of Mine Run was the hardest I ever beheld. Stretching as far as the eye could reach from left to right, on the crest of a low range of hills across the stream, was a continuous line of defenses, upon which and in which could be seen the enemy strengthening their works and preparing to give us a warm reception upon that freezing day.[24] Intervening between our lines and theirs was a low, swampy stretch of marsh, through which Mine Run wound its slow serpentine course, and to make still more difficult a crossing which at any time, under the most favorable circumstances would have been a work of difficulty, they had sharpened stakes and driven the bottom full—thus presenting a barrier a thousand fold more difficult than in a state of nature. Not all was this either. They had dammed the stream in several places and as a consequence an overflow and deepening of its water was the result. Immediately after crossing as you began to ascend the hill towards their works, trees had been felled with topped branches, and these sharpened to a point, presenting a front perfectly impossible to overcome, even though no other impediment was in the way. All along the heights could be seen battery upon battery, some masked while others were clearly peciptible, ready to belch their iron contents of grape and canister into the stiffened, freezing flesh of the best blood of America. As I looked out upon the task proposed to be executed, my heart died within me. Not one who should be seriously, or even moderately wounded could have escaped death in some shape or other. Unable to walk, or imperfectly to get along, not one in fifty but would have frozen before help could be given them.—Strong, vigorous men, upon picket that night, died from frost, and they, even (the only ones) allowed a fire. If these men, in the full and perfect enjoyment of health, froze upon their posts, how could it be expected that *wounded*, half starved ones could stand it? I tell you how it is Louisa, if Meade ever did a noble act in his life, it was when he concluded *not* to fight Lee in his strong hold upon the banks of Mine Run at a temperature of the weather, far, far below freezing. Newspapers blame him and call him coward for not doing so; but let their editors with me have

24. The movement to which Holt refers is the Union move to outflank Lee. Lee was waiting for them. Sedgwick and others considered the line weakly held and unimproved; Holt's eyewitness account may be more accurate. *B&L*, 4:88–91.

seen and felt what I saw and felt upon that occasion, and instead of taunts and ridicules they would bestow words of commendation. Perhaps it was unwise to have thought of and to have attempted to execute such a movement upon such a time, (and I for one think so) but the sequal—proved the wisdom in getting back into camp as soon as possible, leaving Lee to regret our change of purpose.

I do not know, but I shall weary you with a recital of what you no doubt have seen in the papers before this, but coming so closely to me, and feeling, as I did, so keenly all the bitterness of that unsuccessful, cold advance I hope you will put up with it. It was contemplated and arranged that upon the firing of a signal gun upon our extreme left, an immediate artillery duel should ensue, to be followed up in an hour by a charge upon their works. As usual the 121st and 5th Maine were in the *first* line of battle, and as a consequence would receive the first fire and most destructive one of the rebs. From my position I could see every move which was made; and this, perhaps, was one reason why I *did not* relish the dish set before us. Our men, as at Fredericksburg and Rappahannock Station, stacked their knapsacks with guards placed over them to insure their safety, and as they defiled and passed away gave a look, a *last look*, as almost all supposed, upon all their earthly treasure. Not a murmer escaped the lips of our boys—they had made up their minds to obey the order, and in so doing, too to fill the grave of a patriot—the most glorious and respectable of all graves, but which, notwithstanding was anything but to be desired. Talk as we may about *"patriotic fire"* and such like, it is poor pay for a soldier to accept this as the ultimatum of earthly ambitions. If *I am* to die, and die here, let it be in the line of my duty, but if I have a *choice* in such matters, let it *not* be upon a field of blood among mangled masses of human beings, but at home—within the precincts of my own quiet circle of family and friends: *there* let my life, expire sweetened by a sense of having performed my duty well towards my country and my God—there let my last breath be drawn while around my bed, and in the embrace of all I love below, may my passport to the world above be as still and as quiet as the closing breath of a cloudless day.

The firing, as agreed upon, commenced upon the extreme left, at eight o'clock and continued for some time, but not to the extent anticipated. Long before it had reached our right, (and here I was) it ceased and not a gun was fired, except an occasional shot as a signal previously agreed upon. Waiting for a long time for the final order to be given to *"charge"* we were at last made aware that it was *indefinitely postponed* and that a retreat would commence as soon as darkness shut out the view of operations on our side.—This was welcome news—news like the intelligence of life being prolonged by pardoning power, and *all* felt to forgive our leader for whatever we ever saw amiss in him, and being satisfied with what we had instead of trying to better it. Perhaps you have not forgotten what I said of Meade in another letter not long since. What do you think of it now, after you have seen the comments of the press upon *"the situation"*?

All that day we lay, without charge of columns, waiting for the setting of the sun. In the mean while we engaged in chasing each other round in a circle to keep from freezing, and getting under as many blankets as possible, lying *two deep* and *cold at that*. If you or anyone else think it *pleasant* to be a soldier, do not try it as we tried this:—Thanksgiving day upon Mine Run with mercury at twenty or thirty below freezing, and thanksgiving at home with roast turkey and all the good things a bountiful, heaven-blessed country could bestow in home made warm by hickory and anthricite,[25] and glows of friendship which no human agency can extinguish are two very different institutions. However, I presume the Army of the Potomac on this day was more thoroughly thankful that something like common sense had taken the place of mis-guided ambition, than the vast concourses of old men and young men, old women and young women, bond and free who crowded houses of worship on that day telling how thankful they were in being the re-cipients of such blessings as they enjoyed.

I saw more on the night of that eventful day where we left Lee to undisturbed enjoyment of his shelter on Mine Run than I ever saw before, of the cursed institution of slavery. At a house where our division made head quarters for hospital purposes, lived a violent, hard hearted secessionist by the name of *Johnson*. The week previous to our coming among them, he had sold to the rebel army and received his pay for it in confederate rags, about seven thousand dollars worth of leather, and had upon hand, finished and unfinished, about as much more. When *we* came *he* left, going over to the enemy, leaving, how-ever, his family, consisting of a wife, two daughters and several slaves, one of which (a woman with a small unweaned infant at her breast) he paid only a week previously for, the sorry little sum of $1,700. The

25. "Anthricite" meaning anthracite coal.

house we used for a *hospital,* while the outbuildings (negro quarters) our men made use of to keep themselves from freezing. Upon first entering the house, it was found vacant, or rather the family had left it as usual, in charge of female negroes. Not long, however did the daughters—fair specimens of Southern Chivalry—snuff dipping, dilapidated, lantern jawed bipeds of *neuter gender* keep aloof from their hated brethren in blue. Upon entering their domicil, the first sounds which greeted the ears of the Surgeons who composed the operating squad of the division were, *"Who are You?* How dare you come into our house in this way without being asked? You had better leave at once. Your scorn is far preferable to your company, and if you are cold, you had better go among the *Niggars* who appear to be your most particular friends." Much more such choice language was employed, when upon being told by Dr. Bland[26] of the 96th Pa. that we were occupying it as a hospital for the sick and wounded, they exclaimed—"I hope the house will burn down, and every d——d yankee in it!" "As to the *house* burning down," responded the Dr., "I have no doubt but your hopes will be realized; but so far as the d——d yankees are concerned, we shall have them in good quarters before the torch is applied to your dwelling." And so it was. About midnight as the army moved past on its way back again, after securing what was deemed expedient, the buildings (or rather *the building*) was fired and burned to the ground together with its contents of all kinds. Extending to the Negro quarters, they, too feel the angry surging element until all were wrapped in a fearful lurid blaze of light. The tannery too, where this man Johnson had manufactured leather for our foes, shared the same fate. Leather wet and dry, in vats, and out of them to the amount of thousands of dollars, was thus kept from hereafter gracing the heels of graybacks on their retreat from the despised miserable *"Yanks"* who opposed them. In little groups stood old and young Negroes looking on as one after another of their long cherished household goods was consumed by the raging element. The most pitiful sight of all was when all had been swept away, to see these poor suffering sons and daughters of a down—trodden race giving vent to slumbering sentiments of freedom. Thrown out penniless and almost naked upon the world at a season of the year and hour of the night when the hardiest needed a home and loving hearts to comfort, these people

26. Dr. Daniel W. Bland, *OAR*, 3:922.

hailed their deliverance from the hands of their inhuman task masters, as did the Israelites upon the return of the year of jubilee.[27] Cold and apparently freezing, as they stood upon the hard frosty grounds in the month of December, with eyes streaming with tears, they blessed the hand of their deliverer and called upon their God to bless *"de dear gentlemen"* who wrought their deliverance. Contrasting my own with the case of a poor mother who stood before me with two little ones—one an infant at the breast, and the other a little fellow of about two years who stood at her side crying pitteously for a blanket to keep himself warm, I thought how blessed was I, with wife and little ones in a home where every comfort filled the house—where the hand of the oppressor nor pinching grasp of poverty ever entered—where freedom to worship God and govern my household as best I thought—how all these blessings had been vouchsafed me, I was content and resolved never again to grumble at my lot. Oh, Louisa, the sight of these emancipated slaves at that hour, standing bareheaded and barefooted upon the worst night I ever was out, looking forward to the time when families should be re-united—hearts respond to hearts—and the day when their backs should no longer smart under lash of whip was one which I can never forget and never wish to see again.

We placed these miserable creatures in baggage wagons and after conveying them to Culpeper, put them aboard cars for Alexandria, where the government has made provisions for all such as they.[28] God help and bless the poor mortals. I cannot think of them even now, without (as I did then) shedding tears for them. It may be a weakness, but I cannot help it. After *twelve* hours march, in which we made only as many miles, all the time suffering untold miseries by cold, we fairly got started and by night brought up again in our old encampment on Hazel River.[29] We have enough for one season. Let us have no more such as this. If we are to reap glory and win a name in battle by *such* (*I* hardly know what term to apply but perhaps *"advances"*) I for one want

27. "Year of jubilee" is a biblical reference to the Hebrew tradition of freeing all slaves every fifty years, the so-called "year of jubilee." Lev. 2:10 (KJV).

28. Congress passed an article of war on Mar. 13, 1862, forbidding officers to return slaves to their masters. As freedmen and women and escaped slaves all fled to Union lines, various organizations served as social welfare agencies to look after their interests, providing food, medical aid, education, and, in some cases, employment as laborers and soldiers. McPherson, *Battle Cry*, 497, 709–10.

29. Holt's camp at Welford's Ford (also referred to as Welford's Ferry) was about four miles north of Brandy Station on the Hazel River. *Atlas*, plate 23-5.

to be reckoned out. I think it a poor paying business. I will let you know if we so foolishly move again.

Daniel.

Camp of the 121st Reg. N.Y. Vols
on Hazel River, Dec. 15, 1863.

My dear Wife:—

The world is full of wonders, and one of these is, that we are in comfortable quarters—the best of any Brigade of the Army of the Potomac. We crossed over the river a few days ago having permission from General [Horatio] Wright to do so *if we would protect ourselves* from attacks of gurillas, &c.[30] All the rest of the army is on the South side. A more uncomfortable location for a camp could not have been picked out than ours, before coming here. Although upon high ground, it was wet and *muddy* Ah! *such* mud! without a stick of wood for fuel or drop of water for cooking—two very important articles in house keeping. Here we are in the midst of a fine grove which we leave standing, and get our supply from timber adjacent to camp. Water is handy and everything perfect for first rate winter quarters. Log huts, good as any I ever saw, grace our well laid out streets, and now the men are engaged in constructing *side walks* running from Head Quarters to Captain's Quarters, and thence to Hospital, Sutler's tent, &c. The grounds are thoroughly policed. Every man keeps his house in order while company cooks, in houses erected for that purpose, prepare food for the regiment. Evergreens grace the hospital enclosure, as also a walk from thence to my own house. Col. Olcott has in process of erection a *gothic structure* which when finished will be the pride of the Army. Stables for horses and quarters for officers servants are erected in rear of all. Here the Post Office is also located. If left alone, we will in a short time show you how well *men* can get along without the aid of *woman*. But it is *again* reported that we are to move near Fredericksburg. Perhaps so— perhaps not. We will wait and see. I shall come home soon if I can obtain leave of absence for even *ten* days. No leaves have been granted yet in this corps, but no doubt soon will be. Until then wait patiently. I will soon see you,

Daniel.

30. With campaigning over for the season, Sedgwick had returned to corps command and Wright to his division.

Holt's leave of absence, his first in sixteen months of service, was whittled from his requested twenty days to ten days at Christmastime. His father-in-law had died in July 1862 and Holt, as administrator of the estate, was needed at home. He returned by the first of January to the army's winter quarters, having lost his luggage along the way.

> Camp of the 121st Reg. N.Y. Vols
> on Hazel River, Jan. 4, 1864.

My dear Wife:—

After encountering dangers—perils by land, perils by sea, and perils among false brethren, I brought up safely here after my visit home. Orders came on the night of the 31st Dec. to be packed and ready for a start by rail to Washington on the next morning. We got ready and remined so until orders countermanding those previously issued when we once more resumed our old work of cleaning up, &c. The reason of the *alarm* and *not moving* it was ascertained, was on account of disturbance in the Shenandoah Valley.[31] The rebels have made us much trouble in that quarter, and I should not wonder if one of these days we have to send a stronger force there to clean them out completely. The third division of our corps *did* go as far as Brandy Station, and then came back again, the difficulty being for a while settled, I suppose. I am sorry to say that I lost my valise with all its contents while in Washington. After giving it in charge of proper offices to be taken to the Baltimore Depot, I supposed it was all right, and did not find to the contrary until the very moment I was ready to start for the front.— Then I ascertained that it had been taken to the Steamboat Landing to be conveyed to Alexandria. I could not stop as I was not up to time on leave, and so had to leave it with the Provost Marshal to send on as soon as it could be found. I hated to do this, but no alternative was offered—stay over and be dealt with by court Martial or go along on your business and have the confidence of your superiors. I *went on!* It is really vexatious to be shortened as to time, but affairs here are

31. Responding to frequent Confederate raids in the Shenandoah Valley region, Union cavalry under Gen. W. W. Averell attacked the valley from New Creek, about fifteen miles southwest of Cumberland, W.Va., and some forty miles northwest of Winchester at the northern end of the valley. Driven away from his goal of Staunton, Va., by Confederate Brig. Gen. John D. Imboden, Averell instead attacked the Virginia and Tennessee Railroad at Salem, west of Lynchburg, destroying Confederate stores there. *B&L*, 4:480; *Atlas*, plates 82, 100, 135-C.

unlike home matters. Everything goes by rule—line and plumet.[32] My old comrades came about me enquiring what kind of time I had at home and all expressing attachments and feelings for family and friends truly refreshing. I will write again very shortly

Daniel.

Camp of the 121st Reg. N.Y. Vols.
at Welford's Ferry on
Hazel River, Va. January 24, 1864.

My dear Wife:—

I again sit myself down to the pleasant task of writing to you. We are to have a thorough inspection to-day. Gen. Sedgwick and Staff, General Wright and Staff and Col. Upton now commanding Brigade will review the regiment, so I will have to be up and doing. For two or three days past, our boys have been engaged in beautifying the naturally lovely grounds of our encampment, and I am perfectly willing to have *any* man or officer see if we are not looking and doing as well as any regiment in the army. I have just completed my usual round of daily inspection of quarters of the men, and find *nothing* to *condemn*. We are so differently situated and so much more like well drilled and thoroughly disciplined soldiers than we were one year ago, that every one remarks it. At present our camp is full of Herkimer and Otsego visitors. Several ladies are here making visits to their husbands who could not obtain a furlough to go and see them. Among this number is Mrs. Weaver, wife of Lieut. Weaver[33]—a perfect lady, so she appears. I love to visit them in their log cabin and talk of "the days when we went gipseying long time ago." Never since we came out, has a better feeling existed in the army than now. If only they feed us well, pay us well, and *use* us well, we will do all the fighting the North can desire, and think nothing of it: but if instead, we are to go without pay while our families half starve at home, keep back on clothing, and blankets and compel us to live upon salt pork and hard tack instead of fresh beef and soft bread mixed up with a liberal supply of vegetables, you may expect to hear the loudest curses from this naturally happy and contented army that ever startled your listening ear.

---

32. "Line and plum[m]et" meaning precision—an allusion to the straight line drawn by carpenters with a line and plumb. The "plummet" is the weight, also known as a plumb bob.

33. Erastus C. Weaver mustered in as a first sergeant in Co. K, Aug. 23, 1862. He served until his discharge as a first lieutenant on Feb. 14, 1865. *Annual Report,* 198.

The inspection is over and we come out, just as I *knew* we should, with many compliments and praise for neatness and comfort.

Daniel.

Winter quarters allowed Holt the luxury of time to compose long letters home, covering a multitude of topics. The following missive briefly describes actions taken against Lieutenant Colonel Olcott for conduct unbecoming an officer.

> Camp of the 121st Reg. N.Y. Vols.
> at Welford's Ferry on
> Hazel River, Va. January 31, 1864.

My dear Wife:—

I am very tired but will try to say a few words, just to let you know that I am well, and to keep your courage up. I sent for a detail of men to fetch evergreens to beautify and adorn the Hospital grounds. They are all set and present the prettiest appearance conceivable. Inside, as well as outside, (thanks to Christian and Sanitary Commissions) cannot be beaten by any Regimental Hospital. Dr. Holman, (now Corps Medical Director in place of Dr. [illegible] O'Leary set aside), made us a visit and complimented *me,* a simple *assistant* Surgeon upon the order and general appearance of all around.[34] I took the compliment feeling that it was *deserved,* for I have taken pride in making it all we could have it. Clean sheets and pillow cases, neat spreads and warm blankets make a pretty good bed, although *springs* and sofa bedsteads are seldom seen here.

For the first time since my connection with the Army, I have heard a blessing asked at table. I mention it because of the extreme *rareness* of the thing. Not even a *Chaplain,* (so far as *I* am posted) is in the habit of doing it. This most befitting and Christian duty—recognizing the kind interposition of our Heavenly Father in bestowing creature comforts upon His unworthy children—asking the Divine favor and craving a blessing to rest upon us in partaking of His bounty, is never, to *my knowledge* invoked. All seem willing to partake of what is set before them without once acknowledging with thankfulness, the source of the blessed gift—taking it as a matter of course without once rising above

---

34. Dr. Silas A. Holman was medical director; Cornelius B. O'Leary served with the 25th Regiment N.Y. State Militia, and the 145th and 175th N.Y. State Volunteers. *OR,* vol. 36, 1:261; Willard, 26.

animal instincts in satisfying a hungry stomach. I must confess that when Mr. Aldrich (for it was he who had not forgotten his early lessons) closed his eyes and reverently craved the Divine favor and protection, my own eyes filled while my heart reproved the neglected duty. I could not but ask *why* not here, as well as at home, live the life of a consistent follower of the Lamb? taking up the cross and following Him through evil as well as *good* report? It is a hard thing, I admit to stand *alone* in these matters, yet religion and christianity are as highly admired here as at home. There *is* such a thing as being a real christian in the army—but they are few and far between, to judge of the fruit produced. Cox and Lieutenant Henry Walker are, I am glad to say, consistent followers of the Lamb.[35]

I do not know but I have already told you that Major Mather has left to accept a Lieutenant Colonelcy in a Negro Regiment.[36] He was a first rate man and officer possessing the confidence of the entire regiment. Before leaving, however, he preferred charges against Lieut. Col. Olcott for drunkeness, gambling and obscene behavior before the Regiment, citing as witnesses almost all the officers and many of the privates. The result of the trial was a severe repremand and threats of dismissal if further indulged in.—This was very mild on the Colonel, for his character as a *man* is bad enough. He is, I am sorry to say, anything but a temperate, virtuous man. Wine and women are his Gods, and to indulge his appetite in the matter, he has taken to the card table to supply an empty purse. Not an officer in the regiment, and sometimes even enlisted men, have been put under the torture to supply money in shape of *loans* to keep his bottle full, and gratify his lust while on leave of absence.[37]

35. There is no information regarding Mr. Aldrich, who may have been a visitor. Henry B. Walker mustered in as a sergeant with Co. E, Aug. 11, 1862, and as a 2d lieutenant with Co. G, May 4, 1863, where he served until his discharge on Jan. 8, 1864. Cox had been captured with Holt after the battle at Salem Church but was not released until September 1863. He continued to serve in the 121st until his discharge in June 1865. *Annual Report,* 194; Pension and Service Records.

36. Andrew E. Mather mustered into Co. K of the 121st on Aug. 18, 1862. He was wounded while fighting with Co. G at Salem Church and promoted to major. On Feb. 4, 1864, he was promoted to lieutenant-colonel and discharged to take charge of the 20th U.S. Colored Troops. The 20th spent most of 1864 in Louisiana. *Annual Report,* 123; *OR,* vol. 29, 2:623; vol. 34, 4:616.

37. The specific charges against Olcott were that, while drunk, he attempted to force liquor down the throat of Capt. Cleaveland J. Campbell, the Officer of the Day, and that he also ordered a sergeant in his company to drag a sleeping and drunken Captain

It seems hardly possible that more than one-half of our enlistment has expired; yet so it is. If the succeeding one is to be as exciting as the past, we shall witness stirring times. We are about to enter upon the hardest and bloodiest campaign we have ever had, *in my estimation.* When spring opens, and that will not be very long, every energy the Government possesses will be put forth to put down this rebellion. On the other hand superhuman exertions will be made by a dying wicked dynasty to keep afloat another year in hope of intervention of foreign powers. Left alone to themselves, the Rebels all admit that it will be folly longer to continue the unequal contest. I have heard high ones in power among them assert it, and those with no power at all, make the same confession. We at the North, see not a shadow of hope for them on that score, and a worse than foolishness to continue it on any other.—It is my humble opinion that with the settling of the ground, comes the settling of old accounts with the chivalry. They will die hard, *but die they must!!* While they confess to be battling for a *principle,* we do the same thing, and are terribly in earnest in its prosecution. I see not the *first* hope or reason for success on their part. The last man has stepped into their thin ranks—the last dollar long ago has been drawn from an never overstocked treasury, and all that is left is a very small amount of *confidence* in their expiring cause. Were it not that *pluck* constituted the real sum total of what has kept them up these long years of hopeless, unequal contest, long ago I should have been at home, and every other Union man, but this very commodity will keep them alive and kicking long after they should have been entombed.

Daniel.

Constant raiding by Union and Confederate troops took place during the winter of 1863–64. Union general William Woods Averell raided south up the Shenandoah Valley in December; Mosby's Rangers and Stuart's cavalry were constant threats; Union forces tried to draw out the Confederates or to chase after them. Holt's description of the action in early February reflected these actions, albeit incorrectly. On February 6, Union forces demonstrated on the Rapidan to gauge Confederate strength, crossing the Rapidan at several points. Stuart re-

---

Campbell to Olcott's quarters, under orders to call out the whole regiment to aid him in his task if necessary. Olcott was found guilty and punished; Campbell later accepted a commission with the 23d U.S. Colored Troops. Phisterer, 3430; Pension and Service Records; *OR,* vol. 33, 1048.

sponded but did not cross himself. Gen. Judson Kilpatrick did some recon-
noitering and chased off a detachment of Rebels; Brig. Gen. Wesley Merritt's
brigades chased off a Confederate brigade of cavalry. Despite the rumors Holt
heard, there was no major fighting. By the 7th, Union forces withdrew. The
cannonading to which Holt refers was probably a Union demonstration at
Morton's Ford against Jubal Early and the Confederate II Corps.

Camp of the 121st Reg. N.Y. Vols
Hazel River, Feb. 7, 1864.

My dear Wife:—

At last I have something to write about—something to proclaim—
something to feel proud of. The 121st Regiment is no longer what it
was, but now looms up in the distance, the wonder and admiration of
the world. After all the toil and vicessitudes of a protracted war; after repeated applications and as often repeated failures we have been blessed
by an addition to our ranks by *one recruit.* This important addition was
made last night, and whole of the addition was given to Company *"K",*
while the remaining nine companies sat and wept in the silence of the
night watches! Such an important event is well calculated to strike
terror to the heart of our foes and inspire confidence in the ranks of
our men. Rejoice with us. We are happy.—

The weather is balmy and springlike. Our boys go out, dig worms,
and go to the river often returning with a string of nice fish.—I went
one day, but as usual, got nothing. Fish do not like my bait any better
than the men like my pills. Who can blame them? All kinds of game is
abundant. No one disturbs or shoots at rabbits, quails, wild turkeys, and
ducks which astonish one by their tameness. Even *crows,* those most
scary of all birds, devour putrid carcasses of mules, horses and camp
offal with as little concern for man as if he were an inoffensive mouse.

After the war, when evil passions are lulled to rest, this country will
be a desirable one to live in. Northern men and Northern money and
energy will develope its resources, and an unprecedented reign of
prosperity will follow. On some accounts, I should like to live here,
and on some I should not. Heretofore only those of wealth, owning
large plantations and a great number of Negroes, were thought much
of. The *poor* or even small farmers were never taken into the account
when the status of society was reckoned. A new era is to dawn upon
the down troden serfs of Southern Chivalry. *They* are to become men,
while their lords and masters will have to come down and take a back

seat. The *"mud sills"*[38] of a despised North will henceforth teach them real political freedom and instruct in sciences of political economy such as never entered their heads or hearts before. Their baronial estates and mansions will become town halls and seats of villages in which true lessons of life will daily develope the growth and power of Northern freemen.

Very early yesterday morning, we received orders to be ready to start by 8 o'clock on a reconnoisance in force into lands held by rebel hosts, taking three days rations; but here we are yet with the same order re-promulgated, and to *stand ready* until further notice. Well, about 10 o'clock heavy firing (cannon) was heard in front and continued with brief intervals, all day. About sunset, musketry, heavy and continuous, was heard and continued until darkness settled down upon the contending parties. Indeed, so late did it continue, that a man from a tree could not be distinguished two rods distant. Of course we all went to our quarters in a high state of excitement, expecting to be called up at any moment, and impatient to hear the result of the engagement. This morning the firing was resumed about nine o'clock, but at so great a distance as to be scarcely distinguishable. Only a *jar*— heavy, sullen and prolonged, as the echo passed from point to point along the imposing peaks of Blue Ridge. Unlike the sharp, crackling outburst of a thunder clap over head, came that dull reverberation, showing that the conflict had been changed to another and more remote theatre of action. The rattling clatter of small arms could no longer be heard. Death had settled down upon that field of contest, beaming into unfathomed regions of darkness, hundreds of those no better prepared to obey the summons than we, while the Angel of Peace wept over the dreadful carnage. Under cover of Night's sombre mantle, the foe had slunk away leaving the dying to their fate, and the dead to vultures of the air.

It is reported (but of its truth I cannot speak) that day-before-yesterday Stuart with his cavalry attempted to cross the river, and after very slight resistance on our part, was permitted to do so, our pickets and forces giving way before him until he was sufficiently in our power, when Kilpatrick with his band of heroes passed to the other side, cutting off his retreat, while our infantry engaged him in front.

38. "Mud sills" meaning persons of the lowest and least regarded class in society.

Thus surrounded, by his own carelessness, he lost heavily. The number killed I have not heard, but prisoners amounting to eleven hundred, have been sent in. *This is report*, confirmed by three or four different sources; but *I* do not believe it.[39] I *hope* it is so, and very much more; but we shall know soon. No doubt a severe battle has been fought, but I cannot give credit to the *particulars*. It is too soon after battle. No correct tidings can be had so soon.

Daniel.

During late February and early March 1864, the Sixth Corps demonstrated in support of Kilpatrick and Gen. George Armstrong Custer, both of whom were conducting raids in the area. The most substantial raid came on February 28, when Kilpatrick left Stevensburg with four thousand cavalry and headed for Richmond to capture the Confederate capital and free Union prisoners held there. Kilpatrick's raid on Richmond was cut short when a second force under Col. Ulric Dahlgren failed to join him. Kilpatrick withdrew from the outskirts of the city to Union lines near Williamsburg; Dahlgren was killed in action near Walkerton.

Camp of the 121st Reg. N.Y. Vols.
at Welford's Ford on
Hazel River, Va. March 5, 1864.

My dear Wife:—

The Sixth Corps has been on a reconnoisance as far as Madison Court House since I last wrote you.[40] Not a gun was discharged during the four days of our absence from camp—not a rebel was seen, and we

---

39. Holt was right not to trust the reports. Kilpatrick led a force of 1,360 officers and men across the Rapidan at Culpeper, Germanna, and Ely's fords on Feb. 6. He reconnoitered the enemy's position, captured a few pickets, and returned Feb. 7. Also on the 6th, Maj. Gen. Gouverneur K. Warren, temporarily commanding the Second Corps, crossed at Morton's Ford in front of the Confederate position. Exposed to enemy fire and attacked by skirmishers, he withdrew. Brig. Gen. Alexander Hays, commander of the division that made the crossing, thought more could have been done, but Warren disagreed. The Union forces suffered 255 casualties. Merritt's first cavalry division also got into the act; they moved to the Rapidan on Feb. 6 and demonstrated there on Feb. 7 with fifteen casualties, but did not cross in the face of enemy infantry and artillery. *OR*, vol. 33, 140–41, 114–18, 139–40.

40. Madison Court House is in the foothills of the Blue Ridge Mountains, about twenty-five miles northwest of Charlottesville. The Sixth Corps marched over to Madison Court House to support Custer, who was heading for Charlottesville as a cover movement for Kilpatrick's raid. *B&L*, 4:93–98.

had, of course, nothing to do except to *"bout face"* and get home again. I do not know the distance traveled to get here but should think about twenty miles, judging from our starting at sunrise and marching until dark. The country for a greater part of the way was low and in many places covered with water. In *dry* seasons I have no doubt it is sufficiently dry for ordinary farming, but now, it presents in many places, the appearance of overflowed marshes. *Rain* has been the order of the day, *as usual* on this reconnoisance. Had it been *cold* as well as wet, we should have suffered greatly, but as it is, we got along very well. I say *we* I mean *I* for I found dry quarters in the hut of an old Negro, and what was more agreeable was that I was welcome. Two days I was their guest, and those two days I never shall forget for the lively interest all the blacks evinced in matters connected with the rebellion. Here, clear out of the world, you might say, (for the country was very thinly settled, although an old one) where you would naturally expect to find extreme ignorance, I was astonished to find a general intelligence among the poor oppressed beings which thousands of slave owners were not possessed of. One slave in particular—a young man of great manly beauty—strong and well proportioned about three-fourths black who had been born upon the spot, was a perfect wonder to all our officers for the depth of knowledge of causes which produced the rebellion, and the condition of things as they were at present. His master was a Blacksmith—had been a soldier in the last war and served at Norfolk. His *chattel* being the best and most reliable man of the two, was entrusted to transact the old man's business in *every respect.* The old man told me so, saying that *he could not keep house if it were not for Tom.* Yes, Tom kept his books, made purchases, disbursed funds and oversaw the rest of the flock while at work upon the farm.[41] I asked him if he and his young wife would not like to be free and live in the North where he might be thought something of? He replied that he should like to do so, but as long as Massa lived he was bound to stay with him and care for him—that while *he* was young and helpless, old Massa fed and clothed him—used him well and taught him to read and write, and he could not leave so good a man while he was helpless and depended upon him for support. I could not speak against such christian

41. The proportion of slaves, mostly men, who were trained in skilled crafts such as blacksmithing had grown smaller by the nineteenth century. Perhaps 5 percent could be counted as skilled laborers. Eugene Genovese, *Roll, Jordan, Roll: The World the Slaves Made,* 388–92.

sentiments as these and so left him with his kind old Master, one day to find a home in another and more favored land than that, as he himself said he should.

It was upon the 27th of last month that we started out, at 7 o'clock A.M. passing through Culpeper about noon arriving at, or near our old encampment at *Slaughter Mountain* distant from our encampment at Hazel River, fifteen miles, where we encamped in a grove of pines for the night.[42] After breakfast next morning we were again on the move, every moment expecting to be attacked or to attack the enemy. A line of skirmishers and flankers was kept constantly on the watch for hostile demonstrations, but none were made, and so we passed on, destined for Robertson River. *"James City"* came in our way, and *such* a city![43] three or four houses all gone to decay, and the remnant of a former store half fallen, half standing through decay—the sunburst wooly pates of Negroes looking out upon a sight new and strange to them, while our boys made all sorts of sport of the half-frightened, half bewildered inhabitants—all taken together formed a picture worthy to be copied by a first class artist. We arrived at the River about noon, where we remained until 2 o'clock P.M. When finding nothing to fire at, we took the back track and encamped upon the same ground as the night previously. Many of the men gave out entirely from sore feet.— Marching in water, the skin had become blistered and peeled off, and a more distressed company I hardly ever saw. Ambulances were full of them, and the road side was lined with limping raw footed men carrying their shoes in hand while they hobbled along in stockings.— Cox was one of the sufferers. He gave out early in the first day and I had to take care of him by giving his gun and accoutrements to another while he rode one of my horses.

A brisk march next day brought us to our camp on Hazel River where we have since remained and where we are willing to remain until we fairly go to work. These reconnoisances are necessary to find out the exact position of affairs. If we should start upon an expedition not expecting to find opposition and before we had gone a dozen

42. Slaughter Mountain, five miles east of Madison Court House and also known as Cedar Mountain, had been fought over on Aug. 9, 1862, during the Battle of Cedar Mountain.

43. Robertson's River runs just north of Madison Court House, flowing southeast to the Rapidan near Garrett's Mill. James City was located at the foot of Fox Mountain, about halfway between Culpeper Court House and Madison Court House.

miles to be brought up suddenly by an overwhelming force in front, we should feel cheap and be used hard: but knowing the ground, we are better able to meet and contend with a foe. Our cavalry continued its march to Charlottesville where they found plenty of graybacks both infantry and cavalry, but they concluded not to give general battle and so started back again for old quarters which they reached a day after we got in.[44]

Daniel.

---

44. Custer and his two thousand cavalry found Charlottesville strongly defended and thus retreated, escaping an ambush by Jeb Stuart's cavalry on the road back to the Sixth Corps' lines. *B&L,* 4:93–94. Holt's letter of Apr. 4, 1864, concerning the appearance of an old neighbor is omitted.

SIX

More blood has been shed than ever before in a season

April 20, 1864 – July 4, 1864

As the weather warmed in Virginia in *the spring of 1864, the armies came to life. On March 12, Gen. Ulysses S. Grant, hero of Vicksburg, promoted to Lieutenant General and General-in-Chief of the U.S. Army, came east. He planned a coordinated drive against the Confederacy, east and west. Maj. Gen. William T. Sherman was to advance from Chattanooga to Atlanta; Nathaniel Banks was to capture Mobile and push north into Alabama; Benjamin Butler was to push up the Peninsula to cut the Petersburg-Richmond Railroad; Franz Sigel was to occupy the Shenandoah Valley. Grant focused his own work against Lee in Virginia. In preparation for the coming campaign, Grant consolidated the Army of the Potomac into three corps, the Second, Fifth, and Sixth, under Winfield Hancock, Gouverneur Warren, and John Sedgwick respectively, to which the Ninth Corps of Ambrose Burnside would soon be added.*

A strange foreboding fell over the members of the 121st New York. Emory Upton, in a letter to his brother, declared, "We are expecting a stormy campaign . . . ." [1]

Camp of the 121st Reg. N.Y. Vols
on Hazel River, April 20, 1864.

My dear Wife:—

The almost incessant thought of home and its surroundings had driven me again to seek relief in writing. I must confess, that I grow weak and foolish when I let my thoughts wander from this prison house of mine to the free and quiet life which I once enjoyed and hope again

---

1. Emory Upton to Henry Upton, Mar. 26, 1864, Emory Upton Collection, Genesee County Dept. of History.

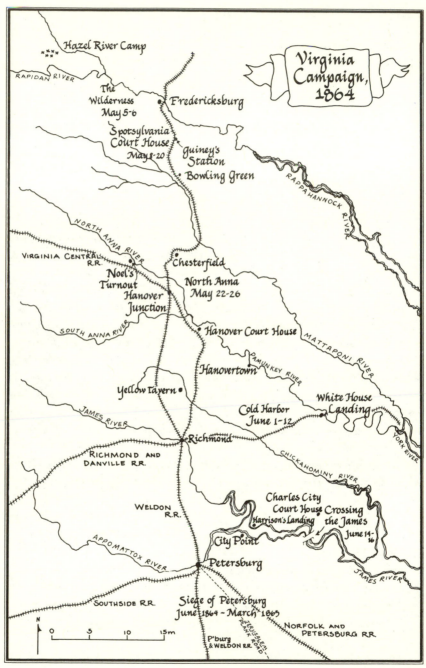

Hazel River Camp

RAPIDAN RIVER

The Wilderness May 5-6

Fredericksburg

Spotsylvania Court House May 8-20

Guiney's Station

Bowling Green

RAPPAHANNOCK RIVER

NORTH ANNA RIVER

VIRGINIA CENTRAL R.R.

Noel's Turnout

Chesterfield

North Anna May 22-26

Hanover Junction

SOUTH ANNA RIVER

Hanover Court House

MATTAPONI RIVER

PAMUNKEY RIVER

Hanovertown

Yellow Tavern

White House Landing

Cold Harbor June 1-12

JAMES RIVER

Richmond

YORK RIVER

RICHMOND AND DANVILLE R.R.

CHICKAHOMINY RIVER

Charles City Court House

WELDON R.R.

Harrison's Landing

Crossing the James June 14-16

City Point

APPOMATTOX RIVER

Petersburg

JAMES RIVER

SOUTHSIDE R.R.

Siege of Petersburg June 1864 ~ March 1865

NORFOLK AND PETERSBURG RR.

N

0   5   10   15m

P'burg & WELDON R.R.

JERUSALEM PLANK ROAD

Virginia Campaign, 1864

MAP BY MICAELA AYERS

to enjoy. I firmly believe that we shall not fight longer than this summer. If we are successful, the rebellion will be ended, and if not, a *peace party* will arise in so great numbers as to compel the Government to recognize the Southern Confederacy, when of course hostilities will cease, but I hope the day will never come when we are forced to acknowledge our weakness to such an extent and bring everlasting disgrace upon a free North. You know *my* feelings upon this matter, and they have not changed. It is imperatively demanded that we make short and thorough work of the job before us. Too many signs, both in Congress and out of it, go to show the impatience which the people are looking upon this prolonged struggle and it is a natural result growing out of the casualties of battle and financial ruin which threatens the Nation. You may depend upon it, there are to be some bloody times before long: but *when* and *where* the blows are to fall, is a mystery to me. All is as quiet as a tomb here as yet, but the heavens begin to lower, and at any hour or minute we may hear the order to begin the campaign. There is no disposition manifested to shrink from the conflict; yet we all feel that when we *do* come together, it will be a death grapple. The atrocities at Fort Pillow and recent disasters on Red River, conjoined with the doubtful advantage gained since the battle of Chattanooga, have exasperated the men and infused within them a spirit of revenge which will tell fearfully when the tide of victory turns in our favor.[2] I cannot but shudder at the thought of the carnage which it seems to me to be inevitable to follow upon the meeting of the two armies. Perhaps *we* shall see but little of all this—perhaps *here* the tide will set and decide the contest. God only knows who among this vast concourse, will live to see wife and little ones again. I will try to set my house in order for either living or dying, and rely upon the strong arm of the Mighty for protection. If I ever needed your prayers, I need them now. Shall not I have them? With eternity so near at hand and the cold waters so nearly in view, we should indeed be hardened if we did not think seriously of an event which we know so closely at hand.

2. The Fort Pillow atrocity took place on the Mississippi River in Tennessee on Apr. 12, 1864, as Confederate cavalry commander Nathan Bedford Forrest and his men captured the fort, then massacred the black prisoners after their surrender. Union General Banks was foiled in an attempt to push up the Red River in Louisiana to expand the Union control over the state. Banks was defeated Apr. 8 and eventually would be forced to retreat downriver. He lost his command by the end of May. McPherson, *Battle Cry,* 748; Boatner, 273–74, 685–89.

I hear but little of the children. I hope they do not think themselves ruled out because I say so little about them. Dear little creatures, I should love to fold them in my arms, and hope to do so *"when this cruel war is over."*

> Daniel.

Camp of the 121st Reg. N.Y. Vols.
Brandy Station, May 2, 1864.

My dear Wife:—

I again write from this point, although I thought this morning it would not be so. Last night we received orders to be ready to leave camp at 7 o'clock this morning, which we did by getting up at 4 o'clock and working hard for a couple of hours. We are, however, within half a mile of the old camp, and once more pitched tents. The cause of this move was to draw our brigade on this side of the river, so that the pontoon bridge might be taken up and removed to the right. I think, however, we shall not remain here long. The whole army is concentrating and getting ready for a move. General Burnside with his command is here and when a thorough organization is effected we shall be ready for a move. I can say but a few words we are all upside down. God bless you,

> Daniel.

Holt began keeping a diary in May 1864. The entries cover the period from the spring campaign of 1864 through his departure from the service. He may have felt that he would be too busy in the coming campaign to write letters regularly to his wife. During the months of May and June 1864, Holt was without the services of the chief surgeon. Dr. Slocum was on duty at the Division Hospital during this crucial time, leaving Holt as the only surgeon on duty with the regiment.

Sunday—May 1st, 1864

Visited the 152nd Reg. N.Y. Vols. in company with Major [Henry M.] Galpin, Captain Kidder and Newton Phelps.[3] Find the boys all well, getting ready for the coming campaign. They have *poor* quarters, com-

---

3. The 152d, recruited in Herkimer County in October 1862, served in the Suffolk campaign in Virginia in May 1863. Sent to Washington July 14, they then transferred to New York City to help police restore order after the July 1863 Draft Riots. The unit returned to Virginia in October 1863 and was attached to the Second Corps in November. John S. Kidder, from Laurens, mustered in as a captain with Co. I, Aug. 23, 1862. He was

pared with ours, and all appear to be glad to leave them. Arrive in camp finding letters from home for which I feel very thankful.

Monday—May 2nd, 1864

Receive orders, pack up and cross over Hazel River preparatory to starting on the campaign. Go into camp upon the same ground we occupied last fall, and use the same chimneys for our tents. It is with feelings of sadness that we leave our comfortable little houses and pitch tents upon cold wet ground. Our division is all together between Hazel and Rappahannock Rivers. Brigade review and inspection—the *last* probably of the season. It is a sad thought that scores of those now moving out in military pride and perfect health will in a short time become food for worms. We must soon engage a foe almost equal in numbers, filled with determined courage. We shall do our duty, come life or death.

Tuesday—May 3rd, 1864

Went to-day with sick from Division Hospital, on the grounds of J M Botts, to Brandy Station.[4] Had a rough time of it generally. Got down there at 2 P.M. and remained until 11 P.M. Saw all off upon the *last* train which left the depot. Had a case of small pox with them.

Wednesday—May 4, 1864

Up at 3 o'clock A.M., strike tents, pack up, eat breakfast, attend Surgeon's Call, mount my horse and off on a march at the early hour of

---

wounded in action at Spotsylvania on May 10, promoted to lieutenant-colonel, and served until June 25, 1865. Henry M. Galpin mustered in as captain with Co. A, Aug. 4, 1862, and had just been promoted to major on Mar. 31. He was wounded in action on Oct. 19 and discharged Dec. 21 as a result. George Newton Phelps enlisted in the 121st while still a minor. He was appointed hospital steward May 27, 1863. Captured with Holt at Salem Church, he was released in August 1863 and assigned to Co. C. *OR*, vol. 27, 3:451, 699, 817; vol. 29, 1:669; vol. 33, 465, 735, 1038; Warner, 93–94; *Annual Report*, 108, 22; Pension and Service Records.

4. John Minor Botts, a leading Virginia Unionist and Whig congressman, stayed in Virginia after secession and wrote against it. He was arrested for his pains in 1861 and imprisoned for eight weeks. In January 1863, he moved to Culpeper County to find warfare literally on his doorstep. He fed hungry soldiers of both sides and entertained officers as well, including General Meade. The only Confederate officer he would not allow in his house was Jeb Stuart, whose troops had destroyed his property and held him briefly as prisoner in retaliation for his Union sympathies. Clyde C. Webster, "John Minor Botts, Anti-Secessionist," 9–37.

4 o'clock A.M. For a wonder, once in the history of the war, we start punctually at the moment disignated. The most perfect order is observed—every Division moves out at the appointed time. Brigades are not behind and regiments vie with each other to be first in line. The best of spirit prevails. We need it. Cross Germanna Ford on the Rapidan at 3 o'clock P.M. and encamp for the night about three miles from old encampment on Mine Run. No incidents of moment occur this first day of the campaign.

The location in which the 121st found itself was aptly named the Wilderness. This dense wood, measuring some twelve miles east to west and six miles north to south, was nearly impenetrable on foot. The Rapidan River served as its northern border, the Orange Plank Road ran along the southern edge, the Germanna Plank Road bisected the wood from the north, becoming Brock Road to the south; the Orange Turnpike ran east to west through its center. There was the tiny crossroads of Wilderness Tavern at its center, but the region was sparsely populated. This was ground near Chancellorsville—a year past, a disquieting memory.

Grant did not want to fight in the Wilderness, where visibility was often less than twenty yards. He was heading for Lee's army, trying to prevent Lee from sending troops either down south to help Johnston fend off Sherman's march against Atlanta, or to the east to go against Butler's troops slowly making their way up the Peninsula toward the railroad. Moving forward by the left flank, Grant's army hoped to push through the Wilderness quickly and meet Lee's men in the clear. It was not to be. Lee's men under Richard S. Ewell and A. P. Hill moved up the Orange Turnpike and the Orange Plank Road, respectively, and met the men of the Sixth Corps on May 5.

Thursday—May 5th, 1864

Letter from wife and Dr. Walker. Under arms at sunrise and advance to Mine Run three miles distant where we engaged the rebel army under General Lee. At 11 A.M. commenced firing and kept up a brisk engagement all day. It was a hard and obstinate fight. As yet, we have gained nothing. I am left alone with the Regiment. Dr. Slocum is at Division Hospital out of harms way. Upon the whole I had rather be here. It is *harder* and *more dangerous* work, but one of excitement and interest. Dressed only about twenty wounds to-day, almost all from other regiments than my own. Encamped for the night upon the field in a log hut about ¼ of a mile from the Regiment, in a cleared field. This is the raggedest hole I about ever saw. No wonder we cannot find or see a reb until we get right upon them. Swampy, hilly, bushes thick as dog's hair, grape vines, rotten logs and fallen trees, make up this pretty picture. A fine place to fight in surely: a perfect quag mire.

The 121st saw even heavier action late in the day on the 6th, when Confederate Brig. Gen. John B. Gordon led a surprise attack on the unprotected right flank of the Sixth Corps, caving in part of Gen. James Ricketts's division and driving it in on the corps' center. Upton sent in the 121st together with the 95th Pennsylvania to help stem the tide, but they too were driven back until Upton rallied some of them and they received reinforcements. The stiffening Union resistance and the oncoming darkness compelled Gordon to call off the attack.

Friday—May 6th, 1864

Lie upon our arms all night. Pickets keep up constant firing during the night. At Sunrise the Rebels make a charge upon our lines and were repulsed. Three times during the day they repeat it, and as often driven back with heavy loss. The fight has become general and hot. General Burnside, with a heavy force of Negroes, has gone to our left.[5] The rebs turn our right, driving us like scared sheep. For *one* I can say that it was hot work just about that time. The first intimation I had of this, was a promiscuous skedaddle from right to left and from front to rear. My horse [named] Frank Halligas had run off, so I ran after the horse. I never made better time, nor ever came nearer being gobbled up. A great many of our men are taken prisiners, some killed and several wounded. Among the *killed* is reported Col. Olcott—shot in the head by a minie ball.[6] After a flight of three miles we rally and form in line of battle. We regain the ground lost, but recover none of the prisoners or wounded. This has been a hard day and night for me—out all night—not a moment of sleep—dressing wounds and sending back disabled of all sorts. I gain a new dress suit entire in this skedaddle, but finding the owner give them up after a while. It was in this wise. Pell mell all were rushing along, horses *with* riders, and horses minus riders. An officer more intent on getting to the rear than to attend to his men, came pushing past my pack horse, and left hanging upon his bit, a carpet bag containing his Sunday suit, &c. It was queer—this transferring baggage

5. Burnside's Fourth Division of the Ninth Corps was made up of black troops commanded by Brig. Gen. Edward Ferrero. William D. Matter, *If It Takes All Summer: The Battle of Spotsylvania*, 4, 359.

6. Five hundred Yankees were captured; although Olcott was only wounded, he was also taken prisoner. He was released three months later and rejoined his unit. Ibid., 3; Pension and Service Records.

but true. My kit was long and protruding and caught the handle just enough to take it off the saddle of—Surgeon Mansen 5th Maine—a *greater* coward if possible, than I.[7] From some cause, troops have been withdrawn from our right and sent to our left all day to-day; and we could see from our front that rebs were being strengthened heavily there. It has been a wonder to a great many beside myself *why* this should be. We now see the folly of it in this skedaddle.

In two days, Grant's army had suffered 17,500 casualties, the most horrific coming as the Wilderness was set ablaze during the battle by small-arms fire. Beginning May 7, Grant pushed south, still advancing by his left flank, seeking to move past Lee's right and open the way to Richmond. Lee quickly blocked him at Spotsylvania, where the campaign would stall until May 21.

Saturday—May 7th, 1864

The 6th Corps is again organized after its scattering of yesterday. Lieutenant Colonel Olcott is reported *wounded* and *captured* instead of being killed. I hope so, for he is a first rate officer even though he *does* sometimes *imbibe*. We are heavily reinforced in the night, where yesterday we were made to leave so ingloriously.[8] It is reported that our *Pontoon train* is captured. I hope not. If true, this is surely a heavy blow—one that we cannot soon recover from. Heavy battle expected at sundown, but *do not get it.* Instead of a fight, we make a flank movement on the Chancellorsville Pike, marching all night, and pass through the place at sunrise.[9]

The Sixth Corps, having made its night march on May 7–8 from the Wilderness to Spotsylvania, took up positions in the Union line, engaging in skirmishes but no major attacks.

Sunday—May 8th, 1864

We are having at present (10½ A.M.) brisk shelling and skirmishing on our immediate front, about four miles from Chancellorsville. Our

7. Surgeon Melville H. Mansen served with the 5th Maine. *OAR,* 1:20.
8. The 121st was reinforced the night of the 6th by Brig. Gen. William H. Morris's brigade (First Brigade, Third Division, Sixth Corps). *OR,* vol. 36, 1:666.
9. Holt's reference to the Chancellorsville Pike is actually the Orange Turnpike, which ran through Wilderness Tavern before meeting up with the Orange Plank Road two miles west of Chancellorsville. *Atlas,* plate 50-1.

brigade in line upon the right where we remained until morning. Several of our boys are killed upon the skirmish line. A great scare and hub bub in the night, caused by disturbed picket line. The Jersey Brigade lose heavily to-day.[10] So far it has been a continuous battle from the time we struck Mine Run until now.

The almost constant fighting from the Wilderness to Petersburg took a steady toll of officers as well as enlisted men. The most significant loss on the Union side was the death of General Sedgwick at Spotsylvania on May 9, which shocked the entire army. The fifty-one year-old West Pointer had led the Sixth Corps with distinction since Chancellorsville.

Monday—May 9th, 1864

Another change to the left. General Sedgwick killed while reconnoitering enemies line. This is an awful loss to us. We had learned to love and obey him as faithful, dutiful children. A general gloom overspreads the Corps. General Wright steps into his place and I hope will *fill* it as well as his predecessor; but I fear *no one* will receive the support and confidence that *"Uncle John"* has with his Corps.[11] We are in rifle pits in front of a batterey, awaiting an attack from the Rebels. We are ready for them and hope they will come along. At seven o'clock P.M. the ball opens briskly. We make no charges upon their works to-day. There is a continual disturbance all night upon our advanced lines, but no general engagement.

The Confederates stubbornly defended their ground at Spotsylvania. On May 10, Upton received permission from his superiors to lead an attack in an effort to break through the "Mule Shoe," a salient jutting out from the Confederate entrenchments, which would soon be dubbed the "Bloody Angle." Placing the 121st N.Y. in position to lead twelve regiments, he broke through and continued to advance. Although reinforcements and support were promised, they never arrived, and Upton had to fight his way back out. He did manage to take one

10. The Jersey Brigade Holt mentions refers to the First Brigade, First Division of the Sixth Corps. The 121st was in the Second Brigade of the same division. The Jersey Brigade lost 789 men between May 8–21. Disturbances on the picket lines caused some of the casualties, but Holt probably exaggerates the losses on May 8. Official reports make little of the Jersey Brigade's losses on that day. *OR*, vol. 36, pt. 1:664–66.

11. Horatio Gouverneur Wright was competent and had been hand-picked by Sedgwick as his replacement. The soldiers accepted him, but they did not love him as they had "Uncle John." Warner, 575–76; Catton, *Stillness at Appomattox*, 116.

thousand prisoners (not three thousand, as Holt states). The twenty-four-year-old Upton was given his brigadier's stars after this performance.

Tuesday—May 10th, 1864

At Sunrise, *"All quiet on the Potomac"!* The Rebels began to shell us, and we them about 10 o'clock A.M. Several wounded brought in. A *very dusty* time around my little flag, called a *"hospital"*. Three times have I been shelled out and three times returned determined to hold my post but was *compelled* by outside pressure to yield to lead and powder arguments. At 5 o'clock P.M., the most awful shelling I ever heard, opened upon the rebels, which continued for about half an hour, when our brigade charged their works, resulting in the capture of three thousand prisoners, but we were obliged to leave the works for want of support.[12] In so doing, we lost heavily, as a matter of course. Not less than three hundred and fifty wounded were sent to the rear where three Surgeons, Dr. Laney (my good old comrade), of the 95th Pa., Dr. Mansen of the 5th Maine and myself dressed *all* their wounds before sending them to Division Hospital.[13] This, to *me* was the *hardest* day of the fight. One man was shot a second time while in my arms dressing his wound, and expired. For an hour bullets, shells and solid shot flew through our midst as thick as hail. I wonder *why we* were not killed. Our Regiment suffered greatly. We paid pretty dearly for these 3,000 rebs and taking of their rifle pits, if such a sight as this day presents, is any kind of pay. At 5 o'clock A.M. get the last load off, and we *"fall into"* our beds (?)!—on the ground.

Wednesday—May 11th, 1864

In line of battle again before the enemies works. Another attempt will be made to carry them. I hope it will prove successful, I hardly know *what* to think of this wholesale slaughter in storming breastworks so well manned and stubbornly defended. *I don't believe it pays.* Rain coming on. We withdraw to camp of last night, where we lie in *very* uncomfortable quarters. Several times during the night disturbed by

12. Upton's forces captured 1,000 prisoners and withdrew with "heavy losses" from the fight. Overall, there were 37,822 Union forces engaged; 4,100 were killed or wounded. No record survives of Confederate casualties. Boatner, 788–89.

13. Dr. Thomas Laney served with the 95th Pa. G. Norton Galloway, *The Ninety-fifth Pennsylvania Volunteers (Goslin's Pennsylvania Zouaves) in the Sixth Corps: An Historical Paper*, 10.

heavy picket and trench firing. We have not charged the works as was expected and understood this morning.

Grant renewed the attack on the "Bloody Angle" on May 12, this time using a much larger force. Lee had removed most of the artillery from the salient on the 11th, believing that Grant was about to make another flanking move, and the guns were not returned in time to oppose the attack. As a result, the initial assault was as successful as Upton's had been, capturing most of Maj. Gen. Edward Johnson's division and overrunning the entire salient. Confederate counterattacks, however, once again forced the Federals back, with both sides suffering heavily.

Thursday—May 12th, 1864

At early dawn, again in line advancing on the enemies works. Carry the first line, capturing five thousand prisoners and eighteen guns. An *awful* day this! Our brigade fell back under a galling fire. Strange it is *how* we live at all. The atmosphere is perfectly pestilential from decaying bodies of men and horses. *One* thing is certain of this campaign thus far, and that is that *more blood* has been shed, more lives lost, and more human suffering undergone, than ever before in a season.[14]

Friday—May 13th, 1864

Rather a quiet day. We dry our blankets and clean up a little. The Rebels evacuate their rifle pits. The 6th Corps once more together. Our Regiment at night stack arms upon the extreme right of the line. The whole number of muskets in the regiment is 118!! *only!* Our Brigade Surgeons were together all day talking over the events and casualties of the week. What changes since we left our quiet homes on Hazel River! At night our Brigade falls into rifle pits and at 5 o'clock A.M., [entry ends]

Holt's diary entry for the thirteenth ended there. He finally had time to write a brief note to his wife, reporting the death of Capt. John D. Fish, killed in action on May 12 as he rode along the line supplying cannoneers with ammunition. "Give it to them boys! I'll bring you the canister," were his last words before he was shot off his horse.[15]

14. Casualty figures for parts of the engagement do not survive. For the regiment, between May 8–21, 49 men were killed, 106 wounded. *OR*, vol. 36, pt. 1:144.

15. John D. Fish mustered in as captain with Co. D, Aug. 23, 1862. The quote is from *B&L*, 4:172. *Annual Report*, 65.

On the field of battle near
Spotsylvania Court House, Va.,
May 13, 1864.

My dear Wife:—

After eight days of the hardest fighting the world ever witnessed, I have an opportunity of telling you that I am still alive and as yet unhurt. Every day since the 3rd when we broke camp, I have been in a fight, and this morning upon the ground waiting for our corps to form again, my mind reverts again to my happy home in the quiet North. No tongue can describe the horrors of the scene around me. Dead and dying men by scores and hundreds lie piled upon each other in promiscuous disorder. God has seen fit so far to spare me, for which I truly feel thankful. I cannot even attempt to give you a *slight* idea of this field of death. All around you lie the unmistakable evidences that death is doing its most frightful work. Do not worry about me. We have driven the enemy at every point, but Oh! at what a sacrifice of life! It is reported that they fell back two miles last night, but in the confusion and disorder which reigns, it is impossible to tell. I am more dead than alive. We have no regiment. It is so scattered that hardly a dozen can be got together. So fearful has been our loss, that it *now* seems we have no place here: but we shall all find enough to do, I have no doubt. Heaven only knows how much longer this battle will last, but I hope not many days. No doubt we shall at last be victims. The rebels fight like very devils! We have to fairly *club* them out of their rifle pits. We have taken thousands of prisoners and killed an army; still they fight as hard as ever. It is such relief to say a few words to you that I can hardly write. Huckans is well and with me. Captain Fish is killed and many, many others! I do not know as you can read the scrawl, but it is the best I can do. Now my dear wife, good bye. We shall be into it again in a few minutes. God bless you, dear one. Kiss the little ones for their father. I will write again as soon as I can. Do not worry for me. He who heareth the ravens when they cry will hear my prayer.[16]

Daniel.

Upton's brigade served as a flank guard on the fourteenth and lost about one hundred men in an abortive probing attack depicted with some humor by Holt.

16. "Heareth the ravens" is a biblical reference from Job 38:41 (KJV).

Saturday—May 14th, 1864

Left and moved more to the right. At 9 o'clock A.M. the Brigade deployed as skirmishers, in the immediate rear of which I took position with my squad. Erected temporary works behind which our brigade took shelter. We are upon the extreme right of the line, four miles from any support in front of Spotsylvania Court House, which is 1½ miles in front. Held position until 4 o'clock P.M., when Gen. Wright in company with Gen. Upton surveys the line and orders an advance. An advance is made of about thirty or forty rods, when we come flying back in all sorts of a hurry. Every man for himself. Here we had *another* run for sweet life. Plenty of grape and canister, minie balls and shot help us over the ground. These arguments are useless. We will get away just as fast as we can without them. From the fact that we ran *so well* and after the command to *advance,* it is henceforth to be known as "Upton's Run!"

Sunday—May 15th, 1864

Again upon the ground lost yesterday. Our Brigade in front as skirmishers. Remain all day. The most quiet one of the campaign, so far. No picket or other firing heard. Encamp for the night in a log cabin, the last of Negro quarters. We burned the large house and outbuildings because the owner was a rebel and upon our evacuating yesterday, fired into our *"demoralized"* ranks. It was a good building and its destruction *helped* to pay for that shot.

Monday—May 16th, 1864

Brigade relieved from picket duty. Six or eight Jerseymen wounded day before yesterday, brought in. Governor Sprague of Rhode Island and Senator Sherman of Ohio, visit the Army.[17] We encamp on the same ground as yesterday. First mail arrives; but none for us.

Still fighting at Spotsylvania
Court House, May 16, 1864.

17. William Sprague was governor of Rhode Island (1859–63), son-in-law of Treasury Secretary Salmon Portland Chase, and the new Rhode Island Republican senator (as of Mar. 4, 1864). John Sherman was the senator from Ohio, and brother of Union general William Tecumseh Sherman. *Biographical Directory of the American Congress, 1774–1989,* 1856, 1803.

My dear Wife:—

I have *another* opportunity of writing to you to-day near the spot where I addressed you before. It is true that we have driven the enemy at every point, still to all appearance their lines are as complete and strong as ever. Advance when you will, you meet the same determination—the same strong works as when we first engaged them. This is the 12th day of fighting: every one of which, except yesterday, has been marked by sanginary conflicts. We are now lying in front within a short distance of the enemy's lines—both armies, apparently sufficiently exhausted to be willing to rest a little. Night before last we were driven from the very spot on which I am now writing, in the wildest imaginable disorder. Never did I make better time in digging to the rear than then.[18] Our entire line gave way, consisting of the 2nd Brigade (ours) and two regiments of Jerseymen. They chased us, firing into our ranks, and hastening a retreat which *I* thought plenty fast and disgraceful enough without any such persuaders. In this flight I lost my mare, but found her again after about six hours, at the Division Hospital, where one of our men had taken her. Trees are perfectly riddled with bullets. Perhaps you will think it extravagant when I tell you that *I have seen* trees at least sixteen inches in thickness, and *oak* ones at that, cut completely off by these leaden messengers. In the advanced rifle pits behind which we fight, every tree is like a brush broom! The dead lie three and four deep in many places, mixed up with wounded who cannot extricate themselves from their former comrades. Some lying between the lines are so completely riddled that it is impossible to raise them. A hole has to be dug side of them and they rolled into it for burial. They were a *complete jelly!* Hundreds of balls had passed through them. We have suffered terribly. Our regiment last night *numbered only 118 muskets!* You see how we have sustained ourselves. Col. Olcott, Capt. Fish, Lieut. Pierce, Lieut. Johnson (son of Dea) and a great many other officers are killed. Among the wounded, Capt. Kidder, Maj. Galpin, Capt. Gorton, and I do not know who all.[19] Our whole brigade is not as large as our regiment was a year ago: but we are not discouraged. We hear nothing from the outer world, and wonder how

18. "Digging" meaning to spur vigorously.

19. Silas E. Pierce mustered in as private with Co. E, Aug. 23, 1862. He was promoted through the ranks and died at the rank of first lieutenant on May 13, 1864, at Spotsylvania. Edward P. Johnson, mustered in as first sergeant in Co. C, Aug. 23, 1862,

they look upon us. I feel that I shall come out safe while thousands shall have passed to their reward. As I said before, this has been the longest and hardest battle on record. He who lives to get through will have a tale to tell which many cannot believe. Human suffering and endurance was never more fully displayed and never more cheerfully borne. But this is no time for gossip, so good bye.

Daniel.

Tuesday—May 17th, 1864

All quiet during the day. We are to leave our position after dark and move to the point where our first charge was made.—*Travel all night! and not go over four miles:* a hard trial on our men.

Wednesday—May 18th, 1864

This morning enter the pits under heavy artillery fire. Came near being sent to my long home by a shell striking under my horse. Prevented the rebels from turning our right and returned to old camp again. Mail arrives. Eight letters from home and friends.[20]

Thursday—May 19th, 1864

Left camp at daylight and advanced half a mile when we commence making breastworks. No firing at 1 o'clock P.M. At sunset a great row going on upon our left. No report of the forces engaged, or the result.[21] Every day finds us fighting more or less but no such heavy slaughter as upon the 6th, 10th 12th, &c. . . *Every* night we are distured for some cause:—if *not* to *fight* it is to support a weak point or relieve others who have been heavily engaged or whose time on picket duty has expired.

---

was killed in action May 10, 1864. Capt. Frank Gorton, mustered in as second lieutenant with Co. K, Aug. 18, 1862, was wounded at Spotsylvania and eventually discharged due to those wounds at the rank of captain on Oct. 5, 1864. *Annual Report,* 149, 102, 76.

20. The Sixth and Second corps were supposed to attack Ewell on the Confederate left after moving the night of May 17. At 4 A.M. on the 18th, the attack began but was abandoned quickly. The corps was reinforced that night. "Long home" meaning coffin or casket. This was the first mail received since the army had crossed the Rapidan River the beginning of May. Boatner, 788; Catton, *Stillness at Appomattox,* 137.

21. Fighting on the left in the afternoon refers to the Harris's Farm battle, when Ewell went against the Union right at Ny River. Ewell lost nine hundred men and withdrew after dark. His goal had been mostly to find out if Grant was moving. McPherson, *Battle Cry,* 733; Boatner, 788.

Friday—May 20th, 1864

Nothing of importance to-day. Left camp at 6 o'clock A.M. and arrive at battle ground where the heavy artillery was engaged last evening. No great loss on our side, the enemy failing to accomplish their object— the possession of Bowling Green pike.[22] We capture eight hundred prisoners. Our loss two hundred and eight, prisoners. Killed on either side slight. A purely artillery duel.

The movements described in the May 21 entry represent the beginning of Grant's next flanking move, this one at the crossings of the North Anna River. Grant and Lee jockeyed for position at these crossings during May 23–27 but did not fight a large-scale battle, and both sides pushed on toward Cold Harbor.

Saturday—May 21st, 1864

Up at half-past three A.M., Breakfast and remain in camp until 9 o'clock A.M. when we move again by the left flank. Picket firing heard in that direction. At 7 o'clock P.M. rebs charge upon our lines and for *once* in their lives, get a belly so full as to cause *puking* and *purging* at the same time—a perfect *emeto—cathartic!*[23] At 10 o'clock P.M. start for Guiney Station. Travel all night making but *five miles*. Our Regiment act as guard to a Supply train.[24]

Sunday—May 22nd, 1864

Bivouacked on a beautiful spot and cook breakfast. Traveled all day towards Bowling Green, where we expected to encamp, but failed to

22. Bowling Green was southeast of Guiney's Station. The Pike presumably referred to the road running south to Hanover Court House, parallel to the railroad. *Atlas,* plate 23-3.

23. "Emeto-cathartic" here is used as a noun meaning a simultaneous vomiting and purging. Since nineteenth-century medicine still used such methods to cleanse the body's system of impurities, Holt's descriptive metaphor is apt. The fight he describes presumably did not involve the 121st, for Upton did not mention it. Russell's division, however, did repulse an attack that day, so perhaps one of the other three brigades was involved. *OR,* vol. 36, 1:192–93.

24. Guiney's Station was on the Richmond, Fredericksburg & Potomac Railroad, several miles southeast of Fredericksburg. Grant moved his supply bases as he moved his army farther south. To maintain reinforced supply lines clear back to the Potomac River would have taken far too many men. So Grant simply used escorts for any supply train that headed south through the guerilla-controlled lands to his army, a method which overcame the supply line problems McClellan had faced in the Peninsular campaign of 1862. Catton, *Stillness at Appomattox,* 57.

reach the place. Encamped after a hard days march, and get our Supper. A wheat field in which we lie, affords provender for weary horses, while the straw makes us a comfortable bed. This night and day marching is tough work on our men. We begin to feel used up, but full of faith that we are *using some one up!* I *hope* it is the rebels.

Monday—May 23rd, 1864

Up at 4½ A.M., and start at 9 o'clock A.M., Draw rations at 2 o'clock P.M., our course towards Hanover Junction.[25] At 7 o'clock P.M., a heavy battle rageing about three miles in advance. We arrive on the ground about 10 o'clock P.M., and encamp for the night. For *once* we *are* lucky in not getting head and heels into a fight. Here a female rebel spy, dressed in male attire is taken. She *looks* well in her Union Soldier clothes. Not in the least daunted here, I wonder how it will be with her when she begins to pull hemp?[26]

Tuesday—May 24th, 1864

Up at 5 o'clock A.M., breakfast and start. Cross the North Anna on canvas pontoon boats, and are now (11 o'clock A.M.) on the ground occupied yesterday by the rebels. We obtained a complete victory over them last evening. To-day hundreds of prisoners are coming in. Heavy firing on our left. My man Walrath confiscated a full blood Virginia racer which I shall try to keep.[27]

Wednesday—May 25th, 1864

Up at 4½. Breakfast at 5 o'clock A.M., 5th Corps in advance. Destroyed Rail Road at Noel's Town and encamped for the night in a pine grove from which we had emerged at 11 o'clock A.M.,[28] Found a nice lot of corn in the ear in a barn. Shelled a bushel for horses. Rain storm at sundown, but pleasant through the night. My man Walrath is bent on stealing all the horses and mules which he can lay his hands upon. Another good one is added to my stock.

25. Hanover Junction was the intersection of the Richmond-Fredericksburg Railroad and the Virginia Central Railroad. *Atlas,* plates 50-4, 81-2.

26. "Pull hemp" meaning death by hanging.

27. John Walrath mustered in as private with Co. E, Aug. 23, 1862, and served until May 27, 1865. *Annual Report,* 195.

28. "Noel's Town" is probably "Noel's Turnout" on the Virginia Central Railroad, about three miles northwest of Hanover Junction. *Atlas,* plate 81-7.

Thursday—May 26th, 1864

Up at the usual hour and breakfast. Re-cross the North Anna, bearing towards Chesterfield.[29] Bivouacked in pine wood at noon and remain until sundown. Take up the line of march, travel all night making seventeen miles.

Friday—May 27th, 1864

On the march and cross the Pamunkey River at 12 M.—At last on the Peninsula.[30] A *very* warm day. Our Division nearly played out. *Never saw so many stragglers!* Encamp on the South side of the Pamunkey. It seems impossible that *so much* can be endured by mortal man. It is fight and run, Run and fight, move to the left *all the while*—get whipped sometimes when we don't know it, and then turn in and whip the rebs the very worst way. So we go.

Saturday—May 28th, 1864

Came to Hanover Town.[31] Cavalry fighting all day in front. Went into camp and had a good old fashioned sleep.

Sunday—May 29th, 1864

Orders came at 9 A.M. to pack up and move, which we did at 11 A.M. On reconnoisance in force to Hanover Court House. (1st Division) destroyed Rail Road, &c. Major Galpin joined the Regiment this afternoon. No supper and no blankets. My man Walrath is off after horses. He had my blankets and rations. I think *this* does *not pay*.

Monday—May 30th, 1864

I *begin* to feel like an old man. No breakfast. In line of battle about a mile and a half from Hanover Court House. Our regiment deployed as skirmishers. Go out with them. At night encamped near the enemy. On the left very heavy firing. Our brigade again all separated. I do not like this a bit. Dr. Laney, my old friend and co-worker gone also. We have become so attached to each other that it seems hard to be separated.

29. Chesterfield is about four miles north of Hanover Junction, northeast of Noel's Turnout, and on the Richmond, Fredericksburg, and Potomac Railroad. *Atlas,* plate 81-2.

30. "12 M." meaning noon. The North Anna empties into the Pamunkey River about five miles southeast of Hanover Junction, and about four miles northwest of Hanover Court House. Ibid.

31. Hanovertown is nine miles southeast of Hanover Court House, along the Pamunkey River.

Tuesday—May 31st, 1864

Dr. Laney came up and joined us. Our brigade once more together. A mail arrives. Letters from home. March all day and at night encamp in a field of corn.

At the end of May began one of the bloodiest battles of this sanguinary spring of 1864: Cold Harbor. Gen. Philip Sheridan had captured the crossroads on the 31st. On June 1, Confederate forces attacked, but Sheridan held on until Union troops came along to push them back. During the night, both sides were reinforced and entrenched, so that by daybreak on June 2, two massive armies faced each other. By June 3, Confederates had laid entrenched works that were virtually impenetrable. Confederate cross fire meant the loss of life in any assault would be staggering. Union attacks were uncoordinated and poorly organized. Within the first half hour of battle for the crossroads, seven thousand Union men lay dead or wounded on the field. The 121st N.Y., its ranks heavily depleted due to the fighting of the preceding weeks, did not play a major role in the Union attacks and consequently lost only seven men; at Spotsylvania it had suffered 155 casualties.

Wednesday—June 1st, 1864

A hard and dusty march. Our division within a mile and a half of Cold Harbor, where we find the enemy in strong force. The cavalry have driven them and hold the ground. We relieve them. A furious battle is now raging in which we hold our own, but are suffering greatly. The 18th corps and one division of the 10th are here. Go into the fight and are severely handled. Our regiment on skirmish line. Find a large number of Zouaves wounded and stop to dress their wounds. It *looks hard* about here. Everything indicates that heavy and severe battles have been fought. Regiment at last emerge from woods, and form line with the brigade in an open field. General Upton, from some cause, *very* wolfish. Threatens to turn *every surgeon in the Division out of office!* I pity the poor fool.

Thursday—June 2nd, 1864

Change Hospital post to front line under protection of rifle pits. Regiment not yet reported. They have been out all night on picket. Constant and heavy firing in front. It is a wonder how men can stand it to fight so long and lose so much. The air and everything about filled with smoke of battle. The wounded as they come to the rear, make a person feel sad. Hundreds are being attended to on every hand. My hands and heart full. At noon our Regiment came in from the left and joined brigade—loss considerable—can't say how much.—Rebels pushing us hard upon the right. They want to turn our right again and see our heels as at Chancellorsville, but are mistaken. Send them back again in double quick. *I like such charges!* The ground covered with graybacks. Twice during the night they attack us, and twice sent reeling back with heavy loss. Let them come again. *We like it!* For twenty-four hours *heavy* fighting. All nature appears to be angry. Everything is in fighting mood. It is a terrible day, full of blood and carnage. God help us in these trying times.

Friday—June 3rd, 1864

The *very worst* day of the campaign! Discord and disorder on every hand. The woods full of dead, dying and wounded men. Literally *heaps* of dead men meet the eye on all sides! Stench like that of putrid carcasses, flavors your food, while the water is thick with all manner of impurities. Cold Harbor, above all places, yet, carries off the palm for *hard* fighting and hard fare generally. On *all* sides, booming cannon and rattling small arms, tell us that the Angel of Death is hovering over us. Two attacks upon our left at Sunset. Driven back with loss. One in the center, with like result. They advance in *four* lines of battle, determined to pierce our centre, but are compilled to retreat with a loss of *thousands*. Never was there such a days work or such wholesale slaughter!

Saturday—June 4th, 1864

As usual, at daybreak are saluted by Parrot guns and Minnie balls. Quite a quiet day after three of such fearful slaughter. All hands appear to be satisfied without further loss to-day. Improve the quiet by burying our dead and preparing for another fight on the morrow.

Sunday—June 5th, 1864

Find time to write a letter home. All nature reposes in quietude this holy Sunday Morning. What grief fills many a heart to-day as they read of the death of husband, son or brother—dying in defence of his country, within a day or two past! Except on picket, not a gun is fired. Read a sermon in the *"Independent"* by H. Ward Beecher.[32] After sun-

32. Henry Ward Beecher was a prominent minister, an abolitionist, and the brother of Harriet Beecher Stowe, author of *Uncle Tom's Cabin.*

down, a furious assault upon our lines the most determined and obstinate of any yet made, lasting over half an hour. *Why* the rebs should thus assault us, I cannot say. They *always* get the worst of it. So too this time, they paid dearly for their night attack, by leaving hundreds of killed and wounded upon the ground. From the extreme left to the extreme right, a perfect pandemonium prevails. Oh how unlike the stillness of the morning hour, when all was so quiet and serene.

Monday—June 6th, 1864

My birth day. Forty-five years have come and gone, for the most part unprofitably spent, I fear. How much longer shall I remain here? God only knows. When I look around and see the sights presented I feel not a great while longer, but of that I know nothing. All quiet at sunrise: all quiet at noon, and now at 8½ P.M. all quiet. A rebel Captain, Lieutenant and eight men came into our lines through mistake, so close are they together.

Tuesday—June 7th, 1864

Quiet prevails throughout the length and breadth of the lines today. At sunset a flag of truce is sent in by the rebs with a request to be permitted to bury their dead. It is granted. I avail myself of the opportunity to look over the field.—A ghastly sight indeed: Do not like it. Stench *awful!* Heavy firing in direction of James River from Gun Boats, no doubt.

In the field before
Richmond, Va. June 8th, 1864.

My dear Wife:—

I do not know *when* I last wrote you or under what circumstances, but perhaps it might afford you infinite delight to know that I am still alive, and thank God, I firmly believe destined to enter the portals of that rebellious city Richmond before whose doors Gen. Grant is steadily knocking for admission. All along, until yesterday we have been under steady fire, but last night a flag of truce was sent in by the rebels with a request to be permitted to bury their dead, which was granted, since which time a lull in the discord has ensued. Intolerable stench from decomposing bodies of men of both sides, who fell between the lines was the cause of asking an armistice.—*Heavy* firing, *but not frequent* is heard upon our left, in the direction of James River; and I have no doubt gun boats are trying to press their way toward the Confederate Capital.[33] These heavy guns with large calibre, cannot be fired as smaller ones. Once in twelve or fifteen minutes, at the shortest, is the time required for a hundred pound parrot or columbiad. Other guns of ten and twelve pound shot and three inch steel guns can be fired as fast as they can be worked, and that is about twice a minute: and they are the ones usually used in field operations, throwing a solid shot or shell three or four miles with accuracy, and velocity sufficient to reduce ordinary works. However, the range of a mile or mile and a half is about the thing. At this distance they can be used with as much accuracy and effect as a telescopic rifle. The art of gunnery is a beautiful one, reduced as it is to perfect mathematical precision. Shot thrown at this distance will completely go through a three foot tree, as hundreds in this vicinity can testify. Our men look on and watch their movement through the air, calculating when it will strike and where, and how long the fuse will burn and the shell burst with as much unconcern as if they were blank cartridges. Yesterday one burst about six or eight rods in advance of where I was sitting, knocking over two men who happened to be going along at that particular moment. One got up not much hurt, while the other flying about fifteen feet in air, alighted as you may imagine—a good deal the worse for handling. He was as fine as snuff, but not one half as dry or good smelling. I am tired to death lying here drinking Chickahominy swamp water in which a thousand dead horses and men are macerating.[34] Truly the decoction is excellent. It is drink this water, eat half cooked fresh beef before it is half dead, run to sink every fifteen minutes, and sleep with stenches under your nose sufficient to cause a turkey buzzard or carrion crow to contract typhoid fever, then up and fight three or four hours and *keep doing it until you get used to it.*—

Generally, I have been well, but have lost *flesh* and once in a while *temper* during the campaign. Do you wonder at it?—Dr. Slocum came to see how I was getting along the other day, and the first words he uttered were, "well, Holt, keep on a little while longer, and all there will be left to send home to Louisa will be your old shoes!" and so I

33. It is difficult to tell what firing Holt heard. There is no record of any naval fire or other action. Holt may have been hearing noise from Sheridan's men skirting Richmond on their way to meet up with Ben Butler.

34. "Snuff" meaning powdered tobacco; "macerating" meaning to soften by soaking in liquid. In medicine, meaning to soften food in the digestive system.

thought. I do not know but that old cough will kill me yet.[35] It is terribly hard upon me sometimes, causing considerable uneasiness. Often I cough for an hour together, which leaves me weak and prostrate enough, I assure you. I have passed through more in the last forty days than I have in the preceeding forty years, so it seems to me, and if I ever live to get out of this scrape, you may shoot me if I ever get into another such. I would not come home *now,* however, if I could. I will wait until the time comes, and then farewell to the Army of the Potomac and all other armies. Nothing has been heard from Phelps yet, but all think him a prisoner.[36] We have but 176 guns in the Regiment. The mean strength of the command embracing officers and *all* is 226. What do you think of my chance of getting home at this rate?—Ed. Cox is now with the regiment. We lost him at Chancellorsville when we first began to fight. He was half crazey and acted like a lunitic which he *was,* and is. He tells dreadful tales of his treatment while in the *"Bull ring"* as he calls it.[37] He wishes you to say to his wife that he is still alive, &c. I will write again as soon as possible and let you know how we get along.

Daniel.

Wednesday—June 8th, 1864

For the *first* time since the opening of the campaign *had my clothes washed!* No firing except picket and an occasional shell up to 5 P.M.—Quiet, for a wonder, the rest of the night. Sleep without being called into the trenches.

Thursday—June 9th, 1864

Another day of rest! Work in front going on steadily and surely. About the same amount of firing as upon previous days. This afternoon

---

35. Holt's cough, which had troubled him for some time prior to this campaign, was tubercular and would eventually kill him. Tuberculosis is an infectious disease characterized by the formation of tubercules, or nodular lesions, particularly in the lungs.

36. Phelps was captured again at the Wilderness and sent to Andersonville Prison where he suffered from scurvy, lost all his teeth, and developed a heart condition. Released in January 1865, he returned to his regiment. The following month he resigned to accept a captaincy in the 114th U.S. Colored Troops. He served in this capacity on the Mexican border until his discharge Apr. 2, 1867. Pension and Service Records.

37. Cox had been captured at Chancellorsville May 3, 1863, and exchanged in September. He was assigned for duty to Brigade Headquarters. "Bull ring" probably refers to a Confederate prison. Pension and Service Records.

several shells sent into camp, doing no harm. Cheering upon our right, *said* to be caused by 4,000 rebels coming into our lines satisfied with what they have got.[38]

The constant difficulty in supplying medical officers in the field was exacerbated in 1864 by shake-ups in the administration of the Medical Department. Surgeon General Hammond had been arrested January 17 and charged with graft, fraud, and exceeding his authority. In reality, he had run up against Secretary of War Stanton, who personally disliked an occasionally arrogant Hammond enough to try to get rid of him. Hammond's trial lasted from January to August 1864. The Medical Department was turned over to Joseph K. Barnes, who eventually succeeded Hammond as surgeon general.

Barnes continued implementation of Hammond's plans to improve the efficiency of the Medical Department but, unlike Hammond, enjoyed the strong backing of Stanton. The prickly secretary of war allowed Barnes a free hand to establish an Armywide ambulance service, based on the work of Jonathan Letterman, who was removed as medical director of the Army of the Potomac and replaced by Thomas McParlin. Both Barnes and McParlin reaped the benefits of the work done by their predecessors.

By mid-1864, the efficiency of the Medical Department had increased enough that Stanton decided to no longer allow the Sanitary Commission representatives to "interfere" with the army's own. This decision was a mistake. True, there was a drop in the disease rate (thanks to more hygienic camps), and the number of patients requiring long-term care was down (again, thanks largely to Hammond's work in speeding the removal of wounded men from the field and providing more intensive patient care closer to the front lines). But when the spring campaigns began, supplies in the field began to run short. As Holt notes below, shortages made it increasingly difficult to treat the wounded in the field after a major battle, and there was little individual surgeons could do about the crisis.

In the field before Cold Harbor
June 10, 1864

My dear Wife:—

I am on the sick list, *all but reporting* myself so. With thousands of others I have the Chickahominy ever to remember with feelings of *gratitude,—grateful because I am not quite dead.* In my last I gave you an in-

---

38. There is no report to sustain Holt's rumor of four thousand Rebels surrendering.

sight into our mode of living and you cannot wonder that I am sick, or any one else. My quarters are constantly besieged with sick men for medicine which if I had (and I have not) would be of little avail so long as they live in the way they do.[39]

General Grant, so it is said intends *another* flank movement upon the enemy, but as for me, I cannot see *where* he is going to *flank* to. We are now in front of Richmond confronting the enemy whose lines in some places are not more than a hundred yards from our own, and we, all the while, constructing works of the strongest kind, and most enduring nature. If we leave all these permanently constructed works, it must be in the very teeth of a foe worthy of the metal opposing him. With our *base* as it is,—receiving supplies from the White House on the Pamunkey we have access to our army at every point with ease and safety. I see no ground to be gained by change of base to James River, but not knowing as much as I might, I am willing to wait and obey orders as usual. We are making slow but sure advances on Richmond, and I suppose that is all we ought to expect, but I feel impatient and want to make *short* work of it. I am satisfied that the days of the Confederacy are numbered, but oh how we have suffered in putting it so far in the back ground!

Night before last, the rebels applied, under a flag of truce, for permission to bury their dead, and remove the wounded in front of our division. It was granted, and I with hundreds of others, went out to look upon the spit from which proceeded the most unearthly stench that ever assailed the nostrils of mortal man. Between the lines (a distance not greater than thirty rods) the ground was as completely torn up by grape and canister as if it had been ploughed by the most skillful ploughman. Stealing out under cover of night, both friend and foe dug little pits just sufficient to cover their bodies and from these they picked off such as exposed themselves in any way upon the works. Here many lay wounded and dead, who could not be reached for removal, and here the ground was a complete sepulchre. Scores of putrid bodies defiled the air—until it became impossible to live so any longer—consequently the flag of truce was sent in. It was a strange sight. Five minutes previously it was worth a man's life to be seen upon the defences, but now hundreds and thousands of both parties swarmed over

---

39. Both food and medical supplies were in short supply during the chaos of this campaign. An influx of forty thousand new, uneducated recruits compromised camp hygiene, as well. Gillett, 232–43.

the neutral ground, conversing in the most kind and friendly manner. No one to see officers and men of these contending armies in so close and friendly intercourse would have supposed that their business here was for no other purpose than that of slaughter of their fellow man. As soon as the little white flag, attended by Gen. Russell and Dr. Holman, Medical Director of the Corps, was seen upon the works, all enmity ceased.[40] Rebel and Loyal officers met and extended congratulations. Stretcher bearers, like ants ran over the ground clearing it of dead and dying. Ambulances, in long trains were conveying the wounded to hospitals for treatment. No shot was fired, no jar, except an occasional long boom of a heavy siege gun upon our extreme right, broke the Sunday stillness of the scene. Upon those long dark lines of threatening works, where nought was seen except protruding muzzles of cannon and muskets ten moments previous, were thousands of their brave defenders, shaking out their dusty blankets and enjoying (for the few short moments of the armistice) the genial sunlight of the hour. After the time had expired for the purpose mentioned, and in less than two minutes after firing the signal gun, not a soul could be seen upon those works: and in less than ten minutes, a friendly shell dropped into our camp by our friendly neighbors reminded us that we had better lie low and keep shady for the rest part of the day.

Daniel

Friday—June 10th, 1864
Nothing unusual to 5 P.M. Wrote a letter home and improved the day by mending clothes &c. Capt. Jonathan Burrel returned from Hospital.[41]

Saturday—June 11th, 1864
We are shelled like perfect fury to-day. Reply, of course. Symptoms of a *left flank movement*. Third division of our Corps leave. I am getting tired of lying here. Almost *anything* for a change.

Between the 12th and 13th of June, Grant moved south again. With a cavalry screen provided by Sheridan, four corps moved overland, one corps by water, all

40. Brig. Gen. David Allen Russell, a hero at the Rappahannock Redoubts, had been given permanent command of the first division of the Sixth Corps. Warner, 416–17.

41. Jonathan Burrell, mustered in as a first lieutenant with Co. A, Aug. 4, 1862, was promoted to captain Apr. 18, 1864. He was wounded in action Oct. 19 at Cedar Creek and died a week later. *Annual Report,* 25.

down to the James River. They then crossed a pontoon bridge and by June 15 were in Lee's rear at Petersburg.

Sunday—June 12th, 1864

Nothing important transpires through the day; but at 10 o'clock P.M. move by the left flank. March all night without being disturbed. Glad to leave the stinking hole of Cold Harbor in the rear.

Cold Harbor June 12, 1864

My dear Wife:—

Here we still are despite the rumor that we were to move day before yesterday. Portions of our corps have been relieved by other troops while we as a division and brigade occupy the same ground as upon our arrival. I hardly think we shall be able to enter Richmond by a direct front movement as we would have obstacles to overcome which would cost one-half our army in so doing. In the first place an endless chain of fortifications are before us, while the Chickahominy rolls sluggishly only a mile and a half away, through swamp and lowlands, like the river of death. On this side of all, the rebel army lie intrenched so strongly that all efforts thus far to dislodge them have proved unavailing. Every few moments shells are thrown into our camp, and the wonder of all is, that so few casualties happen. This morning, for instance at least a dozen have exploded over our heads, scattering their fragments on every hand. Solid shots fifteen or twenty in number have struck within the radius of a dozen rods, and yet no one is injured. It really seems true, as stated, that at least one hundred and fifty pounds of lead is wasted before one man is disabled.

Last evening as I sat with Dr. Laney (my chum of the 95th Pa) beside a tree looking out upon the earth works everywhere being constructed, he remarked to me that he thought me rather imprudent in thus gratifying an idle curiosity, and advised me, with himself, to retire out of danger. I was not quite ready, however, and he left. In less than a minute after he had retired, a shell exploded directly over head, while dirt from a minnie ball (striking within a foot or two of me) throwing gravel in my face, admonished me that his advice was not ill-timed, and I sought my old post behind a little knoll where as yet I have remained unhurt. I wish some of our stay-at-home patriots could be induced to pay us a visit—a *very* short one would satisfy *them* I have no doubt. As for *me,* I am fully satisfied with my experience in dressing stinking maggoty wounds and taking off mangled tagends of what was once arms, legs, &c. I am *satisfied,* I say.

Daniel.

Monday—June 13th, 1864

Cross the Chickahominy at two points on canvass pontoons. Our course *all* points of compass, mainly bearing S.E. We have traveled 25 miles since last night. Encamp for the night on West bank of Chickahominy. Destination—*Charles City Cross Roads.* Picket firing all night.

Tuesday—June 14th, 1864

Up at 4 A.M., breakfast at 5, and move out at 6 A.M. Arrive Charles City Court House at 11 A.M.[42] Encamp within a mile and a half of James River, where we stay for the night. Our Army pretty well together for a wonder. Went to the river and for the first time saw gun boats and transports passing up. This is a most delightful and productive region. Ex-President [John] Tyler's family live here. Their grounds and mansion good to look upon. Nice cherries and strawberries.

Wednesday—June 15th, 1864

At 10 o'clock A.M., still here and waiting. All quiet. Men *happy* from the fact, I suppose, that they are *out of danger.* Encamp near the bank of the James River, upon lands belonging to Ex-President John Tyler, twenty miles below City Point. Get a piece of wood from the tree under which Pocahontas plead for the life of Capt Smith: *a veritable relic.*[43]

> In the field near
> Charles City Ct. House
> June 15th 1864.

My dear Wife:—

Never, since my connection with the Army, have I written under such feeling of gloomy despondence, and if I indulge in strains reflecting that gloominess, you must forgive me. The fact is, we have been *compelled* to evacuate our position before Richmond and are resting away down below *Harrison's Landing* on James River, a point as you will see by

---

42. Charles City Court House lies northeast of Petersburg about fifteen miles, across the James River.

43. The degree of authenticity of Holt's relic is no doubt comparable to that of the pieces of the True Cross.

reference to the map, below where McClellan brought up two years ago.[44] If we have achieved victories, or a *series* of victories, as our Northern friends are pleased to term them, *I have failed to see them!* If loosing sixty thousand men is a *slight* loss, I never want to see a *heavy* one. We, as a regiment, have almost ceased to exist, and if the next six months prove as disastrous to us as the last six weeks have, not a soul will be left to recite the wholesale slaughter which has taken place upon the sacred soil of Virginia. The question naturally arises, "Who is to blame for all this slaughter and want of judgment since crossing the Rapidan?" Everyone has his own thoughts and opinions, and I have mine. A great many say that General [William Farrar] Smith of the 18th Corps, was *behind time* in coming to the front, and not occupying Fair Oaks before Longstreet.[45] That he *was not* up in time to do any good, is as certain as that he got up at all. When the 6th Corps, after thirty-five miles marching, day and night, came within a mile and a half of Cold Harbor, had sent out skirmishers and formed in line of battle, Smith came dragging along from the White House on the Pamunkey, and took position upon our right. We had not crossed the Chickahominy, and at *that* time *could not, because Lee was too smart for us!* From the moment we confronted him at Cold Harbor to the hour of our leaving, *we did not gain an advantage worthy to be called so.* To be sure, we advanced our lines until they almost ran into theirs, so close in many places that conversation (a little loud perhaps) could be and *was* carried on between the two armies. We were constantly under fire, and sometimes terrific, hellish fire, all the while losing men without adequate compensation. The enemy, no doubt, lost equally; but what does *equality* amount to in war where forces are nearly equal? The war *could* and probably *would* continue until *all* were used up. What we want is *decisive victory:* but here we are, far below Richmond, the James River rolling in quiet majesty along as if no contending parties had ever pressed their feet upon its shores. It is a beautiful stream,—moreso I think than the Potomac: and as I sit and look out upon its silvery surface and see transports and gunboats quietly

44. Harrison's Landing was on the north bank of the James, west of Charles City Court House. McClellan had used it as his base after his retreat from the Richmond front in the summer of 1862.

45. Baldy Smith had come east with Grant and was given command of the 18th Corps of Butler's Army of the James. Holt is correct in that Smith did not get up as quickly as he was expected to; this was not, however, entirely Smith's fault. There was inadequate overland transportation from Smith's landing place at White House to the battlefield. Douglas Southall Freeman, *Lee's Lieutenants: A Study in Command*, 3:503–7.

pursuing their way, I almost forget that we are at war, and feel an inclination to take the first boat for home. But *home, sweet home,* when shall I see thee? While I *hope,* I *fear;* and while I fear I doubt if that happy day is in store for me. You know I am always hopeful, and now, even though I cannot see through the mysterious veil which overspreads us, I cannot but feel impressed that we shall ultimately conquer; but *when* that's the question. I often refer to your last letter where you speak of the fortifications around Richmond—of the difficulty of taking them, and the length of time required. It may be, that here with our base upon the river,—a safe and easy supply to the army, we can operate more successfully than where we were. Let us hope so.

As I was riding along day before yesterday in company with Dr. Halsey of the 4th Jersies,[46] we came upon a spot perfectly covered with flowers—those gems of beauty which so completely fill your heart. I remarked, "how Louisa would like to see this." I recalled your words when you expressed a wish that I should send you specimens of the floral beauty of the South. The Dr. gathered a Magnolia blossom and handing it to me said, "Send this to Louisa, with my compliments," which is herewith transmitted. It is a simple little thing, but keep it as a memento of this time and place. The magnolia is a beautiful tree, and just now covered with the sweetest smelling white blossoms you ever saw. The mulberry, too, is a fine tree, from which I have frequent repasts of the blackberry-like fruit which it yields. Ex-President John Tyler's plantation is about a mile and a half distant which I have visited, and can say that *I know* his cherries to be *good.* The mansion, though old and showing evidences of decay, is one of those fine specimins of southern aristocracy, where the F.F.V.'s have so long and luxuriously lived. 120 slaves worked this place a week ago, but now not a dozen all told are here. I would like to live and die in just such a home as this if peace were restored. The surroundings are beautiful in the extreme—old majestic shade trees—clean shady walks and bowers—gardens filled with fruits and flowers—all all calculated to satisfy a man with earth, and fit him for heaven. In this part of the State, everything is different from the Northern and Middle. *Here* the *real chivalry* [dwell?] and here you find that *"marked hospitality to strangers"*

46. Holt's reference is unclear. The only surgeon named Halsey listed in a New Jersey regiment was Asst. Surgeon Luther F. Halsey of the 2d, not the 4th New Jersey, and who was discharged on May 31. *OAR,* 2:707.

of which you read so much. The inhabitants flee from the face of a Yankee as we ought from the devil. Turn your face in any direction and your feet carry you to tenantless houses and deserted fields. All are gone leaving to the mercy of their foes all their earthly store, except such as they can swiftly carry off.

My man has just come in from foraging. The result is, a sheep, a turkey, a quantity of onions, and *lots of apple butter: the* latter *commodity being the only living institution of the South.* I do not know when or how this will get off, but shall send it to corps head quarters for dispatch.

Daniel.

Grant's hopes to seize Petersburg were thwarted when Smith's Eighteeth Corps, leading the Union advance, did not push vigorously enough against the Confederate fortifications on June 16, before Lee's main army had reached them. As the rest of Grant's men arrived on the 17th and afterward, they faced well-manned fortifications and dug in for a siege, which was to continue until the spring of 1865.

Thursday—June 16th, 1864

At 6 A.M., break camp and go to the rear a mile, where we throw up breast works. At 4 P.M. at sound of bugle, pack up. Heavy firing last night and this morning in the direction of Petersburg. All the Army trains over the river. At 11 P.M., take transports and move all night up the river to City Point distant from starting point, twenty miles.

Friday—June 17th, 1864

Arrive at City Point at 6 A.M., Pass the mouth of the Appomattox River and land at Bermuda Hundred. March immediately in the direction of Petersburg four miles and *rest;* where we breakfast. Heavy defenses all along the line constructed by Gen. Butler. Men in fine spirits. Destroyed five miles of rail road yesterday, and were not molested. We are waiting (at 12M) for our supply train. Part of the Corps yet to arrive who did not take transports. At midnight our brigade called up to retake works (which the enemy took from us some time ago,) but did not do so. We came back again after disturbing reb lines.

By June 18, the chance to take Petersburg had passed, but Union forces continued to test the Confederate lines. In one of these moves, Grant sent Brig. Gen. Edward Ferrero's division of black troops against some advance works of the Confederate fortifications. The division, made up entirely of black troops commanded by white officers, had been held out of most of the fighting in May and June. Once in action, they acquitted themselves well, as Holt's comments indicate.

Saturday—June 18th, 1864

Rest all day waiting for our Supply train to come up. We need it. Our boys are out of rations, and *I* out of everything in the shape of food. At length (7 PM), it gets up. The works where we lie are of the strongest possible character, and the neatest made. Negro troops charged upon rebel works and capture 21 guns, after white troops had given up the job as impossible to execute. *"Fort Pillow"* was their watch word, and they well deserve the praise of all. Saw with my own eyes the guns, and the Negro troops who captured them. No mistake about this. Saw Col. Campbell and Capt John Gray with their Negro troops.[47] They are a fine looking set of men. *I* like a Negro soldier.

Sunday—June 19th, 1864

Reveille, sounds *early* this morning. (3 o'clock) Start *immediately* for the environs of Petersburg, distant 7 miles. At eleven A.M. arrive within a mile of the City, where we bivouack. *Saw with my own eyes* the works captured by our Negro troops. They are beautiful and exceedingly strong, situated upon high ground. Not much shelling at 2½ P.M. Expect it at Sunset. If not shall be disappointed. Our brigade goes out on picket duty, immediately in front of the city. Bomb shells with their fiery tails are flying over the doomed city.

Siege combat, while less deadly than pitched battles of the sort fought in the Wilderness, at Spotsylvania, and at Cold Harbor, took a slow but steady toll on both sides. Skirmishing and sharpshooting took place daily, and artillery bombardments, especially from the more numerous and better-supplied Union batteries, were common. None of this activity inflicted much damage on the armies, but it placed a drain on resources that the Union could afford and the Confederates could not. If Grant could keep Lee pinned at Petersburg, both commanders knew that a Union victory was inevitable.

47. Cleaveland Campbell, who had left the 152d N.Y. after preferring charges against Olcott, commanded the 23d U.S. Colored Infantry; John Gray, who mustered in as private Aug. 8, 1862, was promoted through the ranks to serve as a captain in the same unit. McPherson, *Battle Cry*, 740; Annual Report, 28, 78; *B&L*, 4:186.

Monday—June 20th, 1864

This morning is one of the most severe ones we have had, so far as *shelling* is concerned. I believe I was more exposed than ever before. Take up my position with Surgeons of 2nd and 4th Brigade in a ravine through which the road passes to the city. Several wounded from the brigade are brought in, but none from our regiment.

Tuesday—June 21st, 1864

It is pretty quiet to-day, except *sharpshooting*, which *both* sides indulge in. Sergeant [Elias C.] Mathers brought in wounded in the face severely.[48] The day closes quietly, and we are ordered to move together with the corps on the left flank, leaving Petersburg on the North.

Wednesday—June 22nd, 1864

Travel all night and make but 7 miles. Halt towards daylight and sleep two hours, when our brigade forms by divisions and so continue for two hours, after which they advance and engage rebel skirmishers and partially entrench. Private Gagen brought in mortally wounded through the body.[49] The 5th Maine leave for home the time of their enlistment having expired.

Thursday—June 23rd, 1864

Brigade ordered to move out last night, *but did not*. We encamp on the old spot, the Engineers cutting timber for fortifications, most of the night. Up at 4 A.M., breakfast at 5 and are *waiting orders*. *"Remain as you were"*—only we take position in rifle pits a short distance to the right. No firing to-day. The weather intensely hot and sultry.

Friday—June 24th, 1864

Tom fooling all day. Regiment changed position from left to right and right to left—up and down the middle, equal to any French dancing master, and about the same results: finding itself after all its evolutions, in just about the same spot as where the farce commenced. Dissolved mess with Dr. Laney after running it about a month.

48. Mathers would recover and eventually be promoted to command the 20th U.S. Colored Troops. *Annual Report,* 124.

49. James Gagen, a private with Co. B of the 32d Infantry, had transferred to Co. H of the 121st on May 25, 1864. He died June 23, 1864. Ibid., 71.

As part of his efforts to stretch the Confederate forces to the breaking point, Grant extended his lines slowly southward, cutting the Petersburg and Weldon Railroad and forcing Lee to extend his own lines south of the city.

> In the field eight miles
> South of Petersburg on
> Petersburg & Weldon R.R.,
> June 24th, 1864.

My dear Wife:—

I write this while our brigade is busily engaged in fortifying the position which we now occupy. As usual, *flank movements* are the order of the day. At dark, night before last we began moving to the left, marching all night, arriving here at daylight. The distance traveled was only eight or ten miles, but the fatigue was as great as if it had been fifteen or twenty. Halts just long enough to refresh the body are good; but when prolonged to such an extent as to produce sleepiness, are the worst conceivable things on a night march. You sleep, stumble along, half conscious of living and by the time daylight has somewhat chased away the spell, you are in feeling more dead than alive. Oh how many nights have we thus marched and how unwillingly we mount our horses for an allnight jogging along over hills, through streams, and mud a foot deep.

> Daniel.

Saturday—June 25th, 1864

I do not know how this army is to live and do duty these intensely hot days. I have never suffered so from heat as to-day. We are encamped on ground which has been burned over, and completely covered with underbrush.—We are instructed to lay out a camp. A coal pit is as comfortable a place.

Sunday—June 26th, 1864

I hear singing and praying going on in the 2nd Connecticut, but do not feel like leaving my bough house which has been erected with so much care and trouble, attended with so much sweat. We are getting plenty of water from the wells which our boys have dug.

Monday—June 27th, 1864

This day has been one of the most uncomfortably hot ones I ever experienced. For a wonder, all is quiet on the lines. We are all *dying* for *rain!* Oh how I long for the fresh green hills of Herkimer and my dear home in Newport.

Tuesday—June 28th, 1864

Ordered to police and lay out camp. Reconstructed bough house and put things in order generally. Thunder and rain for the first time in weeks. Really refreshing. *Cold* afterwards—*great* contrast from yesterday.

Wednesday—June 29th, 1864

Again laid out camp as if we were to remain forever. Corps review at 7 A.M. Order to *pack up* at 2 P.M. and be ready to march at a moment's notice. *Move* at 3 P.M. down upon the *Jerusalem Pike—Travel all night.*[50] The whole corps in motion towards the left.

Not content to sit idly in his works, Grant made repeated attempts throughout the siege of Petersburg to extend his lines to the south and west and to raid beyond them in order to cut the supply lines to Petersburg and Richmond. In one of these efforts, the Sixth Corps supported Gen. James Wilson's raid designed to destroy railroad lines around the vicinity of Petersburg. While the raid caused significant damage, Union losses were as many as fifteen hundred men.

Thursday—June 30th, 1864

About eight miles South of old encampment on the Petersburg and Weldon R.R. Destroy and occupy it after a very severe battle by the Cavalry under Gen. Wilson, who are ahead of us. Wilson lost 12 guns, six or eight hundred men. Rebel loss heavy—equal to our own. Start back again from this raid at 6 o'clock P.M.

Friday—July 1st, 1864

Come about half way back to old camp and stop. Our regiment out on picket. Letter from wife and [son] George. Went to Division Hospital for first time since the campaign opened.[51] No disturbance through the night.

50. Holt's reference to the "Jerusalem Pike" is to the Jerusalem Plank Road, which ran southeast out of Blandford, the eastern suburb of Petersburg. *Atlas,* plate 40-1.

51. The depot established by the Union army at City Point on June 18 had provided corps hospitals for patient overflow. By July, however, division hospitals were still in field tents near the trenches. As the siege wore on into the winter months, Army of the Potomac Medical Director McParlin would have log shelters build to serve as division hospitals. Gillett, 238–40.

On the Weldon Rail Road, Va.
July 1, 1864.

My dear Wife:—

I write you this morning from a point where I have long wished to be, if I could not address you from the traitorous city of Richmond. Our corps broke camp suddenly on the night of the 29th ult.[52] and after marching until four o'clock A.M., reached the track of the road, which we immediately commenced destroying. As far as we have gone, the destruction is *perfect*—ties are burned—rails warped in such a manner as to be perfectly worthless for re-laying, and the road bed torn up and deminshed. Miles of road are thus destroyed, and a long time must ense under the most favorable circumstances before it will be in running order again. This road has been a channel of supplies to the army about Richmond and its destruction will cripple them more than anything else we could do. The cavalry under General Wilson have the credit of clearing the way for us, and it is reported that he has been roughly handled. A heavy fight has been fought here as large quantities of *debris,* dead horses, &c. testify. We have not yet seen Wilson, but rumor says he is far away in the enemy's country fighting against unequal numbers and nearly surrounded.[53] Fears are entertained for his safety but we hope he will come out all safe. The result of our work is great indeed. We have cut a great artery and the hemorrhage will tell awfully upon rebellion.—Last night we started back, having performed the duty assigned us. We have only come about half way and are halted in a grove of pines. Pickets have been posted, which means, I suppose, that we shall occupy (if we can) for 24 hours at any rate. It is intensely hot. Wood ticks (and the bushes are full of them) flees, lice &c. &c., keep up a counter irritation truly refreshing.

My health generally is pretty good, were it not for that cough which sometimes seems as if it would kill me. I hardly know *what* to think of it. At times I feel but little of it, and at others, when there appears to be no cause for it, I am so violently seized that it perfectly prostrates me. I hope it will soon leave in good earnest.

Daniel.

52. "Ult." meaning ultimate or last. Here meaning June 29th.
53. Wilson, a "boy general" as Upton was, came east on Feb. 17, 1864, to serve as Grant's chief of the cavalry bureau. Grant assigned him to divisional command in Sheridan's cavalry at the start of the spring campaign. His raid mentioned here was successful; he returned to Union lines after destroying the railroad. *OR,* vol. 40, 1:624.

Saturday—July 2nd, 1864

Take up line of march for old quarters, but find them occupied by a division of the 2nd Corps. General Russell remonstrates but in vain.— We are forced to occupy ground upon the left. No policing to-day. Our men justly feel indignant at being obliged to dig wells, lay out camps, build houses, &c., for someone else to occupy.

Sunday—July 3rd, 1864

Our boys in almost a state of mutiny because compelled to make improvement for others to occupy. This is certainly the most disagree-able and stinking hole we ever got into. It has been used as a deposite for the refuse of the Army. However, the boys go to work after letting of the surplus bile, go to work and conclude to make the best of a bad matter. All quiet to-day.

> Behind entrenchments, I don't
> know where, Ten miles South of
> Petersburg, Virginia,
> July 4th, 1864.

My dear Wife:—

We arrived at our present encampment three days ago after our visit to the Weldon & Petersburg R.R., and are now very comfortably situ-ated, after policing the worst piece of ground I ever saw. It had been burned over—everything was *black* from fire and smoke—the ground— a *land* without a spear of living vegetation upon it—*dry* without a drop of water, while the space we occupy had been used as a slaughter pen for the army:—&c. decaying, putrid fragments of cattle, dead horses, mules, all left *above* ground to be buried, and all this by us who had left comfortable quarters not a week before to be occupied by black troops belonging to the 2nd Corps. Our men *did* get mad and swear some I must confess, when they had to put this unsightly stinking hole into decent shape—dig wells, construct houses and *lay out their city*. But one night's good rest and a warm breakfast served to put them into better nature, and so here they are again happy as ever. I wonder a real mutiny does not sometimes break out amoung the boys, when they are so often compelled to work as they do for the benefit of some one else. We get a camp in good order, as this, from an awful stinking cesspool and as soon as made have to give it up to others. Surely it is provoking. I cannot blame them for *thinking* swear, if nothing else. Can you?

The nights for a few days past have been *cold*—so cold that three blankets are not uncomfortable. The days are as *hot* proportionally, as the nights cold. It is a droll country after all. To-day, being the 4th, we ought to have a little music and firing, but not a sound of a gun, except heavy siege guns, fired at regular intervals day and night before Petersburg, breaks the Sunday-like stillness. It is *oppressively silent.* I had rather hear, as we have done all along, the sharp cracking of rifles and reverberating echoes of cannon along the mountain summits than thus to breathe the oppressed atmosphere of a crowded camp, made still more unbearable by drills and dress parades,

Daniel

Monday—July 4th, 1864

The quietest 4th of July I ever saw. *"Rebs"* nor *"Yanks"* dare open their mouths to-day for fear of getting a thrashing. Were it *me* I should hurrah and be joyful, even though a few whistling messengers bade me *shut up!* It is better, perhaps, to remain silent, and not provoke their wrath by usual demonstrations on such a day as this. We are getting a pretty camp after all. Persevering toil will do almost anything.

SEVEN

Into the Valley of the Shenandoah
July 5, 1864 – September 21, 1864

Grant's original plan for the spring campaign had included a thrust into the Shenandoah Valley under Franz Sigel. While Confederate general John Breckinridge had chased off Sigel at New Market, Virginia, on May 15, a larger Union force under Maj. Gen. David Hunter soon entered the valley; by the second week of June it had reached the southern end and was threatening Lynchburg. To meet this threat, Lee sent Jubal Early with the Second Corps to destroy Hunter and, if possible, to threaten Washington and force Grant to detach troops to defend it. Early set out for Lynchburg on June 13, and by the 14th, had Hunter running for refuge in the mountains of West Virginia.

With Hunter out of the way, Early headed north down the valley and toward Washington. Grant paid little attention to Early at first, but when the threat to Washington became apparent, he sent the Sixth Corps to the capital from Petersburg and diverted the Nineteenth Corps, newly arrived from Louisiana, as well. The Third Division of the Sixth Corps left first, arriving in time to help Maj. Gen. Lew Wallace stall Early on the Monocacy River on July 9. The rest of the Sixth Corps and part of the Nineteenth arrived on July 11–12, just in time to keep Early's men out of the Washington defenses.

Tuesday—July 5th, 1864

Worked all day brushing up and *beautifying my tent!* Sent for by General Upton to perform a slight surgical operation upon him.

Wednesday—July 6th, 1864

Wake up at 3 A.M. and ordered to be ready to march in an hour. *Mad* again. We are to remove half a mile to the left in an open dusty field, without a particle of shade or drop of water. Really a cheering thought.

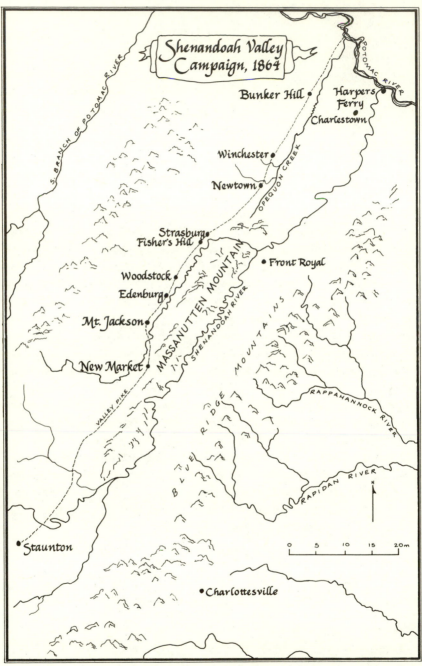

Shenandoah Valley
Campaign, 1864

Bunker Hill

Harpers Ferry

Charlestown

Winchester

Newtown

Strasburg
Fisher's Hill

Front Royal

Woodstock

Edenburg

Mt. Jackson

New Market

Staunton

Charlottesville

S. BRANCH OF POTOMAC RIVER

POTOMAC RIVER

OPEQUON CREEK

MASSANUTTEN MOUNTAIN

SHENANDOAH RIVER

VALLEY PIKE

BLUE RIDGE MOUNTAINS

RAPPAHANNOCK RIVER

RAPIDAN RIVER

0   5   10   15   20m

N

MAP BY MICAELA AYERS

Thursday—July 7th, 1864

2nd and 3rd Divisions ordered to Harpers Ferry. Hot and dusty as ever. Some signs of rain, but none at 3 P.M. It is clearer than in the morning. Visited by Lieut. Quackenbush, who is transferred to Ambulance Corps.[1] Dust a foot deep in tent. *Demoralized to an awful extent.*

Friday—July 8th, 1864

Hot as it can be. No one to blame that I know of, but give the Quarter Master and all hands a blowing up because I have no shade trees drawn to break off the sun from my quarters. I get what I *blow* about. Three army wagons and a gang of hands are at work setting out pine trees *all around my quarters!* It *does* do good sometimes to express a righteous indignation at unbearable evils.

Saturday—July 9th, 1864

Still fixing up quarters. Get *another* load of bushes.— First *dress parade* since the Campaign opened. At 9 P.M. ordered to pack up and move *immediately.* Start at 10 P.M. for City Point. The Rebels throw bomb shells into us as we go. *They heard the word to move out.*[2]

Sunday—July 10th, 1864

1st & 2nd Division travel all night, arriving at City Point at 7 o'clock A.M. Wait all day for transports, and at 8 P.M. embark on board the Propeller *Tappahannock* with the 96th Pa.—the regiment above all others with whom we hate to associate. Slept in a *bass drum* on pilot house roof.—Col. [William H.] Lessig, of the 96th Pa.[3] and one of our boys have a tusstle in which swords and guns are used. Visited Sanitary Commission and obtained a few supplis.

1. George W. Quackenbush mustered in as private with Co. G on Aug. 23, 1862, as second lieutenant with Co. C, May 29, 1863, and transferred to Co. F, July 9, 1863. He fought until his discharge on Apr. 20, 1865. *Annual Report*, 153.

2. Rebels were shelling the Sixth Corps by coincidence; they had made a more convincing demonstration on July 8. Grant ordered the departure of the rest of the Sixth Corps as soon as he heard of Early's defeat of Lew Wallace's force on the Monocacy. *OR*, vol. 40, 3:95–108.

3. The 96th Pa. organized at Pottsville in 1861. Assigned first to Slocum's Brigade in Franklin's Division of the Army of the Potomac, it eventually wound up in the Second Brigade, First Division of the Sixth Corps. They mustered out in 1864. Dyer, *A Compendium of the War*, 1:223; Samuel P. Bates, *History of Pennsylvania Volunteers, 1861–65,* 3:390.

Monday—July 11th, 1864

Passed Newport News at 8 A.M. and Fortress Monroe and Rip Raps at 9 A.M. Lying off Fortress Monroe was the Frigate *Brandywine* and Gunboat *Minnesota,* also an English Man-of-War. The Monitor *Roanoke* on picket above the Fort. Passed several other vessels of note. Passed Point Lookout at 9 o'clock P.M.[4] Turn in on poop deck with about a dozen of our officers, and as many more of the 96th Pa and sleep until morning. Pass a school of porpoise.

Tuesday—July 12th, 1864

Lay at anchor all night above Point Lookout. Passed Mount Vernon and Fort Washington at half-past 11 o'clock A.M. *Did not* feel as badly as I thought I should before reaching the sacred spot. Arrive in Washington at 2 P.M. Debarked in a rain storm and marched as far as Fort Stevens this day.[5] Find the city in a great state of excitement. The inhabitants appear to believe we have saved them from certain death. For *once* we are appreciated.

Upton's brigade arrived in Washington on the afternoon of July 12, marched to Fort Stevens to help confront Early's force, but arrived too late to take part in the limited Union attack launched in that sector earlier in the day. Early, finding the Washington defenses too strong and his own position too exposed, began to withdraw that night, with the Union forces following cautiously behind him.

Lincoln's visit to Fort Stevens, referred to in Holt's letter, very nearly cost him his life. Peering over the parapet in an attempt to see the Confederate position before the fort, Lincoln paid no attention to Confederate sharpshooters who were taking potshots. Sixth Corps captain Oliver Wendell Holmes, later Chief Justice of the Supreme Court, told him, apparently without recognition of Lincoln's identity, "Get down, you damn fool, before you get shot!" Lincoln did.

4. The troops were moving down the James River, around the end of the Peninsula through Hampton Roads, then up the Chesapeake Bay to enter the Potomac. Rip Raps had a communication station (Ft. Wool) offshore one mile from Fortress Monroe at the tip of the Peninsula; Point Lookout, Md., the site of a Union prison, was at the entrance to the Potomac River. *Atlas,* plates 18-1, 18-2, 16-1, 135-A.

5. Fort Stevens was about four miles north of the city center, part of a circle of forts guarding Washington City. Early had reached that sector on July 11 and had planned to attack the fort that afternoon, but called off the attack when he observed Union reinforcements moving into it. *B&L,* 4:497.

In the field under the guns of
Fort Stevens, Washington, D.C.
July 13th, 1864.

My dear Wife:—

Little did I think when I last addressed you clear down below Petersburg, that I should so soon write from this point. Having received orders, we packed up and began our move to City Point on the night of the 9th. Starting at 10 o'clock and continuing until sunrise, we came within sight of the City (a distance of fifteen miles). Here we lay almost all day waiting for the troops who preceeded us to get aboard of transports. The third division of our corps had been some time gone, and now the 1st and 2nd were on their way to join it somewhere near Washington. At length the 96th Pa. (a regiment above all others which we hate) and our own embarked on board the Propeller *"Tappahannock"* and steamed down the James River a few miles where we came to anchor for the night. Next day (Monday) at early dawn, we were on the way, passing Fortress Monroe, at 9 o'clock A.M. An hour previous (8 o'clock) passed Newport News; and the Rip Raps opposite Fortress Monroe at 9 A.M. At 9 o'clock passed Point Lookout, and after seeing all that was to be seen went to *bed!!* entering Chesapeake Bay under fair sail and steam. Yesterday about 2 o'clock P.M. in a driving shower of rain (the first we had seen for six weeks) we landed in Washington and immediately proceeded to this point where we are lying under the guns of Fort Stevens, one of the links of a great chain of fortifications around the Capital.

The trip, taken together was rather a pleasant one—at least it was a change from marching on dusty roads to cool and comparatively shady quarters. Little real comfort, after all, could be taken in such a packed and crowded vessel. Two regiments, without the use of saloons, or State rooms, were piled in promiscuously together—officers and men—upon the decks of an not over-large boat. With eight or ten other officers, I took my position upon the top of the Pilot House, a little affair not over ten feet square, and thus kept it until relieved by arriving at our destination. Having no blankets or bedding of any kind—not even an overcoat, the weather was chilling enough after getting fairly out to sea. No doubt you will be surprised that I should make my bed that night in a *bass drum!*, but so it was. The wind came cutting and cold—nothing over head but blue sky and beneath blue water. I thought if only I could make use of the drum as a *break water* against the windy element it would serve a good purpose. So taking it (one head was out) and placing a small coil of rope for a pillow, I crawled into it and there lay until my limbs became so stiff with cold that I could not stir, and *"let the hurricane roar."* Next day, of course, I paid well for the unusual luxury in a burning fever, and divers other ills to numerous to mention. But as you say *"I never complain"* and so say no more on that score. On our way down we passed Mount Vernon where the remains of our country's father repose in quiet slumber amid the scenes and confusion of a worse rebellion than ever before disgraced the records of a nation's history.—I could not repress the thought that the spirit of the departed Sage, and patriot was tearfully beholding these transports filled with troops, to put down an effort to crush out and extinguish a government for which he battled and bled, and left to generations unborn, the blessed heritage of a freepeople.

All sorts of rumors—vague and ridiculous filled the city when we landed. However, confidence—*perfect confidence* appeared to possess the people that we should save the Capital from spoilation and fire. Never were men more cordially greeted than we. As Saviors and deliverers they looked upon us; and if ever the old Sixth Corps was appreciated and looked up to it was then. Early had *nearly* eaten them up—body and soul, and now we had come to save their carcasses from being strewn to the four winds of heaven.[6] We *were* heroes now, if never before. *Father Abraham* wife and son followed us in a carriage to the walls of the fort and here I lost sight of the good man. We have learned to love him as well as he appears to love his boys in blue, and we all would be willing to sacrifice anything for such a man and such a government. No doubt our business will be active here, but you do not know how pleasant it is to get out of the clouds of dust and the heat which consumed us at Petersburg. Of all places I ever saw, the last quarters of our men were the most unpleasant from dust, heat, dirt, flees, and vermin of all sorts. It cannot be so bad here. Let it come.

Daniel.

6. Holt's estimate of the situation here was accurate in the sense that the Union forces outnumbered Early's, and might very well have defeated them if they had been employed aggressively. But Union commanders were rarely allowed to act aggressively when close to the capital, and even if they had been, most of the intelligence reports coming in at the time heavily overestimated the size of Early's force, some of them even claiming that Lee's whole army was moving against Washington. *OR,* vol. 37, 2:77–204; McPherson, *Battle Cry,* 757.

Wednesday—July 13th, 1864

Lay in camp until 2 P.M. when we move out upon the Tenallytown Road, which place we pass at 5 P.M. and encamp at Poolesville. Wait all day for the rebels to *get out of the way*. We found them thick as huckleberries at Fort Stevens and *ought* to have given them a threshing.[7] Go into camp for the night.

Thursday—July 14th, 1864

Still at Poolesville, at 10 AM. waiting orders. The rebels crossing the river with immense quantities of plunder, so it is said. Witnessed the execution of a spy and deserter at this place.[8] At 1 P.M. ordered to Young's Ferry where we remain all night. Encamp in a corn field. The cavalry cross and reconnoitre.

Friday—July 15th, 1864

Have completely *lost* one day. Cannot account for it but *one day* is gone. Records do not agree. It must be that I slept one day and night and took no note of it.

> Young's Ford six miles from
> Poolesville, Md., July 16, 1864.

My dear Wife:—

As you will see, we are at Young's Ferry on the Potomac, where we arrived to guard it against the passage of rebels who are reported to be in force on the other side. I doubt whether *much* of a force is wanting to get over. Loafing, lying cavalrymen without moral or any other principle, are flying from one point to another circulating all sorts of cock and bull stories, about rebel strength, and how hard pressed they were when they had to fall back after losing half their men, &c. The common expression among our men, when they wish to tell that a person is not to be believed, is to say that *"he lies worse than a cavalryman!"*

7. Poolesville was twenty-five miles northwest of Fort Stevens near Edward's Ferry along the Potomac. Early's troops left the night of July 12; the Sixth Corps slowly followed. McPherson, *Battle Cry*, 756–57; *B&L*, 4:498–99.

8. It is not clear who the "spy and deserter" was. Early's troops burned Postmaster-General Montgomery Blair's house, torched Maryland governor Thomas Hicks's mansion, and destroyed or stole as much as they could carry. They also requested "donations" from towns along the way—two hundred thousand dollars in cash from Frederick, Md., alone. McPherson, *Battle Cry*, 757.

We are ordered, and shall march in an hour or two for White's Ford on the Potomac, fourteen miles up the River where our division is now lying.[9] Only our Regiment and the 95th Pa is here, and all that keeps us is waiting for the Engineers to build a bridge over the Canal on which we may cross.

You do not know how much of a relief it is to us to be once more on free soil. It is like passing from death unto life. I had rather march every day and fight every week here, than to lie in camp and do nothing before Petersburg.—Yesterday I witnessed the execution of a deserter and spy at Poolesville. He had been in the service but a very short time before he killed a lieutenant and private of ours—robbing them after shooting, and then deserted to the enemy. At the North he had been a regular *bounty jumper*.[10] He came into our lines in rebel uniform asserting that he was a deserter from their army, and wanted to enlist in ours. He was detected at once, as it happened he came into the lines where his own regiment was picketing. During the prayer of the Chaplain he displayed the most heathenest unconcern about his situation of any man I ever saw. Looking from the scaffold to those about him—throwing his head from one side to the other, furiously chewing tobacco and in a thousand ways evincing perfect unconcern of all around him. He died of strangling. The neck was not broken, and at least fifteen [minutes] passed before he ceased to live. It was a sad sight but one upon which I looked without wishing it different.

Daniel.

Saturday—July 16th, 1864

The 121st and 95th Pa. have orders to report at White's Ford distant fourteen miles. Start at 9 A.M. take toe path of canal and arrive at the Ford at 3 P.M. Cross over and get dinner. Continue the march until within one mile of Leesburg, and encamp at 10 P.M.

---

9. Holt's reference is unclear. *Atlas,* plate 100, traces the movements of the Sixth Corps and labels their crossing at Conrad's Ferry, located west of Poolesville about five miles. Conrad's crosses the Chesapeake and Ohio Canal and the Potomac River. White's Ford was above Leesburg in Loudon County. Early's forces retreated from Washington over this road. *B&L,* 4:499.

10. "Bounty jumper" meaning a soldier who enlisted, collected the bounty, deserted at his first opportunity, then enlisted again elsewhere to collect another bounty, keeping it up until caught or tired of the game. Robertson, 37.

Sunday—July 17th, 1864

Reveille at daylight. Start at 5 A.M. before taking breakfast. Passed through Leesburg at sunrise. Saw an old preacher and enquired for the residence of Mrs. Morallee.[11] Passed it—a stone house on the Winchester Road. Breakfast one mile from Leesburg on the [Leesburg and Snicker's Gap] Pike. Go into camp two miles from Leesburg.

The Union pursuit of Early was poorly coordinated and largely ineffective. Wright, who had immediate command of the troops marching out from Washington and who was given overall command of all of the other forces operating against Early in Maryland and Virginia, was not aggressive or assertive enough for this sort of assignment. He also faced the added hindrances of having to coordinate the movements of troops assigned to four different administrative departments and of having to deal with a constant flow of orders from Gen. Henry Halleck, now chief of staff, in Washington. While Wright's own men advanced slowly from Washington, part of Maj. Gen. David Hunter's force from West Virginia under Brig. Gen. George Crook attacked Early on July 18 and were repulsed before Wright could join them.

Monday—July 18th, 1864

Awoke at 5 A.M. Commence march at 6 A.M. Pass Hamilton at 8 A.M.—Percellville at 8½. Snicker's Gap at 6 P.M. First firing heard this afternoon. Encamp under fire near the banks of the Shenandoah at 8 P.M. Hunter's men are driven in confusion by the Rebels who are safely on the other side showing their teeth inviting us to the combat. We do not accept the invitation.

> In field on the banks
> of the Shenandoah,
> July 19, 1864.

My dear Wife:—

I have just arisen from a sleep upon the ground in the rear of three batteries which our brigade is supporting on the Eastern shore of the Shenandoah. I believe I last wrote you from Young's Ford on the Potomac, which point we were guarding. It appears that the Division had orders to leave Poolesville at 5 A.M. which they did, crossing

11. Thomas Morallee was apparently an old friend. Holt would stay with him in Washington on his way home after his discharge.

White's Ford at 3 o'clock P.M. all wading the stream which at this point is about half a mile wide and at this time three feet deep. After crossing we bivouacked and made coffee.—Starting again, we traveled five miles and encamped for the night within a mile of Leesburg in Loudoun county. At early dawn we were again upon the move, the Brigade leaving Leesburg half a mile to the left, striking the Winchester Pike about a mile beyond the town, where we halted and ate breakfast. With Capt. McFarland of the 95th Pa. I left the column and passed through the town. The house of Thomas Morallee was pointed out to me and I had the pleasure of seeing his mother, at this early hour, sweeping the steps of her mansion. The village *has* been one of importance, but *now* is utterly gone to destruction. Not a store is open to sell goods—the inhabitants—all secesh *of the very meanest kind*—"gone to the war" while Negroes and broken down old men and women keep the village from following after.

A short march of an hour and a half brought us to the fine little village of Hamilton, where we were for the first time, greeted by cheers and a display of the blessed old Stars and Strips, waved by the hands of fair maidens and lovely children. If these expressions reflect the sentiments of the sterner sex, we have a few sympathizing hearts and friends left in the Old Dominion. Long may they flourish. Long may they live happy and free under its protecting folds.

Still beyond Hamilton a few miles, we pass through the village of Purcellville—*small in dimensions,* but taking the word of the people for it, next to Richmond, which they look upon as being the greatest city of the world, and in the very center of creation, a sentiment I find universally adopted of the Babel of treason, by all half civilized, half-educated bigoted rebels who have never traveled beyond the precincts of their own country or associated with a higher order of talent than the *"human chattels"* around them. Next in order comes *Mulberry Grove,* a place of *one* house, with a score of those beautiful trees to give it a name,—a place of vital importance to its owner and about *five* of the raggedest *Niggars* you ever saw. Husband, wife, children, niggars and all occupy the same room and are sitting (for what I know not) upon the *porch* watching the troops as they pass along. Still a little farther ahead, we enter a defile in the Blue Ridge through which we pass, known as *"Snicker's Gap."* Perhaps you will recollect last year we passed through this same pass in the mountains.—Leaving this rocky defile, we enter a series of hills not unlike those around and about Newport, our own quiet home. Here we meet, for the first time, wounded men coming to the rear—a portion of General Hunter's command, who have been pretty soundly thrashed by our Southern neighbors, who are at present lying over the Shenandoah River, apparently waiting to receive us with open arms "on the other side of Jordan," but whether we shall accept the kind invitation or not, remains to be seen. We sent them our compliments, however, in the shape of a few friendly shells which they returned in the same friendly spirit. One of these gentle messengers fell in a column of Jerseymen who had just "stacked arms" and were lying upon ground within a few feet of me, killing three and wounding half a dozen more. It is needless to say that they were indignant and left. For *my share* I had to dress their wounds.[12]

No certainty attends our movements. So far it appears to be the policy to let the rebels off without fighting them; whether from actual inability to cope with them and overcome them, or whether we *love* them too well, as McClellan did at Antietam, I do not know, but certain it is we have always halted just within sight of them, and after allowing them [to] get safely off, start again in pursuit. I am inclined to believe the report in circulation here, that our Cavalry have overtaken and destroyed a large portion of their baggage train. Some sixty wagons were burned, and they (the Cavalry) say that if they had been supported by infantry, might have captured the whole. In one trunk of an officer was found *seven rich silk dresses,* all stolen from the wives of loyal Marylanders. Another wagon was loaded with *pianos* neatly packed going to grace the parlors of these chivalrous men. Indeed immense quantities of household furniture was being conveyed away— such as sofas, sofa chairs and mahogany bed steads, stands, tables, &c. &c. Bedding rich and costly filled wagons stolen from the people of Maryland and Pennsylvania. Innumerable heads of cattle, sheep, swine, horses and cows were being driven along, all to go to the homes and for the use of these sons of honor and integrity. One hundred thousand dollars in greenbacks and large quantities of silver spoons and plate of all kinds were captured with the rest. *Had we good cavalry,* we should hear a different account. As it is they are the most unreliable men I ever saw, composed of the odds and ends of all commands, amenable to no law, acknowledging no head. In fact they are little

12. The Union casualties were from Crook's failed attack at Snicker's Gap on the 18th. *B&L,* 4:499.

226 · A SURGEON'S CIVIL WAR

better than a disorganized mob—not that fighting material is wanting in many of them, but because they are those who from sickness or other cause have been sent to Washington for treatment, and upon the appearance [of] Early in the Valley, threatening the capital and devastating the country, have been re-mounted and sent out officered by just such men as themselves.—No wonder such men, officered with such officers do not fight but spread disorder and confusion in camp. Better have none.[13]

It has been said that Grant has ordered the 6th Corps to Petersburg again, as soon as it can get there, and that Lee is concentrating his whole army there: that we have been badly whipped at Malvern Hill, as in every encounter with them of late. This *may*, or may *not* be so. We get no mails and hear nothing correctly, but *I* do not believe it. Certain it is that we have not done, as yet what we were sent here for, and I do not think we shall leave until we do. Perhaps we have kept the rebels from making any further advance or doing any more mischief, but we have not *whipped* him for his naughtiness yet, and we must do this or get no credit. You have no idea of the amount of plunder which these vagabonds are driving away. Millions of dollars worth of the very best of *everything* is going off, and we as yet not being able to stop it or recover ever so little. It is too bad. I feel like *fighting* for it.

Daniel.

Tuesday—July 19th, 1864

At 9 A.M. still in camp *looking* at the rebels on the other side.— Hunter's men yesterday sustained considerable loss in killed and wounded. Orders to move, but are countermanded. All sorts of stories afloat in relation to the fall of Petersburg and Richmond.[14] No firing through the day. Hard living. Hard tack and pork.

Grant's standing orders to Wright had been to pursue Early until such time as it was clear that he had retreated into Virginia and no longer posed a threat to Maryland, Pennsylvania, or Washington. With this mission accomplished, the

13. Holt's disparaging remarks about the cavalry were aimed at the troopers of Averell and Brig. Gen. Alfred Duffié from Hunter's West Virginia forces. These men had fought largely as irregulars in West Virginia and the valley since early in the war and were less well-trained, equipped, and disciplined than the cavalry of the Army of the Potomac, which by this stage of the war was quite good. Coddington, *The Gettysburg Campaign*, 64; Jeffry D. Wert, *From Winchester to Cedar Creek: The Shenandoah Campaign of 1864*, 22.

14. These were rumors. At this point the mine for the Petersburg Crater was under construction, but it would not be exploded until June 30.

Sixth and Nineteenth Corps were to go back to Petersburg before Early could get there. Wright advanced until July 20, when he heard that Averell's cavalry had hit Early's rearguard at Winchester and that Early was retreating up the Valley. Considering his mission accomplished, Wright began his withdrawal that evening. Holt and the men around him found the back-and-forth marching tiresome and confusing.

Wednesday—July 20th, 1864

In camp at 8 A.M. At noon, ordered to pack up. Crossed the Shenandoah and bivouack on reb campground. The first thunder storm of the season—a real *ripper!* Get orders at 9 P.M. to report to Chain Bridge as soon as possible.[15] Start at 10½:—cross the river at 12 M.

Thursday—July 21st, 1864

Traveled all night. Breakfast at 8 A.M. near Purcellville. Pass through Hamilton at 10½ A.M. Our men pretty well used up. Pass through Leesburg at 12 M. Gurillas hanging upon our rear. Encamp on Goose Creek two miles from Leesburg.

Friday—July 22nd, 1864

On the march at 7 o'clock A.M. Cross Broad Run at 10 A.M., Difficult Creek at 7 P.M. and encamp for the night.[16] We travel all points of compass to-day.

Wright's forces began to arrive in Washington on July 23, but Wright asked that his men be given two days to rest and refit before embarking on the transports that were to take them back to Petersburg. This was agreed to, and in the interim, on July 24, news arrived that Early had turned about and attacked Crook and Averell at Kernstown and was once again threatening the North. Grant finally agreed to send Wright back to the Valley and began to take measures intended to eliminate the Confederate threat there once and for all. All that Holt could see at this point, however, was a lot of wasted time and effort.

Saturday—July 23rd, 1864

Ordered up at 3 A.M. Breakfast at 4 and leave *instantly,* which we finally do at *8* A.M. Passed through Langley at 11 A.M. and cross Chain

---

15. The Chain Bridge is just outside Washington, passing over the Potomac River.

16. All the small streams Holt mentioned were along the southwest side of the Potomac. *Atlas,* plate 74-1.

Bridge at 4 P.M. Encamp near Tenallytown on grounds occupied by Fort Gaines. A most wild and picturesque spot is that Chain Bridge hanging so high over the rocky bed of the Potomac. If "beauty unadorned" is "adorned the most," then this above any spot on the green footstool is the most beautiful. Instinctively one exclaims as he for the first time looks down upon the wild chasm far below, "Oh how beautiful!"

Sunday—July 24th, 1864

Mail arrives. Letters from home. Answer them. Paid off by Major Robinson. A general rush to Washington by Officers and men, in which *I did not indulge.* Rain heavy and long after night fall. Many visitors from the city. Fast young men and women in abundance.

> In camp near
> Tenallytown, D.C.
> July 25th, 1864.

My dear Wife:—

As you will discover by the date, we are again near Washington, from which place, in a day or two, we are to embark for City Point, and then to our old field of operations near Petersburg. The campaign, thus far, to my mind, has been a disgraceful failure, resulting in nothing decisive in punishing the invaders of free soil, or in recovering a tithe of the vast amount of property stolen from loyal men. "Who is to blame for all this?" I hear you ask. Surely I cannot tell; but rest assured that the rank and file are, and have always been ready to deal a blow deadly and stunning to these unprincipled raiders. We have had abundant opportunities to capture or perfectly disband them but have always let them off until it became the settled belief of all that *fighting* was not in the programme. When we have come, as we have, dozens of times within easy range (cannon) of them we have as invariably halted and let them get a dozen or fifteen miles ahead, and then up and followed on only to repeat former farces and disgrace,—I certainly think, that *so far* Jonathan Rounds would have conducted the campaign better, for we all knew him to be *honest* in politics, whatever he may lack in judgment.[17] Unlike poor Jonathan, many of our officers are dishonest in principle but keen enough in knavery. I cannot write much this time as the mail is about to leave and no one knows exactly what is to become

17. Jonathan Rounds was presumably a fictional character.

of us. I hate the thought of going back again to that awful country about Petersburg. I had rather rough it here every day—through all kinds of weather, than go back again. To me it is like going into prison. Not the first pleasant association is connected with our operations in that quarter. All is horrible to contemplate and sad to endure. Blood, death, carnage and excessive fatigue—these make up the picture on which the mind is prone to dwell when we think upon that unhallowed spot. However, if go it is, go we must, and there is no remedy; but I would it were different.

Daniel.

Monday—July 25th, 1864

To-day the *Regiment* is paid off, very much to its satisfaction.— Ordered to move to-morrow morning with four days rations. Rain continues to fall until 11 A.M. when it clears off *cold*.

Tuesday—July 26th, 1864

Packed up and started at 12 M. Pass through Tenallytown at 2 P.M., Rockville at 7 P.M. and encamp for the night three miles beyond on the Frederick Pike. Stragglers in plenty. *They have been to Washington!* "That's what's the matter."

Wednesday—July 27th, 1864

Start at 5 A.M. Pass through Clarksburg at 12 M. and go into camp at Hyattsville at 4 P.M. A very pretty little town is Clarksburg and like the village of Hamilton, *loyal*. At both of these places beautiful ladies young and old, and little children wave the stars and stripes as we move along, God bless their loyal hearts. I cannot repress a tear as I see such enthusiastic devotion to the dear old flag in this land of treason.

Thursday—July 28th, 1864

On the move at 7 o'clock A.M., passing through Hyattsville at 7½. Urbana 11 A.M. and bivouacked on the Monocacy River for 3 hours.— Passed to the left of Frederick City one mile at 7 P.M. and encamped for the night (12 o'clock) near Jefferson. We are almost tired out.

Friday—July 29th, 1864

Again on the move at 7 o'clock A.M. Pass Petersville at 10 A.M. and enter the gap leading to Harpers Ferry at 11 A.M. Crossed the river on pontoon bridge and entered Harper's Ferry at 12M. Of all the miserable and forsaken holes I ever saw, this caps the climax. A perfect Arabia Petra.—A habitation for bats and owls. John Brown was a fool to make so much of the town as to ever set foot in it.[18] Encamp on the heights three miles beyond. It is hard to see the *point* of this ceaseless routine of marching and counter marching, when no rebels are in sight or hearing. We are all getting tired of it.

Saturday—July 30th, 1864

Ordered to start at precisely 10 o'clock P.M. Men allowed to go to the river and wash themselves and clothes. Orders come to move while thus engaged. Go to Bolivar Heights and remain an hour. Pass into Harpers Ferry and remain until 10 o'clock P.M. when we cross the river and encamp at 2 A.M., within a short distance of Petersville. An intensely hot day. Many cases of sun stroke and all apparently, for *nothing!*[19] What *does* this tom fooling mean! If *any* body can enlighten us we should be pleased to know.

Sunday—July 31st, 1864

Last night we were ordered to march precisely at 7 o'clock this morning. Still in camp at 9 A.M. It seems to me perfectly outrageous to march our men as has been done ever since coming North. I have lost all confidence or respect for our commanders. They either do not know *what* to do, or they are unfit for their commands. *Midday* and *midnight* marches is the rule. Yesterday and day before, men fell down with sun stroke like a bullock under the butcher's cleaver. Granted more passes to Ambulance and fall out, than for a month previously. If this does not soon end, the army will halt without the command to do so. Men *cannot* stand such devilish treatment. There is no humanity in it. *I* will not blame a man for disobedience to *such* orders as we are daily receiving. We are willing to do what *men do,* but to be used and treated like *dogs is not* human. Met a Missouri friend in the Village of Harpers

18. Holt's reference to "Arabia Petra" is to the ancient city of Petra, a rocky and uninviting place surrounded by cliffs, much as Harpers Ferry was. John Brown's raid on the Federal arsenal at Harpers Ferry in 1859 was widely credited with exacerbating sectional tensions that led to the war.

19. "Sun stroke" or heat stroke due to excessive exposure to sun and heat is marked by excessive body temperature, dry skin, and eventually coma or death. Some men may have instead suffered from heat exhaustion, which is when the body goes into shock, resulting in a lower body temperature and fainting. It is less deadly than sun stroke.

Ferry, who invited me to his house where he gave me refreshments, *&c.* He was a revenue officer—true and faithful.[20] Start at 12 M. *without dinner.* Lie at Harper's Ferry waiting for the Corps to cross until 9 P.M. Cross over, march all night and finally stop a mile and a half from Frederick, more dead than alive at sunrise.

Monday—August 1st, 1864

All day in camp. Make a long credit mark for it. The men resting as well as their weary bodies can.

The constant moving and marching, together with regular medical duties, were beginning to show their effects on Daniel Holt. Unbeknownst to him, however, something was being done to straighten out the command problems hampering the forces arrayed against Early. Plans were in the works to combine all the Union forces into a single command under Maj. Gen. Philip Sheridan, whose aggressiveness, Grant hoped, would be a match for Early's. Sheridan would not assume command for several days, though, and in the meantime, the army continued to wait.

On the march, at camp at
Frederick City, August 1st, 1864.

My dear Wife:—

I write you this time being so tired and worn out that it seems to me I cannot follow the regiment much further. Since my last, we have traveled over two hundred and fifty miles, over the dustiest roads, in the hottest sun and dryest time I ever saw. I wish I could fully convey to your mind the sufferings which our men endure in thus keeping up a continual tramp, day and night, when to appearance (to *us* at least) there is no need of it. Often have I fallen from my horse, as nature giving way to sleep, I was unable to keep the saddle any longer. After all, night marching is the most pleasant were it not that night was made to sleep in, and no constitution can endure protracted fatigue and wakefulness without the eyes closing in deep heavy sleep. As I have dismounted for coffee, often I have fallen more like a dead than a living man, and only because *I am worn out.* Oh dear, how has this poor old body been tortured with pain and parched with thirst as I have rode mile after mile in dust so deep and thick that you could not see the

20. "Revenue officer" meaning tax collector.

fifth file ahead of you. Cavalry, trains, infantry and all moving on the same dusty road keep the atmosphere full of dirt, getting into your mouth, lungs, ears,—penetrating clothing, making the body more like the skin of an elephant than that of a human being. But enough of this complaint. It is not *soldierly*—it will not do to think of a dear wife and little ones—*you must be a man*—let no such weakness as *"homesickness"* come across you, I have come to *fight,* not to weep; but unbidden, in spite of me, I cannot forget that I *have* a *home* and a good one, too, thank a most kind and indulgent God; and I do not count it unmanly to prize it and to love it. We have passed through Leesburg, into the Valley of the Shenandoah, thence back to Georgetown, thence to Frederick through Harpers Ferry, and then back again to Frederick City where we now lie. This state of things cannot always endure. The last *"fall in"* will be heard—the last tap beating to quarters through our thinned ranks, the last bugle call to *"march"* will sound, and like poor old John Brown, our souls will keep marching on.[21] Until then good bye

Daniel.

Tuesday—August 2nd, 1864

Start at 4½ A.M. Orders countermanded and we encamp for the day about a mile from last night's encampment in a grove of white oaks.

Wednesday—August 3rd, 1864

Start at 4½ A.M. Cross the Baltimore and Ohio R. R. at Lime Kiln Station, leaving Frederick City on the left, at 9 A.M. and cross the Monocacy River near Buckeyestown at 10 A.M., where we encamp.

Thursday—August 4th, 1864

A still quiet morning. Bands everywhere playing their sweetest strains. This is the day set apart by the President to be observed as a day of thanksgiving, humility and prayer,—a day whose observance ought most religiously to be observed. If *ever* we needed the divine protection and influence it is now, in the dark hour of our National distress. Major Ellis died suddenly this morning of heart disease.[22] He was attached to

21. Holt's comment regarding John Brown refers to Julia Ward Howe's hymn, "Battle Hymn of the Republic," set to the popular tune of "John Brown's Body Lies A-Moulderin' in the Grave." One of the lines of the hymn was "our souls are marching on."

22. William Ellis had been wounded at Spotsylvania while leading a charge against the Mule Shoe. A gun ramrod had gone through his arm and bruised his chest. He went

General Russell's staff. An imposing funeral cortege conduct the body to Frederick City in an ambulance—the body wrapped in the flag of his regiment. The weather intensely hot. Our men improve the halt by bathing and washing clothes in the river. A real luxury.

Friday—August 5th, 1864

Nothing new. Not even a dead Major to relieve the monotony of this hot weather. Encamped in a field on which wheat had been grown. The *stubble* makes a first rate bed to lie upon. Orders to leave at 10 P.M. Cross the Monocacy and travel all night.

Saturday—August 6th, 1864

Pass through Buckeyestown at 1 A.M.—through Petersville at 7 A.M. and breakfast at 8 A.M. Travel through heat and dust all day, the men falling out like exhausted sheep. Pass through Knoxville and the Gap, continue the route to Harpers Ferry, cross the river and encamp four miles beyond. We cannot make out what this all means.

Sheridan assumed command officially on August 7 but did not immediately order the army to move out from Harpers Ferry. Holt continued to grumble.

> In camp four miles West of
> the village, *Harpers Ferry,*
> August 7, 1864.

My dear Wife:—

Were it not duty (conjoined with inclination) I should not now address you. To tell a plain, unvarnished tale of truth, I am feeling almost used up. The hand and eyes run along the lines, to be sure, but my mind wanders over confused scenes of sun stroke—exhausted men lining the road sides and path ways,—broken down wagons—dead horses and mules—the sun pouring down its burning rays like liquid fire upon our defenseless heads.—Never, no never, has any army suffered like this for a few weeks past. I am perfectly inadequate to portray the real misery of the men from excessive heat and toil: and when you

---

home to recuperate but returned to active duty before fully recovering. He served on the staff of General Russell, commander of the First Division. George T. Stevens, surgeon with the 77th N.Y., autopsied Ellis and discovered that a splintered rib had pierced the heart, causing him to bleed to death internally. George T. Stevens, *Three Years in the Sixth Corps,* 385–86.

consider the *results* accomplished by such over work, you fail to recognize one single advantage gained to the Union cause, unless by losing hundreds of the best troops we have, thus cutting short the war from want of material. Last night when we encamped, not one-third of our men were able to stagger to the stack to place their guns; and this is true as regards the whole command. I feel myself fortunate in belonging to so small a regiment, for were it as it was when we entered the service, *I should not attempt* to do the business of it. Dr. Slocum is off all the while and therefore *as usual* I am alone.[23]

Had you kept an account of our *wanderings,* (and no other word will express the idea) since we arrived at Washington, until now, you would have seen us going every point of the compass in twenty-four hours, passing and repassing places, whose pronunciation would endanger the life of a common man, finally bringing up in pretty nearly the same spot we left in the morning, reduced in strength and numbers, demoralized to an extent fearful to behold. Unless the 6th Corps speedily redeems itself, it will become a stench in the nostrils of the Nation and all loyal men. We *must* do something soon, or we are forever ruined as a corps. I am inclined to think that we are acting under restraint from Washington. *I hope so.* I do not wish to have the blame rest on us, for we are and have been willing to wind up this business at any time, *and we are able:* mind that. You must be content with *short* and *far between* letters.

Daniel.

Sunday—August 7th, 1864

At 9 A.M. still in camp, nearly used up. We are beginning to think of leaving in a body for home unless we are better used. Hundreds of our men have died from over-exertion, heat and sun stroke. It is too bad. No enemy in sight or army where about that *we* know of. I feel the spring of youth fast flowing from these weary limbs. My old body cannot stand this much longer. I am giving out in lungs and vital parts. Soon this pilgrimage will end with me if I stay here. Whatever comes, I will try not to disgrace the flag of my country by cowardice or neglect of duty. While [I] am in the service I will be true to it. Even though I die in it.

23. Surgeon Slocum was detailed to the First Division Hospital during May and June 1864 and most likely was still there. Pension and Service Records.

Monday—August 8th, 1864

In camp, feeling very faint and weary. It is hard upon so weak a frame as mine, but I do not wish to complain. I feel ashamed of expressions of impatience such as I have indulged in of late. I enlisted expecting toil and privations instead of luxurious ease. I will try to be reconciled, although with my feeble eyes of faith I cannot see clearly the star of freedom shining brightly in the background. I still have confidence that all will end well, but Oh how these awful marches through dust and scorching heat—day and night, tell upon us poor soldiers, while our brothers and fathers remain at home the recipiants of every earthly blessing.

Tuesday—August 9th, 1864

Still in camp. Letters from home. Were it not for these missives of tender love, we should truly feel deserted. They come as dew on the wilted flower—refresh and restore the beauty—give life and animation and unite in bonds indissoluble the heart with the sacred altar of home. Orders to march again at 5 A.M. Approve passes for several Captains and prepare for another tedious march.

With his forces assembled and organized, Sheridan advanced on August 10. Early pulled back to Strasburg without a fight. Sheridan halted before him on August 13, having heard reports of a large Confederate force threatening his rear, and withdrew to Halltown in stages during August 15–26, where he would remain on the defensive for the next month.

Wednesday—August 10th, 1864

On the move at 5½ A.M. Pass through Old John Browns town (Charlestown) at 9 A.M. Visited the jail and Court House where the old hero was incarcerated, and the spot upon which he died.[24] This *has been* a very pretty town, but now presents a sad dilapidated appearance. A great many of the bricks and other materials of which the jail is composed, have been carried off as relics, until it sure looks hard enough. In the center of the Village on the main street opposite the Court

24. Brown was arrested after his raid on Harpers Ferry and held in the Charlestown Jail. His trial began Oct. 25, 1859. Found guilty of murder, treason, and fomenting insurrection, he was hanged on Dec. 2. Nevins, *Emergence of Lincoln,* 70–97.

House—the most conspicious object of the town, it is the most disgusting spectacle which can be conceived of. It is a fair specimen of Southern Institutions—full of holes, frowning grates and bars, chains, bolts and tumble-down pillars and colonades. Encamp at 6 P.M. on the road to Winchester about eight or ten miles from Charlestown. No dinner to-day. Weather about as hot as it can be.

Thursday—August 11th, 1864

Move at usual hour 5½ A.M. pass through no town, leaving them all on the right. Bivouack for three or four hours on the bank of Pepper Creek, and start again after heat of day is over. *Of all weather I ever saw* this is the very hottest. It seems as if eggs would cook in the sun. Encamp for the night on Pepper Creek near an old stone mill. This day has been one of *real bodily* suffering, but many others are worse off. I am thankful for what I *do* enjoy.

Friday—August 12th, 1864

On the move at 7½ A.M. Pass Newtown and Middletown, and go into camp at 8 P.M. one mile South of Middletown. The weather seems to grow *hotter* instead of cooler. Wonder if they are having such awful weather up North. Not a breath of air stirring. Our men falling out and being captured by gurillas as they never have before. Rain is needed more than anything else. We are all praying for it to lay the dust and cool the air.

Saturday—August 13th, 1864

Move at 7 A.M. Cross Cedar [Creek] and march to within a mile and a half of Strasburg, *and return at night to old camp* of yesterday! For a wonder find the Rebels ready to meet us on strongly fortified naturally defensive ground, on the other side of the town.[25]

Sunday—August 14th, 1864

All day in camp. We (the Brigade) are encamped on half an acre of ground made as filthy by human excrement as half an acre can be. It is disgusting and insulting to a decent body of men to place them upon such ground when other can be had. Horses, trains—everything all

25. This refers to the Confederate position on Fisher's Hill, where Early was prepared to stand while waiting for reinforcements. *B&L*, 4:502.

mixed up together. We dare not offer battle. It looks too pokerish in such a place as this.[26] Supply train and mail arrive. Supplies from Harpers Ferry, *our base.*

Camp of the 121st Reg N.Y. Vols.
near Strasburg, Va., Aug. 15, 1864.

My dear Wife:—

Here we are clear up the Shenandoah Valley, halted by the rebels in a mountain pass through which the Shenandoah River makes its way one branch continuing up the Valley bearing its name, and the other the Luray Valley. It is oppressively hot, and I am sitting on a cracker box—shall I say it?—*shirtless!* Our baggage trains are at Winchester, far out of harms way, and I have no clothes except what I have on. Tom (a perfect *jewel* if ever a man was a jewel, and as good a friend as I have upon earth) is washing his and offered to wash mine too: so I am sitting waiting for it to dry and to improve *every minute* am writing to you. Do not tell any one that I am so short of clothes for really I have part of another if I could only get it!

Our cavalry have started out full tilt some where I know not where, but expect it is to gobble up the whole concern which they can do if so disposed, for we really have something like cavalrymen now.[27] General Sheridan (who is in command) having his old reliable troops in the saddle, and he personally overseeing every movement. I like him first rate, and so do all. He is a stirring officer, wide awake and alive to all around. Only set him on, and I believe he will make short work of Early and all the rest of the rebels in this Valley; but I fear he is crippled by powers at Washington, as every commander in this department has been from the first. Not so in the Southwest. *There* the Generals in command do as they see fit. *Here* every Congressman and every Department clerk thinks himself competent to command and *to* give orders. It is said that we are to start back again in a short time for Harpers Ferry. The old story of going back to Petersburg is again revived, but appearances are anything but favorable for such a move. We have enough to do here for a little while if they will only let us do it. If I *ever complained* I would tell you how that tormented old cough keeps me going, and

26. "Pokerish" meaning causing fear or alarm.
27. The Union cavalry had been turned into an effective force in 1863, and by 1864 had the Confederates outgunned, outhorsed, and outnumbered. Wert, 22.

how I fear I shall have to resign if I calculate to live out half my days, but *"I never complain,"* so good bye.

Daniel.

Monday—August 15th, 1864

Move camp about half a mile to South West. Write letters home in reply to those arrived yesterday. Our camp upon the crest of a hill with fair view of Blue Ridge and Alleghanies,—beautiful sight. Nature in all her wild loveliness lies stretched out before us. These views are enough to inspire any heart with heavenly emotions.

The Sixth Corps, together with some of the cavalry, covered Sheridan's withdrawal down the valley. Early followed closely, picking off stragglers and harassing the rear guard.

Tuesday—August 16th, 1864

Remain in camp all day expecting orders to fall back, as almost all have left except this corps. Orders came at 8 PM., to fall in at 10. P.M. which we obey, passing through Middletown at 10½. Follow the pike and pass through.

Wednesday—August 17th, 1864

Newtown at 2 A.M. Pass through Pleasant Town at break of day. Halt for breakfast at 7 A.M. one mile South of Winchester where we are at 8½ A.M. Pass through Winchester at 12 M. The rebels chase us up while we run with all our might. I cannot see into these things yet, but suppose all is right. *I* should stop and fight and *whip* or *get whipped.* The Jersey Brigade mostly captured here. Encamp near Sulphur Springs on the Opequon.[28]

Thursday—August 18th, 1864

Up at 3 A.M;—form line of battle on the Opequon Creek. Remain in line two hours, when we take "route step" and pass through Berryville at 10 A.M.[29] The remains of Army wagons, still smoking, in large num-

---

28. The Jersey Brigade had been part of the Union flank guard under Brig. Gen. Alfred T. A. Torbert, when on Aug. 17, Early hit it and inflicted some three hundred casualties. *B&L,* 4:503.

29. "Route step" meaning "route march," a military march used to cover long distances easily. It requires neither silence nor marching in step nor precision in carrying arms.

bers are all about scattered over the place. We lost heavily in transports at this place. Rebels begin to think of giving *us* battle if we do not them. Day rainy. Rebs pressing close. Encamp at 6 P.M.

Friday—August 19th, 1864

Remain in camp all day. We are about four miles from Charlestown on a small creek, do not know the name.[30] The Jersey Brigade came in yesterday not half as badly off as was represented; only one regiment gone. Guns and revolvers found on the premises of the owner of this land. The people *all* disloyal.

Saturday—August 20th, 1864

Still in camp at 8. A.M. Col. Olcott expected to-day. He was one of the loyal officers who were placed under fire in Charlestown. He was exchanged and is to be here soon.[31] We are *foraging* to an awful extent. All kinds of *varmints* are eating us in retaliation. Bought a grey colt of Walrath for $50.00.

Early, who was badly outnumbered and knew it, adopted the strategy of demonstrating as aggressively as possible to keep Sheridan off balance and on the defensive. In one such move, he sent Maj. Gen. Robert Emmett Rodes's infantry division against the Sixth Corps on August 21 near Summit Point. The Union forces withdrew the next day, a move that had been part of Sheridan's plans even before the attack, but which annoyed Holt greatly.

Sunday—August 21st, 1864

Expected to move camp to-day; but instead, the *long roll* sounded.[32] Early is down upon us like mad. Get into line and off in ten minutes. It is astonishing how quick a regiment can up and off, when necessary. We sally out in double quick to repel the attack. They come almost into our tents before we know of their presence. On our way out Lieutenant Van Scoy was shot in the leg. This was intended for *me* as he was close

30. Holt probably camped near or on Cameron Run, which becomes the main waterway through Charlestown. *Atlas*, plate 82-6.

31. After Olcott's injury at the Wilderness, where he was struck in the head by a minie ball, he was captured by Confederates. He was released three months later and rejoined his regiment. His wound had long-lasting effects; after the war, his father had him committed to the New York State Lunatic Asylum for insanity said to be brought on by his wound. Pension and Service Records.

32. "Long roll" meaning military drum roll, sounded as a call to action.

by my side, I mounted, he afoot. The only shot fired just then. They expected an *officer*, but did not get the one they calculated for, so *I* think. Our regiment on picket all day: lost 2 killed and 5 wounded.[33] My stretcher bearers and stretchers *all* gone. The drum corps have to bring off the wounded and bury the dead, an unheard-of thing, so far.[34]

Monday—August 22nd, 1864

Left picket line at 2 o'clock A.M, travel until daylight. Pass through Charlestown. Rebels press closely and attack cavalry at this point. We go into our old quarters on Bolivar Heights and pitch tents. Are ordered out again at 2 P.M. to support the 8th Corps who are engaged with the enemy about a mile from Halltown.[35] Remain all night under arms.

Tuesday—August 23rd, 1864

Have had orders to be ready to march at 4 AM., but at 8 AM. are still in camp. Lieut. Col. Olcott returns to the regiment and assumes command.—A complete overthrow in regimental matters of discipline. Glad to see it. We were getting *demoralized,* I am afraid. Change camp camp and lay it out in regular order. Invited to share tent with the Colonel as I have none. Finally go in with the Quarter-Master Sternberg.[36]

In the following diary entry, Holt records that his health is still failing. He does not mention this condition to his wife in a letter dated the same day. Instead, he relates many events of the fighting near Summit Point.

33. This action, when Confederate General Rodes attacked Sheridan, resulted in 250 Union, 160 Confederate casualties. Hiram Van Scoy mustered in as sergeant with Co. K, Aug. 23, 1862; as second lieutenant with Co. H, May 29, 1863; as first lieutenant with Co. F, June 11, 1864. He recovered from his wound and transferred to Co. G, where he served until discharge (June 25, 1865). Wert, 35; *Annual Report,* 192.

34. Such practices were not entirely unfamiliar in the army, despite Holt's disclaimer. During battles, for example, musicians might work at division hospitals to help set up the tents, carry supplies, and bury the dead. Gillett, 234.

35. Charlestown is southwest of Harpers Ferry. Bolivar Heights is directly west of both Harpers Ferry and Bolivar. Halltown is just north of Charlestown.

36. The demoralization of the Sixth Corps had worried Sheridan since the early days of his command. The losses at Spotsylvania; the apparently aimless wanderings all over the western part of Virginia and Maryland in late July; the heat, dust, and humidity of the marches—all had taken their toll. Sheridan's arrival as commander helped some, and a trickle-down of returning discipline began. Theodore Sternberg mustered in as first lieutenant with Co. E, Aug. 23, 1862, and as quartermaster on Jan. 5, 1863. He served with the 121st until discharge (June 25, 1865). Catton, *Stillness at Appomattox,* 280–81; *Annual Report,* 117.

Wednesday—August 24th, 1864

Feel thankful that we have *less* than a year to serve. What great events have transpired during the two we have been in the service! Who of us will come out alive? Never felt much worse, bodily. My lungs and chest almost used up. I shall have to get out of this soon or lie as thousands do here in the soil of a slave state. Nothing in military line during to-day.

> Camp of the 121st Reg. N.Y. Vols
> near Halltown, Va.
> August 24th, 1864

My dear Wife:—

As you see we are again clear down the Valley a hundred and fifty miles from Strasburg, the last place from which I addressed you. Shall I say that we *retreated* before an inferior force? It looks like it, surely, for all the way down here, they were poking their jokes at us in the shape of shell and shot in a very provoking way. Perhaps it was *strategy* which impelled us to withdraw. I think it was; for of all hard looking places to assail and carry, this was the capshief.[37] It appeared to be as utterly impossible to route them at Strasburg as it is impossible to pass through life and sin not. We did not come directly here, but encamped for a day or two at Charlestown, a place made memorable by the trial, conviction and execution of old "Ossawattamie John Brown," whose soul despite Governor Mason *et. al.* of secession proclivities, keeps moving on.[38] Here Early had the audacity to make a dash upon us in broad day about ten o'clock one Sunday morning when we were washing, shaving, &c. causing us to get up and dash instantly. In less than fifteen minutes, tents were down, horses packed and we in line of battle ready to receive the distinguished stranger. On our way out to meet him, a shot was fired, as I always supposed for me, (being on horseback) and struck Lieutenant Van Scoy in the thigh who was marching close beside me. I sent him to the rear and kept on after dressing his wound. By this time we had got beyond the rebel line, and had to fight our way back again when we established a picket line and held it until that night when we

37. "Capshief" meaning "capsheaf," summit or finishing part.
38. "Governor Mason" was Virginia senator James Mason who questioned Brown after the raid and later demanded a congressional inquiry into the incident. He became Confederate minister to Great Britain and was captured, along with John Slidell, in November 1861 during the infamous *Trent* affair. Nevins, *Emergence of Lincoln*, 86, 115; McPherson, *Battle Cry*, 389–90.

decamped and came to this place of two or three houses, and a depot on the rail road running from Harpers Ferry to Winchester. Ever since we got here, we have been heavily engaged in skirmishing but no general engagement has resulted. The rebels, embolden by our *non-intervension,* have become quite annoying, and they will have to be whipped pretty soon or they will whip us. We have been supporting a part of the Eighth Corps, which as yet have done all that has been.[39] We lost ten killed and several wounded at Charlestown.

Daniel.

Thursday—August 25th, 1864

Still in camp, hardly able to hold up my head. Letters from home. Answer them. Several hard showers to-day. Our tent leaks like a riddle.[40] Completely wet through. Everything soaking wet. General turning in of all extra horses, mules, &c.

Friday—August 26th, 1864

Expected to move early this morning but are still in camp at 9. A.M. A furious attack upon our lines at 5 P.M. but without success on the part of rebels.[41] Heavy storms of rain and wind at night. *Very* sick to-day.

Saturday—August 27th, 1864

Hardly life enough to keep journal or make out weekly report of sick &c. However it is done and sent to Brigade Head Quarters to Dr. Plumb.—I shall have to go myself to General Hospital or get better here, as it is I am very nearly used up—a fit subject for doctoring and nursing—fast breaking down in lungs and bowels.

Sunday—August 28th, 1864

Ordered to break camp and move at 4 A.M. Up at 3 ready to start, but do not move until 7½. Move out towards Charlestown about two miles, and halt until 4 P.M. Heavy guns about six or eight miles in ad-

39. The Eighth Corps, also referred to as the Army of West Virginia, once under Hunter's command, was now under the more capable leadership of George Crook. The corps had originally consisted of the troops of the Department of the Middle, based in Baltimore, but had been expanded to include the forces in West Virginia in 1863. Boatner, 191–92, 549.

40. "Riddle" meaning a coarse-meshed sieve.

41. On Aug. 25–26, Early withdrew from Charlestown, leaving Anderson behind to mask his withdrawal. He moved up the Potomac to try to draw the Union troops away

vance. Take position on (or very near) our encampment of last Sunday, two miles and a half beyond Charlestown.[42] Encamp for the night.

Monday—August 29th, 1864

All day in camp. A battle in front between our own and the rebel cavalry and Breckenridge's Corp (reb) They drive us about 7 miles. Send support and halt them about two miles in front. Our loss must be quite considerable. A barn and contents burned at 11 P.M. Six loaded guns go off in quick succession. This is the place where other guns were found a week ago.

Tuesday—August 30th, 1864

This day in camp. Regimental wagons come up at 12 M. Major Galpin obtains 20 day's leave of absence to go North to excite enlistments for this regiment.[43]

Wednesday—August 31st, 1864

Wall tents erected: for *what* purpose I do not know. We shall have to pull them down again in twenty-four hours, or I am no prophet. Sickness on the increase in the Regiment mostly of a dysentaric character. Still about as sick as I can be without entirely giving up.

Thursday—September 1st, 1864

Nothing important to-day. Mail arrives and bring letters from home. The weather continues hot, although not so insufferably hot as a week or two ago.

As the standoff in the lower valley continued, Holt's health slowly deteriorated. The war, especially the hard fighting in May, the frustration in front of Petersburg, and the grueling marches of the summer had not helped his morale. Even so, his views of the upcoming elections and the possibility of victory showed that he had not lost heart completely.

from the valley by threatening another invasion of Maryland or Pennsylvania. The ruse did not work. By Aug. 27, Early returned to Bunker Hill. Wert, 38.

42. Sheridan's troops were now following Early as he moved south and west. The action here was primarily skirmishing between cavalry. Ibid., 38.

43. On July 18, Lincoln had issued a call for five hundred thousand volunteers in hopes of avoiding another draft before the November elections. Not completely successful, the call for volunteers did provide fresh recruits from August on. McPherson, *Battle Cry,* 758; Allan Nevins, *The War for Union: Organized War to Victory, 1864–1865,* 225 n. 15.

Camp of the 121st Reg, N. Y. Vols
near Charlestown, Va.
Sept. 2nd, 1864.

My dear Wife:—

Last night brought two very welcome letters from home,—one from yourself and one from Gertrude. It really makes me homesick when I hear you talk of home affairs and invite me to dine with you. Nothing would afford me greater pleasure, and to feel sure of doing so without disturbance by those discordant commands to *"fall in!" "pack up!" "march!"* Sometimes I think the time will never come, but I find that day succeds night—the wheels of time keep steadily revolving, season succeeds season, and soon my pilgrimage here will end. Yes, indeed, two years have wrought changes wonderful in me, as in all others now alive after so much excitement, toil and peril. When I entered the service I felt as if I was able to do a great deal for my country, but now the tables are turned and I am (so far as *feelings* are concerned) the mere wreck of a man. As the season advances I have less and less power to cope with its changes, and the cold nights which succeed intensely hot days, produce sad effects upon me. Last night I thought I never should get to sleep for the cold. I have but one blanket, and that a poor, thin one, and to sleep in the open air with nothing over you but the walls of a flie[44] and the blue dome of heaven, dew falling like rain upon you, tells more sensibly upon me this fall than ever before. For ten days past I have hardly been able to hold up my head; but this morning feel some better, and hope to continue to gain. My heart and lungs labor hard to do their work, and my bowels are so deranged as to induce constant desirse to go to stool. This has, as is always the case with me, produced hemorrhoids painful and irritating enough in itself to disqualify me from duty. I only mention this so that you may understand the reason *why* I am, to all appearances, *so demoralized.* Perhaps I have sufficient excuse—perhaps not, at any rate, I feel nearly ready to give up. Dr. Kelly, Medical Director of the Division advises me to go to General Hospital; but no such institution receives one unless it is to act as a stepping stone for discharge from the service; something by the way which I *have* thought of, if I cannot obtain it in any other. I shall make an effort to get out *early,* for I feel confident that a *fall campaign*

44. "Flie" meaning fly—a tarplike canvas protection.

will prove ruinous to my health. Duty, I think, does not require that I should *die* in the service.[45] I think that even *now* some of the officers would consent to my discharge, but as so much uncertainty hangs over our future movements, I suppose the thing impossible at present. Our Corps is expecting to be ordered to City Point again, but no order has reached us to that effect. If I am doomed to Petersburg again, I almost wish I might die now and go to glory; for all places I ever sat foot upon I think this the most repulsive. God spare me from such an event.—I believe I should almost be willing to desert before going there again.— Not one single solitary cheering feature relieves the odious aspect of all things connected with that spot. I shall ever look upon it, as in the Wilderness:—the hell of all my earthly experience. Dear me, what have I not heard, seen and felt upon those fields of carnage. It almost chills my blood, now after months are fled, to look upon it again. Never, no never, let my eyes rest upon that soil again. It is like dragging from the grave the festering, mouldering carcass of your victim and making it your bedfellow. I am, perhaps too sensitive upon the matter but I cannot help it. God has given me the feeling.

The nomination of McClellan for President at the Chicago Convention was expected here, and he will get many votes, but not a majority.[46] Lincoln, for some cause, is not quite as popular as when first elected, but no one can say *why*.—For *my* part, *I* see no reason to change my views with reference to the honest "father of his country," and shall give him my vote and heart as fully and freely as ever. I want peace as much as any other man, but not a *dishonorable* one. We had better fight a year or two longer than submit to disgraceful compromises. The army is receiving *now* what it ought long ago to have received—*men* instead of *money*. I hope another call for 500,000 will be

45. Of the twelve thousand medical officers serving the Union army, over three hundred died during the war. For Holt's resignation to be accepted, he would have to have another physician declare him unfit to serve. Gillett, 275; Pension and Service Records.

46. McClellan's nomination by the Democrats came as no surprise. As the most popular Democrat in the country, McClellan hoped, as did his party, that his days of army glory would translate to political victory. But the Democrats split over the question of pursuing the war. McClellan, who refused to dismiss the army's four years of service as a failure that required new leadership, ran on a Democratic peace platform which did precisely that. McClellan lost. In the end, he looked too much like a Copperhead, peace-at-any-price candidate. Soldiers did vote for McClellan in large numbers but as a whole were even more likely than the general public to vote for Lincoln. McPherson, *Battle Cry*, 760–62, 774–76, 803–6.

made *immediately* upon the heels of this, and the rebellion crushed out this fall. It can be done in three months as well as three centuries if it is only handled as it should be.

Daniel.

Friday—September 2nd, 1864

An addition of about a dozen men to our regiment, eight or ten from hospital and two deserters from other commands, sent here to serve out the balance of their enlistment.

Saturday—September 3rd, 1864

Broke camp and started at 4 A.M. Dispatch read at 10 A.M. that Sherman had taken Atlanta and achieved a most perfect and glorious victory over [Maj. Gen. John B.] Hood—the enemy flying in every direction.[47] Glorious news! The skies begin to brighten. In the eagerness and fullness of my soul, I call upon all that is within me bless the name of God. I will patiently wait the end which cannot be long. At 10½ halt at Clifton and go into camp for the night. This cheering news is enough to make a sick man feel well again. It has so affected me. I feel as if I could endure any hardship if only we see favorable results follow the efforts we put forth to put down this rebellion.

Sunday—September 4th, 1864

Occasional firing upon the left. Constructed breastworks and remain in camp all day. We are much comforted over the news of yesterday. The clouds appear to be breaking. I wonder how a *doubt* could have ever entered on poor desponding hearts as to the final glorious result of the war we are waging to establish the government in righteousness. God pity our poor feeble natures.

Early and Sheridan continued their war of nerves, leaving Holt at a loss as to what would happen next. Early, convinced that Sheridan's inactivity was a sign of lethargy, continued to demonstrate against him, while Sheridan, still believing Early to be stronger, waited for him to send some of his men back to Lee.

47. Atlanta fell to Sherman on Sept. 2, 1864, one day after Hood evacuated the city.

Camp of the 121st Reg. N.Y. Vols
near Clifton, Va., Sept. 5, 1864.

My dear Wife:—

Again we have changed quarters, and again in line of battle. We have been ready for and expected to be attacked at daylight this morning; but at this hour (9 o'clock, A.M.) all is quiet in front. We have been here this makes the third day, and have been twice beset and twice driven them off. Last night the 65th N.Y. (recently added to our Brigade) came near being taken, every man. The regiment had been taken out upon a reconnoisance in the afternoon and proceeded about three miles when they were completely surrounded and cut off from the rest of the Army. The Adjutant came into camp last night reporting the regiment *"gave up,"* he having escaped by leaving horse, *sword,* &c., &c. crossing defiles, woods, fields and every unheard-of place. However, in a short time one after another came dropping in until morning, when at roll call, almost all answered to their names. I think we have no business here. In the first place we are too far from our Stronghold at Charlestown, and the base of our supplies at Harpers Ferry. Our rations are out to-night, and we must either fall back or be supplied by trains coming up; an enterprise, in my opinion fraught with danger, from the fact that our right is wholly open and unsupported, and the direction, above all others, which Early would most naturally take to surprise or give us battle. He has now, after being reinforced, superior in numbers, and has the advantage of position—two points of great importance to an army acting on the defensive. However, he begins to act upon the *offensive* now, since we have played the fool with him until he really thinks we *dare not* attack him in earnest. Perhaps not. We shall see before long. General Sheridan will not risk a battle unless sure of success. It would be killing to have a damper thrown upon the good news from Atlanta. Just now we need *victories,* not *defeats.* But I am no General, and cannot decide such matters. I am feeling a little better than when I last wrote, but still ought to be upon the sick list.

Daniel.

Monday—September 5th, 1864

In camp all day. Nothing new. Raining. Surely *we are* thankful that the dry and parched land has been moistened by *"the tears of heaven."*

All animate nature responds to the genial influence. The fields are clothed in the brightest emerald.

Tuesday—September 6th, 1864

Spent the day as yesterday. All quiet. Supply train arrives from Harper's Ferry and bring mail. Letters from home. Answer them. It is a little *cold*. Fires not uncomfortable yet all are pleased with the change.

Wednesday—September 7th, 1864

Raining. Regimental inspection. Move camp about 40 rods. Letters from wife and Gertrude. It is getting rather uncomfortable in our little shelter tents, but the skies will soon clear and we shall be quite happy again.

Thursday—September 8th, 1864

Pleasant. Nothing new. Hospital attendants cut down from 10 to 4 by order of Col. Olcott. A big breeze in consequence. Those at Division Hospital sent for by a guard. Doctors all protesting. I lose Powers by the operation. Very well. It is strange that *military* men cannot let *medical* alone. We have the Power and *will* have our own way yet. This game has been tried before by Col. Olcott and failed. *It will now.*[48]

Friday—September 9th, 1864

Still in camp with no orders indicating a move. We begin to feel anxious for a move in spite of all we have passed through. What a strange mortal a soldier is, never content—never satisfied.

Saturday—September 10th, 1864

Rainy weather. Time hangs heavily on our hands as we lie thus in camp. We need rest, but *motion* is just as necessary. It does seem to me that a life of inanition is demoralizing to a soldier.[49] A strange and complex creature is man. I hardly have faith in my own sanity.

---

48. Sheridan's medical director, James Ghiselin, had put together a medical organization in the valley based on Letterman's work with the Army of the Potomac. Surgeon-General Barnes was quite cooperative in meeting Ghiselin's requests for supplies. The major problem was a shortage of ambulances, and, as Holt points out, unnecessary interference by military men regarding medical staffing needs. Gillett, 242.

49. "Inanition" meaning lethargy.

Sunday—September 11th, 1864

It is *Sunday* to the Christian world, but not to us. As *such Sunday* does not come to us. I long for the time to come when I shall once more visit the house of God with my family. Raining again to-day.

Monday—September 12th, 1864

The supply train arrives bringing the mail, but *nothing for* me. Cold and rainy. Put up bunk in tent. Feeling some better than a week ago, but still *not* well.

Tuesday—September 13th, 1864

The 2nd Division have gone on a reconnoizane to the front. The enemy reported to have evacuated Winchester. *Very* cold for the season.—Fires needed. We capture about 200 rebs. Any amount of sheep, cattle, pigs and turkeys are driven into camp.

Wednesday—September 14th, 1864

The utmost quiet prevails. No one can conjecture what is to become of us. Some suppose we shall be sent to Petersburg, but *I* cannot see it.

Thursday—September 15th, 1864

The day comes and goes like all the rest—*nothing* to do but to sit in a cold tent and find fault with everything around you.

Friday—September 16th, 1864

Reverend Dr. Adams reports for duty as Chaplain of the regiment.[50] He formerly belonged to the 5th Maine. He is a *good* man and a *smart* one at that. We feel fortunate in securing his services. The 5th Maine is now nearer our hearts than ever. We have always affiliated with them and they with us. Whatever one did was right in the eyes of the other. We shall have better times.

Saturday—September 17th, 1864

Dr. Adams mustered in as Chaplain of the 121st Reg. N. Y. V. Nothing new transpires in the regiment or Army. Never knew *such* a hell in *such* stirring lives as we have had.

50. Sixty-two-year-old John Adams mustered in as chaplain with the 5th Maine. When that regiment had served its term, he was asked to serve with the 121st. He did so until the end, mustering out with the regiment on June 25, 1865. Phisterer, 3428–29. Adams's letters were published in 1890.

Sunday—September 18th, 1864

For the first time in a long while a little stir in camp. Ordered out. Struck tents and prepared to move, but the order was countermanded. Chaplain Adams prays at undress parade. Write several letters to friends.

By September 15, Sheridan had won his waiting game. Kershaw's division and Maj. Wilfred E. Cutshaw's artillery battalion left for Petersburg that morning. Sheridan learned of the move almost immediately and began to plan his attack. He struck Early at Winchester on September 19, catching the Confederates with their divisions strung out over too long a front. Despite the Union's advantages in numbers and position, Sheridan nearly lost the battle due to poor planning and Early's quick response. Only the commitment of Russell's division, his last reserve, saved the day, and with Upton and his brigade in the lead, it broke the last Confederate attack and started Early's army on a retreat that would not end until the Confederates reached Fisher's Hill. Casualties on both sides were heavy, but Sheridan could bear them. Early could not.

Monday—September 19th, 1864

Up at 2 A.M., having orders to march at 3 A.M., Were ready but do not start until 5 A.M. Pass by the right of Berryville and engage the enemy about six miles from Winchester. Whip them the worst they ever were whipped in the world. General Russell killed and General Upton wounded.[51] Drive them six miles—a perfect rout. Capture any quantity of rebels and break them up completely. Never had such a time dressing wounds and running to keep up with flying rebs. Of all skedaddling ever witnessed, this took the lead. Our men *ran* with all their might, charging the demoralized panic stricken set. For once in their lives they *know* they are whipped—yes *skinned alive.* They leave *everything* which can in the least hinder them in getting away from the "d——d Yanks." Glory enough for one day. I am nearly dead with overwork and excitement but can afford to die for such a result.

Tuesday—September 20th, 1864

Start on the war path at 4 A.M. The Jonnies in full retreat up the Valley toward Richmond. They have got enough of *"My Maryland"* this

51. Russell was killed by a shell fragment in the heart; Upton, commissioned brigadier general to rank from May 12, after his courageous work at Spotsylvania, was knocked off his horse by a shell. He refused to go to the hospital and was instead carried about the battlefield on a stretcher so he could continue to direct his men. Warner, 417, 520; Catton, *Stillness at Appomattox,* 297–98.

time.[52] Just to keep them moving we keep our cavalry and light artillery throwing grape and canister at them. It is an awfully exciting time. All we know now, is to *"sail in."* Every man for himself. Thousands of prisoners are brought in or rather we overhaul and send to Winchester. The country is full of graybacks. Every house has more or less concealed. In one house we caught a general in a *case of drawers!* "Upstairs, downstairs, in the Ladies Chamber" we find them stowed away by their loving female friends.[53] It is good to have such just men. After chasing them as no army was ever chased before, through Newtown, Middletown and all the rest of the places, from pure exhaustion and unable to move any longer, we encamp within a mile and a half of Strasburg: our old ground, and what is left of Early's men, are in their old quarters beyond the town.

> Camp of the 121st Reg. N. Y. Vols.
> near Strasburg, Va.
> Sept. 21st, 1864

My dear Wife:—

Here we are again at this old spot, but in very different circumstances from our previous occupation. At that time we were a dispirited and almost broken hearted army of men; but to-day, thank God, one general and universal shout of joy pours from the mouth of all. Once more in truth we can exclaim, "we have met the enemy and they are ours!"[54] The battle of Winchester, fought on the 19th, in which we all participated, will long be remembered as the most signal rout of the enemy and success to our arms which has resulted since this war began. It was a *hard* contest, yet still easy. God appeared to strike terror into their disorganized and shattered columns, and in their flight of miles in which we followed them, they appeared to be intent on one object only, and

---

52. The popular song "Maryland, My Maryland" had two versions of lyrics, one for each side: "We won't succumb to Yankee scum" for the Confederates; "The despot's heel is on thy shore" for the Yankees. Irwin Silber, ed., *Soldier Songs and Home Front Ballads of the Civil War,* 60–61.

53. "Upstairs, downstairs" is part of a Mother Goose nursery rhyme. "Goosey, goosey, gander/whither dost thou wander?/Upstairs, downstairs, in my lady's chamber./There I met an old man/Who would not say his prayers/I took him by the left leg/And threw him down the stairs."

54. Holt was probably trying to impress his wife with the quote made famous by War of 1812 hero Oliver Hazzard Perry. Louisa's father, Charles Willard, had been a veteran of that war.

that was to get out of our way as fast as possible. Oh! Louisa, my life is little worth, when such results follow. With mine, let your heart ascend in grateful praise, to that great and good God who presides and rules over us, that the day star has arisen and the dark clouds of treason driven back. The skies are once more clear. "From the North, from the South, from the East, from the West," one general shout of joy and praise arise. I am *tired* but *happy*. For forty-eight hours my eyes have scarcely known sleep; but I *cannot* sleep; Every fibre of my body and every nerve of my system is alive to the fact that at last we have done something to call out the praise and gratitude of the Nation; and it *has* been acknowledged. The Secretary of war has just telegraphed to us, that the President appreciates it, and thanks us for the effort and sacrifice and has ordered one hundred guns to be fired in Washington to-morrow in commemoration of it. Immediately upon the heels of this, comes an order from our brave and beloved General Grant that one hundred are to be fired in each corps in this department at the same time as those in Washington. What can more thrill and make glad the heart of the poor soldier than this? My heart is full, my eyes are full and I am full to over-flowing. Praise God for it. To Him alone belongeth the glory. We have waited so long and yet so impatiently, and at length the God of Jacob has given us the victory. Let all that is within us praise His holy name. Short sighted, weak and sinful, we have doubted His power and willingness to lead us over the sea of rebellion into the light of freedom. I cannot sufficiently extol and magnify His name, nor with sufficient humility prostrate myself before Him. Forgive me, oh my Savior, for ever distrusting Thy power, or ever rebelling against Thee. My eyes have been beclouded, and my heart has been chilled so that I could not see Thy glory; but today, with clearness Thy hand is seen and my own moral imperfections are made manifest. Let us no longer live in darkness but walk in light, obeying His word as dear children.

It is impossible *now* to state with accuracy the number of prisoners and arms taken; but *thousands* have fallen into our hands, and are still coming in. Since daylight this morning until now. (11 o'clock. AM) General Sheridan has captured one thousand nine hundred, and so it goes.[55] I have seen people run and run hard, but never, since I first

55. Official casualties for Confederates, exclusive of cavalry, were 199 killed, 1,508 wounded, 1,818 missing. Federal losses were 697 killed, 3,983 wounded, 338 missing. Wert, 103.

drew breath, have I seen such panic and confusion take hold of an army. They threw away *everything*—blankets, knapsacks, haversacks, guns—yes, *everything* which could in ever so small a degree, impede their flight. For miles in length the ground was strewn with the most promiscuous assortment of *Yankee*(?) notions.[56] I cannot give you even a slight idea of the *panic* on one side, and *enthusiasm* on the other. Our men worked and fought, and fought and worked, and ran and fought until they could scarcely stand, and only gave over the chase when it became so dark that you could not distinguish between friend and foe.—Wounded men appeared to forget their wounds and sick men their sickness. Everything that had life, upon that day of ours, was full of happy enthusiasm. A wounded Sergeant of ours, as he was being carried to the rear on the shoulders of his comrades, exclaimed as I passed him on my way to the front, that he was shot and might die, "but Oh! Doctor, I am willing to go now! They are all gone! You cannot find them," and with a toss of his cap and a lusty hurrah, he continued on his way. Such was the feeling of all. Not a desponding heart—not a face beclouded by disappointed zeal, but a universal good will and spirit of heroism inspired every breast. As I said at first, we are in our old quarters and the rebs in theirs; but when we shall make an advance, I cannot say. Perhaps to-day, and perhaps not at all; but one thing is certain, and that is, that when we *do* go, it will be with a will and energy not to be outdone. They are in a very strong position and well fortified, and to take it if they hold it as they can, will cost us many a good and loyal life. I understand that a mail will arrive and leave to-day; so I have snatched this opportunity to let you know that I am alive and well. *Just at this very instant* orders have come to be ready to march at a moment's notice, and I must up and pack. So good bye for this time, and God bless you. I will write again the first opportunity.

Daniel.

56. "Notions" presumably meaning small household items such as needles and pins—all in short supply among Confederates. Rebels stripped these items from Yankees who had been imprisoned or killed.

EIGHT

Just about used up

September 21, 1864 – October 21, 1864

*S*heridan intended to follow up his Win-
chester victory by smashing the Confederates who had regrouped at Fisher's Hill.
After advancing as far as Strasburg on September 20, he deployed the Sixth and
Nineteenth corps in front of Early's positions on the 21st, meanwhile sending
his cavalry off to threaten the Confederates' supply lines and positioning Crook's
men to launch a surprise attack the next day. The only fighting at Fisher's Hill
consisted of an attack by several Union regiments, mostly from Gen. James B.
Ricketts's division, against a small knoll in front of the Confederate position
where Early had posted some skirmishers.

Wednesday—September 21st, 1864

But little done to-day, except to establish our lines. The rebs hold the
Pass and will no doubt show fight. Averell's Cavalry have gone around
them, and we shall see what we shall see. At 2 P.M., we the 1st Division
move to the front and form in line of battle. The 19th [Corps] take
position upon our left. 1900 prisoners with 4 battle flags brought in this
morning.[1] Great depression of feeling among the people of the Valley.

*Sheridan attacked Early's overstretched lines at Fisher's Hill on the afternoon of
the 22d. Crook's men hit the exposed left wing of Early's force in the flank and
Ricketts's men attacked it from the front. Maj. Gen. William Emory's men
attacked Early's right on the hill itself and then the rest of Wright's corps,
including the 121st, hit the center. Outflanked and outnumbered, Early's little*

---

1. The 1,900 prisoners referred to are either those captured at Winchester or the
product of a rumor. The action in front of Fisher's Hill on the 21st was little more than
a skirmish; no action between Winchester and Fisher's Hill would have netted such a
large number of prisoners. Wert, 107–15.

army caved in quickly and retreated, falling back first to New Market and then to Brown's Gap and Port Republic, giving control of the valley to Sheridan, who reached Harrisonburg, ten miles to the northwest of Port Republic, on the 25th.

Thursday—September 22nd, 1864

Just at daylight came up with the Brigade which moved to the right at 12 o'clock last night. Lost our way on account of guide not staying to pilot us. *Reduced him to the ranks* in consequence![2] At 12½ rapid and heavy firing heard in the rear of the enemy. No doubt it is Averell and his men rapping for admission.[3] We shall *pitch in* soon, I have no doubt. Remain in camp until 5 o'clock P.M., when a general forward movement is ordered. We go. We drive them out of their holes as a weasel would a rat. No order on their *going!* What little is left from Winchester will be gobbled up at Strasburg. *Such* grounds and such works a thousand men ought to hold against 50,000; but Jacob's God is with us. He is fighting our battles, and to Him I bow in humble reverence. No, not to *man,* but to *God* belongs the glory. We capture 20 guns of all calibre—from a three inch steel gun to a 32 [pounder] siege piece. Our loss as a regiment, during both fights cannot be much. We are fortunate indeed for we were in the very teeth of all. I halt that night in the hollow at a brick house beside a grist mill. Find many wounded and dress their wounds. Among them two likely boys from the 122nd N.Y.[4] They are badly wounded and pray to be put out of their misery by bleeding or any other means but of course I cannot do it. I dress their wounds as well as I can and send them to the rear in the morning.

Friday—September 23rd, 1864

Early this morning, before light, take up the line of march to overtake the regiment which continues its pursuit all night. Had good luck last night in obtaining *bedding cheap.* Pass a station on the rail road at 10, through Maurytown at 11 AM., and Woodstock at 12 M. Found the regiment halted at a stream just outside the town. At 2 P.M. again on

2. "Reduced him to the ranks" meaning demoted an officer to the rank of an enlisted man. In this case, where Holt referred to a guide, it may simply mean dressing him down or relieving him of his special status.

3. Holt is presumably referring to the flanking move Crook was to execute. Averell's cavalry took part in that maneuver. Wert, 117–20.

4. The 122d N.Y. was from Onondaga County, organized at Syracuse. Phisterer, 3439.

the move and encamp for the night at Edenburg.[5] We are constantly picking up men, destroying their arms, and sending them to the rear. Just about used up all of us.

Saturday—September 24th, 1864

Again on the move at 6 A.M. We have an object to move for now, and it is not so disagreeable as when to all appearance, we had none. At 9 AM. passed a reb burial ground of 300 graves, belonging to hospitals at Mount Jackson, which we pass half an hour later. Here we find our friends waiting for us: but a few shots sets them whirling again and we follow up fast as we can. Arrive at New Market at half-past three, the rebs in full run up the Valley trying to save what little there is left. Shell them. They skedaddle fast as their legs can carry them. Our men marched *six* miles without a halt, and some of the time on *double quick* at that. *"No time for chat"* as the demoralized soldier said at New Orleans, during the last war. Never since I was born, did I have such *real sport* in following up a band of disorganized flying rebels. It pays for all our hard marches and sleepless nights. Caryl came near getting killed by a shell.[6] Never saw a man turn *quite* so white as he. He says he will not follow me up so close again. Encamp for night on picket line.

Sunday—September 25th, 1864

Rebels far away on the—road—not below as we expected last night. Our men in *high* spirits. General Torbert reported to have whipped the rebel cavalry in Luray Valley.[7] At 8½ Pass through Sparta, and Harrisonburg at 3 PM. Encamp for the night on a hill half a mile to the East of the town. The rebs have somehow got away from us, and we are letting them run as the boy did the molasses. Our men have a great time in *foraging!* is that the word. I should think so by the quantities of tobacco, &c, &c. which they bring in. *Dry goods,* some how or other get into their hands too.[8]

5. Edenburg is on the Manassas Gap Railroad, halfway between New Market and Strasburg.

6. Mose H. Caryl, mustered in as sergeant with Co. I on Aug. 23, 1862, served with the 121st through the end of the war. *Annual Report,* 30.

7. Gen. Alfred Torbert was sent with most of the Union cavalry to advance up the Luray Valley to the east and cut off Early from the rear. While Torbert was able to drive the Confederate cavalry before him and advance up the valley, he did not do so quickly enough to catch Early in the rear, much to Sheridan's disgust. Wert, 130–32.

8. "Dry goods" meaning textiles, fabrics, notions. It is unclear if Holt means this or is using slang for another term.

Monday, September 26th, 1864

    A day of *rest* in every sense of the word. In camp all day. We need it.

In the Shenandoah Valley
at Harrisonburg [Va.]
Sept. 26, 1864.

My dear Wife:—

    I last wrote you while lying before Strasburg after our battle at Winchester. I now write you from this place, after *another,* if anything more decisive and important at Strasburg. Thursday, September 22nd will be memorable, as well as the 19th for a successful engagement— an engagement wherein the loss was almost entirely on one side—that of the rebels. The situation at Strasburg was one of the most perfectly fortified places by nature I ever saw, while the works thrown up were such as ought to resist a long and heavy siege if properly manned and defended. *Our* army could have held it against the combined attacks of the entire Southern army. Because they were demoralized to such an extent that a Regiment of old women with broom sticks could have driven them out, not because they were really *compelled* to leave, did we set them to flying like wild sheep over the country. At five o'clock P.M., a general forward movement was ordered and in a short time the report of rifles upon the right gave notice that the ball had opened in that quarter. Soon the action extended along the whole line, and as we pressed forward a shout, such as always heralds a charge, rose upon the air. Here the excitement became intense, as all knew that to carry these works, defended both by nature and wit, as none others were, would require a courage, skill and determination worthy the spirit of the Revolution. But the last hours of the Rebellion are drawing nigh. God has struck terror into the heart of our foes, and we are driving them everywhere before us. Upon the right, upon the left, in front and all around, rises that unmistakable cheer of victory! Scarcely is the signal given for a charge before they turn and flee as if pursued by the avenging arm of the Almighty. Guns loaded to be used against us are captured and their deadly contents thrown with un- erring precision into their terror stricken ranks. Men dismayed and seeking safety in flight, throw down their arms and cry for quarter! Generals in vain rally their men, and for a moment stand against the shock; but in the next, a broken straggling mass is all that is left of the *flower of the South.* The mountain gorge becomes filled with detached portions of artillery, cavalry and infantry. Broken down wagons, as they attempt to escape over the turnpike road, dismounted cannon with caissons obstruct the passage while our men hasten on the retreat and more perfectly complete the panic by firing into the frightened, hungry throng, the missils intended for our own destruction. Surely, *such* a sight is seldom seen. Scarcely in the history of man has such complete wreck been made of an over-confident rebel army. Thousands more are added to those men we captured on the 19th at Winchester.—It seems to me that *now* they will get out of here as quickly as possible and join their comrades at Richmond, which they can do if so disposed. Our loss, as a Regiment, thus far in the Valley, is not much:—not more than fifty in killed, wounded and missing, while we have gained a name and character in the army of which any command might well be proud.[9]

In spite of all I could do, being mounted at that, the brigade got ahead of me as much as six miles during the night. I stopped at a house in a deep ravine where the wounded were brought and dressed their wounds until two o'clock in the morning, when I stretched myself to rest under the stoop of the house. Here the captured rebels were brought also, and placed in the barn yard *with the rest of the cattle* and a guard placed over them. Shall I tell you how *I* captured a rebel Major? Well, I certainly brought one in, captured or not. I found him skulking among the rocks and bushes, and supposing I had a right, walked him into quarters. "Who goes there?" I exclaimed, it being dark, and I seeing that his uniform indicated being rebel. No answer was returned until repeating it, he answered, "a Confederate Officer wounded in the foot." "How came you here?" He replied "damn this old horse and this rocky hole, if it had not been for them, you would not be asking me that question! My horse fell and threw me off among those rocks, and came near breaking my neck. As it is I reckon my foot is smashed." After a few more words I took him into the kitchen, placed a guard over the Major (for so he proved to be) and proceeded to dress the wounds as they came in.

My man Halligast did a pretty thing for me this night.[10] As you recollect, I told you that my blankets were old and worn, and I was

9. The 121st lost fifteen men at Winchester and five at Fisher's Hill. *OR,* vol. 43, 1:112–20.

10. "My man Halligast" is unclear; Holt seems to be referring to his resident horse thief and man (servant), John Walrath. Holt's horse's name is given as Frank Halligas (see May 6, 1864 diary entry); Walrath provided Holt with a number of purloined horses. See also Oct. 15, 1864, diary entry.

sleeping cold on these frosty nights. It is the usual custom on such occasions as this, to look around a little and see if there is nothing which will be of benefit to you.—So going down cellar (unbidden), he came back reporting it filled with all manner of goods, packed in bales, boxes and bundles. "Are there any *blankets* there?" says I. *"Yes, lots of them!"* "Then get me two or three." This he did, handing through the window (this was the way of ingress) a pair of nice new woolen coverlets warm and comfortable just the thing for a [chilly?] night like this, and not bad ones to bring home as relics of the Rebellion.—It proved that the cellar *was* full indeed; for here were bales of quilts and blankets stolen from the people of Maryland on their raid into that State. Saddles, harness and almost everything of that sort was here, all once the property of loyal men. This being the case, we thought it no robbery to appropriate six large loaves of beautiful bread about the size of a half bushel, a roll of new butter, five apple pies, a jar of apple butter, a jug of Sorgum syrup and a *wash board*. From the Mill (for this was the house of a Miller) we got a sack of wheat flour, and one of Graham to make pan cakes of. All this for *my* mess; while the boys went in for their share, while I fear after helping themselves to, will leave but a small portion for the family when they get back, as most of them have fled, and I do not know as I can blame them after witnessing what they have of the valor of their men. The citizens believe, and they cannot be persuaded otherwise, that our force is at least as great as one hundred and twenty thousand and this force led by Grant in person.[11] They assert that *no other* man man could have driven Early out of the Valley. All manner of excuses but the right one, are made, for the mortifying event, and all kinds of evil prognosticated of us. The women are particularly hostile and wolfish.

This Valley is one of the most lovely the eye ever rested upon. For miles and miles away, almost a garden stretches out before you.—If ever a people *ought* to be happy and prosperous, it is the people of this region. No richer or better soil can be found, and no signs except those of thrift and easy luxury can be seen. At Mount Jackson, our boys did an act which must be condemned by every lover of humanity. They burned a hospital in which there were a few sick men. Of course the sick were removed, but the act of destruction of their hospital building

11. Sheridan's troops in the Valley campaign numbered 37,000 when his attack on Winchester began, versus Early's 15,000. By Strasburg, Early had lost 4,000 men. McPherson, *Battle Cry,* 777.

ought to be punished by death.[12] None but heathen will thus mar the beauty of civilization. Stonewall Jackson had endeared himself to his people, and won our respect by erecting five comfortable structures like the one destroyed, and in burying the dead in well laid out ground.

Daniel.

Tuesday—September 27th, 1864

Still in camp at 11 o'clock AM. Supply trains arrive but no mail. We have to haul supplies 150 miles by horse and mule power. Receive orders at 10 P.M. to be ready to start to-morrow morning at half-past four. We are about equal distance from Washington, Richmond and Harpers Ferry.

Wednesday—September 28th, 1864

Up in time and ready to start at the hour designated last night, but at 6 still in camp. General orders read in Regiment relative to maurauding.[13] Orders for marching countermanded and we pitch tents again. Orders again at night to be ready for a move at 5 to-morrow morning.

Grant's original orders to Sheridan had been to destroy Early's army and then to lay waste to the Valley, to eliminate the major source of foodstuffs for Richmond and the Confederate army at Petersburg. Following Winchester and Fisher's Hill, the remnant of Early's force was no longer a serious threat, and Sheridan set about the business of destroying crops, tanneries, mills, and anything potentially useful to the Confederate war effort.

Thursday—September 29th, 1864

Strike tents at 6 A.M. and move out upon the Staunton Pike. We move five miles to Mount Crawford and suddenly bring up on account of bridges being burned by the citizens. In retaliation, we burn their stacks, houses and fences. A prettier or more fruitful Valley never lay

12. Mount Jackson is about twenty miles south of Strasburg, along the Manassas Gap Railroad and the North Fork of the Shenandoah River. There was a cavalry action there on Sept. 24, and Sheridan's report mentions finding several Confederate hospitals in the area full of wounded, but it does not mention burning any of them, nor do the reports of the cavalry commanders or of the Confederates. *OR*, vol. 43, 1:27.

13. Grant's order came on Aug. 26, 1864: "Do all the damage to railroads and crops you can. If the war is to last another year, we want the Shenandoah Valley to remain a barren waste." Ibid., 1:917.

stretched out upon the face of the Earth than this. It goes to destruction by order of General Grant.

Friday—September 30th, 1864

Remain in camp all day waiting for bridges to be built. It might in truth be said that we are *foraging* to an awful extent. Nothing that lives and is used as food or in anywise conduces to the comfort of men, is left behind. We take *all* we can and *burn* what we cannot get away. The entire drum Corps march a circle with a rail upon their backs for one hour after taps, for being tardy in sounding calls.[14]

Saturday—October 1st, 1864

Start on the back track at 4 P.M. Arrive at Harrisonburg at 5 P.M. and encamp. Supply trains arrive with mail but not distributed.

Probably the most controversial event of Sheridan's Valley campaign was the death of Lt. John R. Meigs. He was the son of Q.M. Gen. Montgomery Meigs of the Union army and during the Valley campaign was attached to Sheridan's staff. Reported killed in early October, it was thought at first that the twenty-two-year-old Meigs was murdered by guerrillas. It was not discovered until the war was over that he died trying to evade his captors. Nonetheless, Sheridan ordered the burning of every house and barn for five miles around the village of Dayton, Virginia, in retaliation for Meigs's death. Sheridan quickly thought better of this and countermanded the order in time to save the village itself, but a number of houses and barns had already been burned.

In camp at Harrisonburg, Va.,
October 2nd, 1864.

My dear Wife:—

I have just received a letter from you dated on the 18th of last month, for which accept thanks. No recent letters arrived owing to the length of time necessary to transport supplies from the front. Here we are, one hundred and twenty miles up the Valley, and all the army have to be fed by food hauled from Harpers Ferry, in wagons. Our trains keep running all the while and to guard them requires quite a little army. You can, perhaps form some idea of the magnitude of

---

14. Holt refers to a common method of punishment, carrying a heavy split log rail around on one's shoulders. Billings, 144.

feeding this vast concourse of people, when I tell you that *one train* was *eight* miles in length, and of necessity have to move slowly. Gurillas are constantly hanging on our outskirts picking off stragglers and doing such mischief as they can. No longer ago than day before yesterday, a party of Mosby's men came down upon the train as they were on their way in, and killed *nine* of our men by shooting. After robbing and stripping them naked, they cut their throats and left them on the road side, a spectacle horrible to behold by all who might chance to see them. About the same time, Captain Meigs, (son of Quarter Master General Meigs,) Dr. Ohlenschlager and a Major whose name I now forget, were shot and killed by these same men. Riding in front of the train a short distance, suspecting no evil, they were suddenly beset by a gang who lay concealed, and commanded to surrender. Throwing the lines over their horses necks they were commanded to give up their arms. Having none they of course could not comply, when these villians deliberately shot them through their heads and after robbing them, left for the mountains. Dr. Ohlenschlager lived to get into camp, but the others died instantly.[15] What is to be done with such a heathenist set? The country is full of such lawless miseries. An order from General Grant has been issued to General Sheridan to lay waste and utterly destroy everything which can support an Army. In the execution of this sentence, the Cavalry are at work burning barns, stacks, mills and factories of all kinds. Yesterday one regiment burned no less than 119 barns, besides firing every stack of grain which lay in their way. You can form no idea of the gloom which overspreads the whole region. One heavy, black cloud of smoke hangs over the Valley like the pall of death. Lurid streaks of flame dart up through the pitchy blackness relieving for a second or two the stately building which is being devoured by hungry flames.

One village, *Dayton,* has been burned, and every house within five miles of it, in retaliation of the murder of the three officers whose death I have just mentioned. Thousands of head of cattle, horses, sheep, &c., are being driven off, and such as cannot be thus conveyed away, are shot upon the spot. The inhabitants look on like doomed culprits while their property is destroyed before their eyes. A stoical indifference appears to have taken possession of them as regards their fate. No resistance is

15. Holt's account of Meigs's death may have combined more than one Confederate ambush. Sheridan reports the death of Meigs on Oct. 7, but reports the attack on Ohlenschlager as having happened on the 11th. *OR,* vol. 43, 1:30–32; Wert, 145.

made to any act which we see fit to commit. They appear to think that
their day has come, and nothing but death or starvation is in store for
them. It is hard to look upon this wholesale destruction—laying waste
the most beautiful Valley the sun ever shone upon in a tract a hundred
and twenty miles in length from six to twelve in beadth. Here the rebel
army have found a garner[16] for their corn, wheat, oats, &c., and here
the Union Army have met with more serious and frequent disasters
than in any other part of the Confederacy.

The hardest feature in this universal confligration is, that many real
innocent and Union-loving people suffer. These, as everywhere, are
poor—less able to stand the pressure than the more opulent.
Hundreds of such are leaving their homes in groups of a dozen or
twenty. Some in better circumstances than others, pick up their little
all, and placing it in an old rickety democrat wagon, drawn by an
animal pitiful to behold, while the greater part come straggling on
Gipsey like, fed by our boys from provisions in their haversacks; sometimes riding in a Government wagon, sleeping out as none others can,
with scanty covering, either of bedding or clothing. One family followed our regiment all through the Valley. They appeared to have
adopted us, and we them. This family consisted of Father, Mother and
six children—one a grown up daughter who carried in her arms her
little nursing sister, while the mother led by each hand a wee bit of a
half-naked, hatless, shoeless boy, just able to keep from under the
wheels of passing ambulances, batteries, &c. This was a fair specimen
of *"poor white trash"*—a set of men and women far less attractive than
the poorest Negro.[17] Snuff-dipping, tobacco-chewing and smoking
creatures filled with domestic whisky when they can get it—trading
with and consorting with slaves who look upon them as inferiors, such
as they *really* are.—No people, or set of people I ever met with, so de-
serveve our pity, or need the influences of religious instruction,
conjoined with free schools.

Our hearts were made happy by good news from our brothers at
Petersburg. General Grant has telegraphed his success to us, and now

16. "Garner" meaning a granary.

17. "Poor white trash" meaning poor, uneducated, nonslaveholding white Southern-
ers. In the social hierarchy of the South, poor white trash were above all blacks but below
all other whites. For many black elite slaves, however, poor white trash were socially
unacceptable and below even the slaves. Charles Reagan Wilson and William Ferris, eds.,
Encyclopedia of Southern Culture, 1138–39.

we begin to feel that the days of the rebellion are numbered.[18] It may, and probably will live for a death struggle, but that struggle will surely come before long. A strong man dies hard. Fearful will be the contortions to witness, but the strong arm of the Republic will shield us from harm.

As a matter of course, you are fully posted as to our operations in this department. I cannot tell you any better than has already been done. If others do as well as we, it will not be long before Davis & Co. will knock for admission into the circle from which he has debarred himself. Let the blows come thicker and faster until the deed is done. If even at this hour, we shall succeed in the accomplishment of the great object for which we waged this war, it will be the proudest day in our history. And *I* believe we shall. A year from to-day will see the volunteer arm of the Army mustered out of service, and then if we have accounts to settle with England or France, bring them forward.[19]

Daniel.

Sunday—October 2nd, 1864

Rations distributed. Mail opened. Letter from wife and Gertrude. Answer both. Preaching in the afternoon by Chaplain Adams. Prayer meeting in the evening. Adjutant Weaver takes a part in the exercises. I am glad of it.

Monday—October 3rd, 1864

Orders came last night to move this morning at half-past five o'clock. The orders countermanded, and we remain in camp all day. Rainy, as it has been for three days past. Capt. Meigs, Dr. Ohlenschlagger and a Major whose name I have forgotten, killed by gurillas as they (the officers) were riding a short way in advance of the supply train. A cool unprovoked murder after they had surrendered.

---

18. In order to prevent Lee from detaching more troops to the valley, Grant launched a new series of attacks on Lee's lines at Petersburg during Sept. 29–Oct. 2. These attacks resulted in limited gains, which were probably significantly exaggerated in the early reports reaching the Union army in the valley. Wert, 142.

19. Holt's opinion that England or France might still intervene in the war was by now insupportable. Once the Emancipation Proclamation went into effect, England's working classes would not allow the British to support the South with its attendant institution of slavery; the French would not act unilaterally to support the South. The Union's victory at Gettysburg had put the nail in the coffin for both British and French proponents of the Confederacy. McPherson, *Battle Cry,* 552–57, 650–51.

Tuesday—October 4th, 1864

Regiment detailed to go on picket, the first time in a long while. The country laid waste for five miles around in retaliation of the murder of Capt. Meigs and party. They were on General Sheridan's staff.

With the campaign apparently over and victory in sight at last, Holt allowed himself to make his first move in an effort to terminate his enlistment with the 121st New York. His health was no better, and he felt he must leave the army at this point or die in the service.

Wednesday—October 5th, 1864

In camp all day, feeling of *all* men the most miserable.— Sent for Dr. Plumb to give me a certificate of disability on which to base an application for discharge from the service.[20] Did not come, but promised to do in the morning. Fitted up camp. Orders to move at 5½ in the morning.

Having completed the devastation of the lower end of the Valley, Sheridan began a slow withdrawal northward, destroying everything of military value along the way. Grant had hoped that Sheridan would take a bolder course and move on the rear of Lee's position at Petersburg, but he failed to talk Sheridan into it. Instead, he agreed to Sheridan's plan to lay waste to the Valley and then bring most of the Union forces over to Petersburg via Washington.

Thursday—October 6th, 1864

Move out at 6 A.M. Pickets drawn in. Passed Mauryville at 9½. Sparta 10½ A.M., New Market at 3 P.M., and encamp three miles north of the town. Paymaster Robinson here, and pays off the men in the evening. He is evidently very glad to get rid of his money as the gurillas are sadly in need of greenbacks.

Friday—October 7th, 1864

Ordered to be on the move at 7 A.M. Move out at the hour, but wait three hours to let the 8th and 18th Corps cross the river. Pass through New Market at 10½. The whole Valley in a blaze. Heavy dark clouds of smoke hang over it like a funeral pall. Cannot [help] but [feel] compas-

20. Dr. S. Hiram Plumb, an assistant surgeon with the 24th N.Y., was later promoted to surgeon of the 82d N.Y. Willard, 10.

sionate [for] the case of the poor deluded people.—Pass through Hawkinsville at 11½ A.M., Edenburg at 3 P.M. Gurillas burn a bridge over the river causing considerable delay in crossing. It only makes our work the lighter. Took dinner just outside the town. Passed through Woodstock at 6 P.M. and encamp two miles North of the town.[21]

Saturday—October 8th, 1864

Started at 7 A.M. Arrive at Hawkinsville at 10 A.M. Reach old quarters at Strasburg about 12½ and encamp. I had no idea of the *natural* strength of the position until now. Started resignation papers. Strasburg is a miserable delapidated town, fit only for snuff-dipping tobacco smoking females such as inhabit it. The first *snow storm* of the season. Mail arrives bringing letters.

> In camp at Strasburg, Va.,
> October 8, 1864.

My dear Wife:—

I have just time to say to you that we arrived here this afternoon and we are encamped for the night. It is very cold—a storm of *hail* and *snow!* flying. We probably shall start again on our way up the Valley, in the morning. The paymaster has come and gone, much to the relief of our boys who were in the need of greenbacks.—Our march from Harrisonburg to this place was one of disagreeable coldness. The weather is becoming decidedly unpleasant. I hope we shall soon finish up and go into quarters for the winter, if that is to be. If not, "let the hurricane roar—it will the sooner be o'er," and we shall be among our friends again. The thought is refreshing after two years and a half steady marching and counter-marching. Perhaps we shall make a *flank movement* into New-York State before you are aware of it. If the entire Army does not, it may well be that *I* shall be thus transferred. I shall try for it, as my health is very poor. My lungs are *very* sore and a cough distressingly severe is a constant attendant. I *must* leave the service soon, or die in it. There is no use disguising the fact that I am daily running down. My friends advise the step, and I cannot look upon it with disfavor. I have spent the time in faithfulness to my men, and now that there appears to be a lull in war matters, I think I had better turn my thoughts homeward while I have the

---

21. Woodstock is located five miles north of Edenburg.

strength to do so. I am writing this by fire light on my knee, and if you cannot make out the pencil marks, believe it comes from the same old hand and heart. I will inform you if anything important transpires. The mail is about to leave and I must close. How you can endure such letters is a mystery to me, written as many are, when the body is full of suffering, but after all there is a pleasure in it. Give my love to mother and the little ones. I hope it will not be long before I shall be able to tell you that my resignation has been accepted and I [am] about coming home.

Daniel.

Sunday—October 9th, 1864

All day in camp. Weather intensely cold. Wind blowing a gale from the North West. Chaplain Adams preached a short sermon. Almost frozen.

Monday—October 10th, 1864

6th Corps began its move to Front Royal at 8 A.M.[22] Start without previous notice. *Some* lose their breakfast, *others* stay to get it. *I* had mine. Arrive at our encampment 2 miles this side of the village at 2 P.M. Marched 12 miles. Company *"C"* for cheering derisively, are made to carry rails upon their backs for two hours, while some are tied up by their thumbs.[23] Colonel Olcott must look out how he orders a whole company to be thus punished. Weather awfully cold.

Tuesday—October 11th, 1864

A report prevails that we have captured four guns from the Outlaw Mosby, killed fifty-nine of his murderous gang. *No prisoners were taken!*[24] Our men in fine spirits—every one a host in himself. Remain in camp all day.

22. The Sixth Corps' move to Front Royal was intended to be the first leg of its trip to Washington and Petersburg.

23. "Tied by thumbs," usually to a tree limb overhead, was a common punishment. The prisoner would gain relief only by standing on tiptoe, since his arms were usually stretched out to their limits either overhead or to the side. Robertson, 133.

24. Holt's report is probably a rumor or an exaggeration. While Mosby's men suffered occasional checks in the valley, the only time when a large group of them was routed was on Sept. 23, when a party attacking a supply train unexpectedly ran up against an entire brigade of Union cavalry. Several of his men were captured and later executed, leading to reprisals and counterreprisals over the following two months. Wert, 150–55.

Wednesday—October 12th, 1864

Still in camp at 12 M. No move indicated. Raining and unpleasant. Regimental inspection at 1 PM. Trains arrive and rations issued. The gurillas to-day kill several officers after surrender, and seven cavalrymen.[25] Head Quarter mail captured. Ordered to move at 6 o'clock to-morrow morning.

Contrary to Sheridan's expectations, Early had not yet given up the fight. Having been reinforced by Kershaw's division, Cutshaw's artillery (the same units withdrawn before Winchester), and a small force of cavalry under Brig. Gen. Thomas Rosser, Early had shadowed Sheridan back through Strasburg, and on October 13 took up a position opposite the Union encampments at Cedar Creek, causing Sheridan to bring the Sixth Corps back the next day.

Thursday—October 13th, 1864

Up at 4 AM. Breakfast at 5, and start at 9 A.M. We are to be rear guard. Pass through White Post at 12 M. and arrive at Mill Wood, near Manassas Gap at 4 P.M., where we were halted and face about and encamp at Mill Wood. Couriers arrive ordering this move. All our trains are up, having started from Winchester to join us on the march for *I* think Washington, and from thence by transports to Petersburg. An unaccountable order surely. We hear heavy firing at Sundown in the direction of Strasburg.

Friday—October 14th, 1864

Start on the back track at 3 A.M. and march until 9½ A.M., when we halt for breakfast. At 12 M. arrive at Newtown and at 2½ at Middletown and encamp one mile South of the town near our old encampment when we first entered the Valley. Saw several boys from Newport who were newly enlisted in the heavy artillery, among whom were James Herendeen and Henry Brown.[26]

25. Both Union and Confederate forces committed their share of atrocities during this campaign, although some of the reports, including the one of Meigs's death, were inaccurate or exaggerated. Gen. George Custer's cavalrymen shot and hanged suspected guerrillas without trial; Mosby promised retaliatory executions, a promise approved by Lee and Confederate Secretary of War James A. Seddon. Mosby never would be captured. He and his Rangers served until they disbanded Apr. 21, 1865. Wert, 152–55.

26. Neither James Herendeen nor Henry Brown appear in the official registers of the war.

Saturday—October 15th, 1864

Remain in camp all day. Frank Halligast, my man, went out foraging and was captured by Provost guard—his plunder all confiscated, and he sent under arrest to Corps Head Quarters. *I* thought the gurillas had him together with two of my horses, and all their accoutrements. The horses are given up at last, and he released.

Holt's medical leave was finally approved in mid-October, and he was able to settle his accounts and join the newly discharged 95th Pennsylvania en route to Washington on the first leg of his journey home.

Sunday—October 16th, 1864

The 95th Pa goes home to-day, their term of enlistment having expired. I wish I could get off with them. *I finally go!!!* Resignation papers come in at 9 and I start at 10½. Sold my riding horse to Lieut. Weaver for $250. Settled up mess [a/c?] with Dr. Slocum and then put out pell mell on the road for Winchester. Stop with Quarter Master Sternberg over night. Came near being gobbled up by gurillas as the regiment had the start of the three hours, and the country open. It was hard work to overtake them twelve miles out of camp.

Monday—October 17th, 1864

Started at 7 A.M. Escorted out of town by a band playing home sweet home. Bid farewell to Army friends and Army life.—It is hard to part with them all after so many mutual hardships and reverses. Pass through Bunker Hill at 12 M. Take dinner at a secesh house near Darkville and arrive at Martinsburg at 5 P.M. Travel 22 miles to-day. Sleep at a hotel and find the room full of rats. Cannot get transportation on my resignation papers. The 95th Pa encamp for the night near depot. Martinsburg is quite a city—equal to Utica—more of a place than I imagined. It does not seem possible that I am now a *civilian* in soldier's clothes.

Tuesday—October 18th, 1864

Load my baggage on board the cars at 6 A.M. Get breakfast, pay for lodging and start from Martinsburg at 7 A.M. Arrive in Baltimore at 7. P.M. Put up at 92 E. Baltimore Street. Send trunk and baggage home. Remain in the city all day and encamp for the night.

Wednesday—October 19th, 1964

Start from Baltimore at 10 AM. Arrive in Washington at 1 PM. Put up at National. Go to Surgeon General's Office and get blanks necessary to settle up my accounts with that department. Go to R. L. Ream's in the evening. Do not see Morallee. I think Washington the meanest hole I was ever in, for one of such consequence to the world.

Thursday—October 20th, 1864

Up and dressed at 6 A.M. and am writing this at that hour. Now for breakfast. Settled all my accounts at the Surgeon General's Office and receive final pay $162.00. Pay bill of $5.50 at National and spend the evening and night at the house of Thomas Morallee. I am finally clear of the army in every respect, and ready to go home.

Friday—October 21st, 1864

Take the 7½ o'clock Express for New-York bidding farewell to all in Washington and the army, and bring up at my home in Newport after an absence of two years and three months, very much to *my own*, if not to that of others satisfaction. Adieu to hard tack, salt horse and stone pillows.

When he returned to the Mohawk Valley in late October 1864, he was simply "Dr. Holt, Physician." Setting his sword and green sash aside, he wanted only to take up again the role he had played in the community twenty-six months earlier—a country doctor. Unfortunately, Holt's health prevented him from resuming medical practice.

Finding it difficult to support his family, he applied for a government pension in 1867, blaming his troubles on those dreadful days and nights at Rappahannock Station in November 1863, followed by the Mine Run campaign in December. Bronchial and lung trouble, along with an "impaired function of the Alimentary Canal," had left Holt bedridden.[27] By June 1867, when he made a sworn statement for his pension, Holt described his sufferings with the classic symptoms of tuberculosis: night sweats, coughing up blood and pus, and the formation of frequent abscesses. For a year a throat infection made his voice so faint that talking could only be accomplished through low whispers. Although he wrote in his pension application that the warm weather had brought enough improvement to his health that he was in hopes of a partial recovery, he died a

27. Daniel Holt, Deposition for Pension, Pension and Service Records.

little over a year later on October 15, 1868, at the age of forty-seven. He was buried in the family plot in the Protestant cemetery in Newport, New York.[28]

Holt's sword now hangs on display at the Masonic Lodge in Newport. The plaque with it reads:

This sword which was once the property of the late Daniel M. Holt, M.D. was taken from him when a prisoner during the War of the Rebellion, May 4, 1863. During his ten days imprisonment he made the acquaintance of General Robert E. Lee, who was a Mason, and who, upon becoming aware of the fact that the prisoner was also a member of the Order, released him. He also returned all his personal belongings including this sword which Dr. Holt, upon his return home, presented the Newport Lodge No. 455 F. and A.M. of which he was a member.

Mary Louisa Holt, who saved the letters Daniel had written to her, and who cared for him during his illness, collected from the government a widow's pension of seventeen dollars a month. She died on November 9, 1894, at the age of seventy-one. Their only son, Willard, entered the medical profession and set up practice in Newport. He died at the age of thirty-five, on January 17, 1894, eleven months before his mother's death. Isabel Holt, Louisa and Daniel's daughter, married Raymond Ferguson, a Methodist minister from Dekalb, New York.[29] *Before her death in 1930, at the age of seventy, Isabel presented to the Herkimer County Historical Society the bound volume of her father's remarkable letters, guaranteeing their survival so that Daniel Holt's original goals would be met—that his letters survive, that the facts be related, that times such as these might never be seen again.*

28. Pension and Service Records; *Herkimer Democrat,* Oct. 28, 1868.

29. Pension and Service Records; *Herkimer Democrat,* Nov. 9, 1894, Jan. 31, 1894; Willard and Walker, 289.

Bibliography

Manuscript Collections

Daniel Holt Papers. Herkimer County Historical Society, Herkimer, N.Y.
Clinton Moon Papers. Herkimer County Historical Society, Herkimer, N.Y.
Emory Upton Collection. Genesee County Department of History, Batavia, N.Y.

Primary Sources

Board of Supervisors 1856. Ilion, N.Y., 1857.
Board of Supervisors 1857. Herkimer, N.Y., [1858].
Board of Supervisors 1862. Little Falls, N.Y., 1863.
Boyd, Belle. *Belle Boyd in Camp and Prison*. Ed. Curtis Carroll Davis. New York: County Clerk's Office, [1865].
Davis, George B., Leslie J. Perry, Joseph W. Kirkley, and Calvin D. Cowles, eds. *Atlas to Accompany the Official Records of the Union and Confederate Armies*. Washington, D.C.: Government Printing Office, 1891–95. Reprint. *The Official Military Atlas of the Civil War*. New York: Fairfax Press, 1983.
Herkimer County Census for 1855. Herkimer, N.Y.: County Clerk's Office, [1856].
Herkimer County Journal
Herkimer Democrat
Holt, Daniel. "In Captivity." Ed. James Greiner. *Civil War Times Illustrated* (August 1974): 34–39.
Johnson, Robert Underwood, and Clarence Clough Buel, eds. *Battles and Leaders of the Civil War*. 4 vols. New York, 1887.
Mohawk Courier
Official Army Register of the Volunteer Force of the United States Army for the Years 1861, 1862, 1863, 1864, 1865. 9 vols. Gaithersburg, Md.: R. R. Van Sickle Military Books, 1987.
Syracuse Standard
United States. Department of the Interior. Pension Records, Military Service Records. National Archives, Washington, D.C.

The War of the Rebellion: A Compilation of the Official Records of the Union and Confederate Armies. 128 vols. Washington, D.C.: Government Printing Office, 1880–1901.

Secondary Sources

Adams, George W. *Doctors in Blue: The Medical History of the Union Army in the Civil War.* New York: Henry Schuman, 1952.

Adams, John Ripley. *Memorial and Letters of Rev. John R. Adams.* Cambridge, Mass.: University Press, 1890.

Alotta, Robert I. *Civil War Justice: Union Army Executions Under Lincoln.* Shippensburg, Pa.: White Mane, 1989.

Annual Report of the Adjutant General of the State of New York for the Year 1903. Ser. no. 36. Albany: Oliver Quayle, 1904.

Baker, Jean H. *Mary Todd Lincoln: A Biography.* New York: W. W. Norton, 1987.

Bartlett, John Russell. *Dictionary of Americanisms: A Glossary of Words and Phrases Usually Regarded as Peculiar to the United States.* 3d ed. Boston, 1860.

Bates, Samuel P. *History of Pennsylvania Volunteers, 1861–65.* 5 vols. Harrisburg: State Printer, 1869.

Benton, Nathaniel S. *A History of Herkimer County, Including the Upper Mohawk Valley, from the Earliest Period to the Present Time: With a Brief Notice of the Iroquois Indians, the Early German Tribes, the Palatine Immigrations into the Colony of New York, and Biographical Sketches of the Palatine Families, the Patentees of Burnetsfield in the Year 1725.* Albany, N.Y.: J. Munsell, 1856.

Best, Isaac O. *History of the 121st New York State Infantry.* Chicago: Lt. James H. Smith, 1921.

Billings, John D. *Hardtack and Coffee: The Unwritten Story of Army Life.* 1887. Reprint. Chicago: Lakeside Press, 1960.

Biographical Directory of the American Congress, 1774–1989. Washington, D.C.: Government Printing Office, 1989.

Blustein, Bonnie Ellen. "'To Increase the Efficiency of the Medical Department': A New Approach to U.S. Civil War Medicine," *Civil War History* 33 (March 1987): 22–41.

Boatner, Mark M. *Civil War Dictionary.* New York: David McKay, 1959.

Brodie, Fawn. *Thaddeus Stevens: Scourge of the South.* New York: W. W. Norton, 1966.

Catton, Bruce. *The Coming Fury.* New York: Doubleday, 1961.

_____. *Glory Road.* New York: Doubleday, 1952.

_____. *Mr. Lincoln's Army.* New York: Doubleday, 1951.

_____. *Never Call Retreat.* New York: Doubleday, 1965.

_____. *A Stillness at Appomattox.* Garden City, N.Y.: Doubleday, 1953.

_____. *Terrible Swift Sword.* New York: Doubleday, 1963.

Chapin, Lt. L. N. *A Brief History of the Thirty Fourth Regiment N.Y.S.V.* N.p., 1903.

Coddington, Edwin B. *The Gettysburg Campaign: A Study in Command.* New York: Charles Scribner's Sons, 1968.

Coggins, Jack. *Arms and Equipment of the Civil War.* New York: Fairfax Press, 1983.

Coryell, Janet L. *Neither Heroine Nor Fool: Anna Ella Carroll of Maryland.* Kent, Ohio: Kent State University Press, 1990.

Donald, David Herbert. *Charles Sumner and the Rights of Man.* New York: Alfred A. Knopf, 1970.

Dyer, Frederick Henry. *A Compendium of the War of the Rebellion.* 3 vols. New York: Thomas Yoseloff, 1959.

Edwards, William B. *Civil War Guns.* Harrisburg, Pa.: Stackpole Co., 1962.

Field, John James. *Abridgements of the Patent Specifications Relating to Firearms and Other Weapons, Ammunition and Accoutrements, 1588–1858.* London: Holland Press, 1960.

Flexner, Stuart Berg. *I Hear America Talking: An Illustrated History of American Words and Phrases.* New York: Simon and Schuster, 1979.

Fox, William F. *Regimental Losses in the American Civil War.* Albany, 1889.

Franklin, John Hope and Alfred A. Moss, Jr. *From Slavery to Freedom: A History of Negro Americans.* 6th ed. New York: Alfred A. Knopf, 1988.

Freeman, Douglas Southall. *Lee's Lieutenants: A Study in Command.* 3 vols. New York: Charles Scribner's Sons, 1942–44.

Freemon, Frank R. "Lincoln Finds a Surgeon General: William A. Hammond and the Transformation of the Union Army Medical Bureau," *Civil War History* 33 (March 1987): 5–21.

Galloway, G. Norton. *The Ninety-fifth Pennsylvania Volunteers (Goslin's Pennsylvania Zouaves) in the Sixth Corps: An Historical Paper.* Philadelphia, 1884.

Genovese, Eugene. *Roll, Jordan, Roll: The World the Slaves Made.* New York: Pantheon, 1974.

Gillett, Mary C. *The Army Medical Department, 1818–1865.* Washington, D.C.: Center of Military History, U.S. Army, Government Printing Office, 1987.

Gray, Wood. *The Hidden Civil War: The Story of the Copperheads.* New York: Viking Press, 1942.

Hardin, George A., ed. *History of Herkimer County, New York.* Syracuse, N.Y.: D. Mason, 1893.

Leech, Margaret. *Reveille in Washington.* New York: Harper and Brothers, 1941.

Long, E. B., and Barbara Long. *The Civil War: Day by Day.* New York: Da Capo Press, 1971.

McClellan, George B. *McClellan's Own Story.* New York: Charles Webster, 1887.

McNamara, Owen. "A Surgeon's Civil War Adventures." *Legacy: Annals of Herkimer County* (Summer 1986): 3–6.

McPherson, James M. *Battle Cry of Freedom: The Civil War Era.* New York: Oxford University Press, 1988.

―――. *Ordeal By Fire: The Civil War and Reconstruction.* New York: Alfred A. Knopf, 1982.

Mathers, Mitford M., ed. *A Dictionary of Americanisms on Historical Principles.* Chicago: University of Chicago Press, 1951.

Matter, William D. *If It Takes All Summer: The Battle of Spotsylvania.* Chapel Hill: University of North Carolina Press, 1988.

Maxwell, William Quentin. *Lincoln's Fifth Wheel: The Political History of the United States Sanitary Commission.* New York: Longmans, Green and Co., 1956.

Mitchell, S. Weir, et al. *Gunshot Wounds and Other Injuries of the Nerves.* Philadelphia, 1864.

Nevins, Allan. *The Emergence of Lincoln: Douglas, Buchanan, and Party Chaos 1857–1859.* New York: Charles Scribner's Sons, 1950.

_____. *The War for the Union: The Organized War 1863–1864.* New York: Charles Scribner's Sons, 1971.

_____. *The War for the Union: The Organized War to Victory 1864–1865.* New York: Charles Scribner's Sons, 1971.

_____. *The War for the Union: War Becomes Revolution 1862–1863.* New York: Charles Scribner's Sons, 1960.

Phisterer, Frederick. *New York in the War of the Rebellion.* Albany, N.Y.: J.R. Lyon, 1912.

Rein, David M. "S. Weir Mitchell, Pioneer Psychiatrist in the Civil War." *Topic* 2 (Fall 1961): 65–71.

Robertson, James I., Jr. *Soldiers Blue and Gray.* Columbia: University of South Carolina Press, 1988.

Ross, Ishbel. *Rebel Rose.* New York: Harper and Brothers, 1954.

Sanders, Col. C.C. "Chancellorsville," *Southern Historical Society Papers* 29 (1901): 171–72.

Sears, Stephen W. *Landscape Turned Red: The Battle of Antietam.* New Haven, Conn.: Ticknor and Fields, 1983.

Siepal, Kevin H. *Rebel: The Life and Times of John Singleton Mosby.* New York: St. Martin's Press, 1983.

Sifakis, Stewart. *Who Was Who in the Civil War.* 2 vols. New York: Facts on File, 1988.

Silber, Irwin, ed. *Soldier Songs and Home-Front Ballads of the Civil War.* New York: Oak Publications, 1964.

Stevens, George T. *Three Years in the Sixth Corps.* Albany, N.Y.: S. R. Gray, 1866.

Thornton, Richard H. *An American Glossary: Being an Attempt to Illustrate Certain Americanisms Upon Historical Principles.* 2 vols. New York: Frederick Ungar, 1962.

Warner, Ezra J. *Generals in Blue; Lives of the Union Commanders.* Baton Rouge: Louisiana State University Press, 1964.

Webster, Clyde C. "John Minor Botts, Anti-Secessionist." *Richmond College Historical Papers* 1 (June 1915): 9–37.

Wert, Jeffry D. *From Winchester to Cedar Creek: The Shenandoah Campaign of 1864.* New York: Simon and Schuster, 1987.

Willard, Joseph and Charles Wilkes Walker, eds. *The Willard Genealogy.* Completed by Charles Henry Pope. Boston: Willard Family Association, 1915.

Willard, Sylvester. *Regimental Surgeons of the State of New York in the War of Rebellion, 1861–3.* Albany: N.p., [1863].

Wilson, Charles Reagan, and William Ferris, eds. *Encyclopedia of Southern Culture.* Chapel Hill: University of North Carolina Press, 1989.

Wood, Ann Douglas. "The War within a War: Women Nurses in the Union Army." *Civil War History* 18 (1972): 197–212.

Word Mysteries and Histories: From Quiche to Humble Pie. Boston: Houghton Mifflin, 1986.

Young, Agatha. *The Women and the Crisis: Women of the North.* New York: McDowell, Obolensky, 1959.

Index

Main headings are alphabetized in letter-by-letter order; subheadings are arranged in page-number order.

A Surgeon's Civil War

was composed in 10/13 ITC New Baskerville
on a Macintosh with Linotronic output
by Books International;
printed by sheet-fed offset
on 50-pound Glatfelter Supple Opaque Natural stock
with halftones printed on 70-pound enamel stock,
notch case-bound into 88-point binder's boards and Kingston
Natural cloth, and wrapped with dustjackets
printed in three flat colors on 100-pound enamel stock
finished with polyester film lamination
by Thomson-Shore, Inc.;
designed by Will Underwood;
and published by

The Kent State University Press

KENT, OHIO 44242